CAPITALIST SUPERHEROES

"*Capitalist Superheroes* peels back the glamorous façade and shows us what fantasy characters like Batman, Superman and Iron Man truly are: the horrific embodiments of neoliberal capitalism. By making us sympathize with powerful but all-too-human billionaires, these films legitimize the power of the Berlusconis and Rupert Murdochs of the world. Dan Hassler-Forest strips down the superhero fantasy to show us that this new emperor is wearing no clothes – or rather: that what is hidden behind the superhero's colorful costume is in fact the true power of Capital."
Slavoj Žižek

"This brilliant and lively book shows that the superhero films so familiar to us as Hollywood blockbusters are by no means just innocent entertainment; on the contrary, they engage, in quite malign ways, some of the fundamental political and socio-economic issues of our time. Superheroes of one sort or another are as old as literature itself, but no one has done more than Dan Hassler-Forest to help us understand the pre-eminent modern versions of the type: Superman, Batman, Spider-Man, and the like. Though his book will immediately find readers among everyone with a particular interest in superhero film and fiction, it deserves a much wider audience as well."
Carl Freedman, author of *Critical Theory and Science Fiction*

"Stylish, perceptive, and engaging, Hassler-Forest's *Capitalist Superheroes* reminds us that even in the glimmer and glow of new technologies and special effects, movies are still permeated with politics and ideologies."
Timothy Corrigan, author of *A Cinema without Walls: Movies and Culture after Vietnam*

Capitalist Superheroes:

Caped Crusaders in the Neoliberal Age

Capitalist Superheroes:

Caped Crusaders
in the Neoliberal Age

Dan Hassler-Forest

Winchester, UK
Washington, USA

First published by Zero Books, 2012
Zero Books is an imprint of John Hunt Publishing Ltd., Laurel House, Station Approach,
Alresford, Hants, SO24 9JH, UK
office1@jhpbooks.net
www.johnhuntpublishing.com
www.zero-books.net

For distributor details and how to order please visit the 'Ordering' section on our website.

Text copyright: Dan Hassler-Forest 2011

ISBN: 978 1 78099 179 5

A CIP catalogue record for this book is available from the British Library.

Design: Stuart Davies

Printed and bound by CPI Group (UK) Ltd, Croydon, CR0 4YY

We operate a distinctive and ethical publishing philosophy in all
areas of our business, from our global network of authors to
production and worldwide distribution.

CONTENTS

Acknowledgments

This book constitutes the end product of period of research and development, in which I was fortunate enough to benefit from the knowledge, insight, and feedback from a variety of friends, colleagues, and students who either shared an interest in my field, or who were kind enough to let me impose upon them with endless questions and opinions. I feel compelled to single out a few of them for special mention.

The graduate conference "The Politics of Superheroes: Renegotiating the Superhero in Post 9/11 Hollywood Cinema," organized at Yale University in January 2009 by Jeremi Szaniawski and Victor Fan, was an invaluable source of new ideas related to my topic, in large part because it introduced me to a number of brilliant people from around the globe who have become highly valued contacts. For their stimulating conversations, blog articles, and Facebook chat sessions, I wish to thank Jeremi, Jean-Guy Ducreux, Ryan Vu, and Gerry Canavan for their generous feedback and insights.

While working on this book, I have been fortunate to be surrounded by a network of smart and interesting people in Amsterdam to whom I am grateful for their support and feedback. Although there are far too many to list each name individually, I would like to express my heartfelt thanks to the following people: David Nieborg, René Glas, Thijs van den Berg, Paulina Aroch, Ernesto Illescas-Pellaez, Jaap Kooijman, Jan Teurlings, and Johan Hartle.

For helping to proof-read sections of this book as it came close to its final stages, my thanks goes those who were kind enough not only to devote precious time to these chapters, but for adding generous ideas of their own as well: Jefferson Robbins, Matthew Barron, Melinda Jacobs, Sarah Faict, Ryan Aston, and Pier van Loon. Special thanks as well to Joyce Goggin, Jason Dittmer,

Thomas Elsaesser, Bill Chambers, Walter Chaw, Carl Freedman, Timothy Corrigan, Slavoj Žižek, and extra special thanks to Darko Štrajn.

Above all, I wish to express my deepest gratitude to Christoph Lindner, my colleague and former PhD supervisor who has always been extremely supportive, forthcoming, and practical while the project took initial form as my doctoral dissertation. I have learned more from this process than from anything else, and much of it from Christoph.

Finally, my love and thanks to my family, who have been nothing but encouraging and surprisingly interested in my work; to Noah and Joshua, my two boys who both love super-heroes in their own way; to my cat Boris, for providing a reliable source of distraction by tossing items off my desk while I was writing; and to Mariecke, who has stood by me throughout the writing process with warmth, affection, a healthy dose of skepticism, and a bottle of champagne on hand for every milestone along the way.

Introduction

On 18 February 2002, German weekly news magazine *Der Spiegel* ran a cover featuring American president George W. Bush and four of his most prominent cabinet members depicted as comic book superheroes and action movie icons like Batman, Rambo, and Conan the Barbarian. The headline read: "Die Bush Krieger: Amerikas Feldzug Gegen das Böse" ("The Bush Warriors: America's Crusade Against Evil"). As the Bush administration was at the time attempting to generate European sympathy for its plans to invade Iraq, the editors of *Der Spiegel*

The Bush administration in the guise of Hollywood action men and super-heroes (18-02-2002).

expected a response from the White House. The message they received, however, was hardly the outraged indictment they had expected. Instead, the U.S. ambassador visited the editorial office to report that "the President was flattered," and subsequently requested thirty-three poster-sized enlargements of the cover for the White House (Lawrence and Jewett 2003: 43). Apparently, the notion that there was anything offensive about the depiction of American heads of state as bloodthirsty action movie icons and vindictive superheroes was completely alien to the Bush admin-istration, nor was the ironic headline "America's crusade against evil" perceived as derogatory or sarcastic.

This should have come as no surprise. If the cartoonish image on the German magazine cover is an exaggeration of the way American neoliberal politicians have tended to present themselves on the global stage, it is only a slight one. The notion of the United States as a heroic and benevolent "world police" has intensified incrementally from the 1980s onward, with a new form of American global hegemony emerging "as the center that supports the globalization of productive networks and casts its widely inclusive net to try to envelop all power relations within its world order" (Hardt and Negri 20). This shift from 20th-century nation-state imperialism to global Empire has been accompanied by a growing conflation of politics with enter-tainment and celebrity culture. Increasingly, American political figures have associated themselves with film stars and fictional characters, from Reagan's frequent references to Rambo and the Terminator to George W. Bush's *Top Gun*-inspired appearance on the deck of an aircraft carrier in premature celebration of the end of the War in Iraq.

Like the action men of popular Hollywood cinema, the neoliberal agenda of the Bush Doctrine presented itself as a heroic force that operates in the arena of global geopolitics in the same way that superheroes regulate their fantasy worlds. Just as Batman and Superman fight evil forces strictly on their own terms, the Bush administration forcefully resisted international forms of regulation, instead adopting the heroic slogan "you're either with us or against us" in its quest against the new evil. This correspondence between the geopolitical superpower of the United States and the global popularity of superheroes in the neoliberal age deserves closer analysis, and serves as the primary focus of this book.

9/11 and Intensified Neoliberalism

The development of neoliberal policies alongside neoconserv-ative values has informed the rise of capitalism as a global paradigm that no longer seems to allow for any other options. Since the end of the Cold War, alternatives to capitalism no longer appear to be viable or even imaginable, which has given rise in the affluent West to a sense of living outside of history. Neoliberal capitalism, rather than one system among many, has become not just the default model, but the only available option in our political vocabulary. After the years of false security of the 1990s "Pax Americana," the economic system of neoliberalism (described by David Harvey as early as 1990 as "flexible accumulation") underwent a radical intensification following the terrorist attacks of 11 September 2001. In response to these attacks, the neoconservative American government seized an opportunity to reinvigorate older notions of national identity that revolve around a strict duality of good and evil. Drawing on rhetoric that is familiar from the Manichean simplicity of popular fantasy narratives, the Bush administration labeled its new enemies in similar terms an "Axis of Evil," launching a long military campaign that further stimulated the deregulation of business and the privatization of government functions on a previously unimaginable scale.

This aftermath transformed the attacks of 11 September 2001 into something more than a mere historical event: the impact of 9/11 came to be experienced as the kind of epochal singularity that resulted in a sense of historical rupture. In the decade that followed, the term "post-9/11" became a form of shorthand for an indicator of a politics, an ideology, and a Western culture that has redefined itself in terms of geopolitical power and identity. As this new form of cultural and political discourse took shape, American popular culture saw the emergence of narratives and genres that reflected these shifts. The superhero movie, which has established itself as the dominant genre in 21st-century Hollywood cinema, is one of the clearest articulations of the many contradictions, fantasies, and anxieties that inform this age of neoliberal policies alongside neoconservative values.

Over fifty high-profile Hollywood films featuring superhero characters were released in the ten years from 2002 to 2012, generating global box office revenues of more than fifteen billion dollars in that period alone (source: boxofficemojo.com). The extraordinary resilience of the genre as a global box-office force during this age of intensified neoliberalism is unusual, and indicates a shift in cultural and ideological concerns as well. As David Harvey has stated, "the difficulty under capitalism ... is to find a stable mythology expressive of its inherent values and meaning" (1990: 217). The main argument of this book is that the superhero figure in fact represents in many ways the kind of "stable mythology" that expresses fundamental beliefs of neoliberal capitalism, as well as some of the anxieties that have accompanied it. By looking at the highly specific ways in which the contemporary cycle of superhero movies reflects equally specific core aspects of neoliberal capitalism, I aim to show that this genre of popular fantasy articulates, sustains, and –occasionally–critiques the cultures of 21st-century capitalism. By staging a confrontation between some of the most popular superhero films and the conceptual tools of critical theory, this book offers a fresh perspective on the ideological agenda of this popular genre.

The central concern of this book is therefore the intersection of American politics and entertainment, focusing on the superhero figure as a potent placeholder for the conflicting fantasies, anxieties and desires that typify the age of intensified neoliberalism that was ushered in under the George W. Bush presidency. Traditional distinctions between fact and fiction, news and entertainment, and the real and the virtual have become increasingly tenuous in the post-9/11 years, as the conflation of politics and entertainment grew even more intense than it had become during the Reagan era. This continued erosion of once-stable boundaries points towards the hypothesis that the 9/11 attacks have caused an intensification of cultural attitudes and perspectives associated with postmodernism as our "cultural dominant." As contemporary critical theorists such as Fredric Jameson and Slavoj Žižek have argued, the political and cultural shifts that have occurred in the aftermath of the terrorist attacks represent neither the end of irony nor the end of history, but rather an intensification of the cultures of late capitalism on a global scale.

Within this context of globalization, American forms of entertainment have become more ubiquitous than ever, with Hollywood's branded franchises appearing routinely across a wide variety of platforms, ranging from video games and comic books to theme parks and endless merchandising products. This larger framework of global commodity culture facilitated the 21st-century renaissance of the superhero as the dominant figure in postclassical cinema. On the one hand, the commercial success and sustained appeal of characters like Batman, Superman and Spider-Man can be related to their iconic status as pop-cultural figures that are instantly recognizable to millions of consumers around the world. In a fully globalized cultural economy, it obviously makes sense for multimedia conglomerates to invest in recognizable and marketable brands that appeal to multiple audiences and fit easily into multiple paradigms, such as the summer blockbuster movie, role-playing games, toy production, etc.

But besides their status as global brands and narrative franchises with built-in audiences, superheroes are also "co-constitutive elements of both American identity and the U.S. government's foreign policy practices" (Dittmer ch. 1). Their rise to the foreground of international popular culture during the years of the George W. Bush presidency must therefore also be considered in terms of their ideological content and the genre's connections to American nationalism. The superhero as an operative paradigm in a world of neoliberalism and globalization therefore provides the perfect embodiment of Hardt and Negri's definition of Empire, which operates "not on the basis of force itself but on the basis of the capacity to present force as being in the service of right and peace" (15). As superhero characters like Superman and Batman have been embraced with such abandon by global audiences, the question how this reflects upon attitudes towards post-9/11 American politics and the War on Terror becomes unavoidable, especially when one considers the Bush administration's efforts to act out just such superheroic fantasies of "punishing evildoers" and defeating an "Axis of Evil."

The Post-9/11 Superhero Movie

The superhero has been a very visible part of popular culture since Superman appeared on the pages of the first issue of *Action Comics* in 1938. After this character's breakthrough success, costumed superheroes soon became the defining fantasy of the comic book form, soon also extending into other popular narrative media like radio and film serials. While the novelty of the superhero as a specific trope in popular fantasy first arose in the late 1930s, this figure's roots can be traced back to older forms of American genre fiction, most notably cowboy figures like The Virginian, and the heroes of pulp novels from the 1920s and early 1930s. Many different motifs from American popular literature thus converged in the figure of the superhero, which was subsequently aligned more explicitly with nationalist iconography during World War II. Several previous studies of the superhero have taken a structuralist approach to the genre, focusing on the most common narrative patterns that appear in superhero comics.

In this book, I offer no absolute definition of the superhero, nor do I attempt to provide an exhaustive summary of the figure's many historical incarnations. Instead, I approach the figure as flexible and adaptable figure who serves to unite a diverse group of texts that are extremely diverse, but which do demonstrate certain common tendencies that allows us to group them roughly together. Where many other studies have been preoccupied with formulating a general definition of the superhero figure, my work instead is invested in the specific elements that connect these texts to historical developments in postmodern capitalism. In my selection of primary texts, I have focused primarily on the historically specific phenomenon of the big-budget Hollywood superhero movie. The A-list superhero movie first appeared in 1978 with the blockbuster *Superman*, with occasional further iterations throughout the 1980s and 1990s, and it has been one of the mainstays of American mainstream cinema from the early 2000s onwards, with no signs so far of relenting.

Although it seems evident that such a thing as a "superhero movie genre" exists, it is important to acknowledge that genres should not be considered stable categories, nor can their boundaries be distinguished by analyzing single texts, or even large groups of similar texts. Genre is in fact a slippery concept "because of the static, merely classificatory intellectual framework that it seems to imply: the various genres are understood as a row of so many pigeonholes, and each literary text is expected to fit more or less unproblematically into one of them" (Freedman 20). In order to use the term productively, we must therefore first acknowledge that genre is not so much a classificatory tool as it is a way of grouping diverse texts together, frequently in order to increase their commodity value.

I approach the term therefore not so much as a way to distinguish superhero movies from other texts that make up the larger genre of popular fantasy and science fiction, but in terms of its use value. Genres are defined neither by producers nor by consumers of texts, but through the complex process of interaction between constantly changing groups of interacting users. Any theoretical use of genre, therefore, requires an approach that:

- addresses the fact that every text has multiple users;
- considers why different users develop different readings;
- theorizes the relationship among those users; and
- actively considers the effect of multiple conflicting uses on the production, labeling, and display of films and genres alike (Altman 214)

It is therefore far more important to consider how, why, when, and by whom a term like "superhero movie" is used than to attempt any kind of text-based analysis that would help us forge a theoretical definition of a superhero.

Following Altman's approach, this book will employ the term "superhero movie" as a genre that is recognized as such by general audiences.[1] My discussion of the genre will remain limited to those popular narratives that are clearly identifiable as such on three basic levels: semantically (by the appearance of costumes, masks, superhuman powers, etc.), syntactically (narratives in which heroes save cities/worlds/communities from destruction by evil), and pragmatically (texts that are written and talked about *as* part of an existing superhero genre).[2] Moreover, the films of which I offer detailed discussions in this book have been selected in large part on the basis of their popularity, with many of my case studies giving new interpretations of some of the most successful films in recent Hollywood history.

If my reading of this genre takes this form of popular fantasy seriously, it attempts to do so as a deliberate response to a general tendency to take such texts seriously in an entirely different way. Fan culture has gained a strong hold on film criticism, and many volumes and myriad articles have been written in defense of the genre as a "serious" art form. Since this book is neither a work of film criticism nor an investigation of fan culture, I refrain throughout from giving value judgments on the aesthetic merits of any particular film. Instead, I focus on ideological criticism, working from within a framework provided by the traditions of Marxist critical theory and psychoanalytical theory. My analysis offers one particular way of understanding these texts, based on the historical-materialist point of view that their meaning is ultimately determined by the economic systems of which they are the product.

And while there are obviously other popular genres that could be interpreted in similar ways, I believe the superhero figure provides the strongest distillation of the fantasies, discourses, and anxieties that have shaped neoliberal capitalism over the past few decades, and most specifically in the years since 11 September 2001. In part, this is because "superheroes are not reflections of, but are instead (along with many other elements) co-constitutive of the discourse popularly known as American exceptionalism" (Dittmer ch. 1). As I will argue in this volume, these discourses of American exceptionalism have played a decisive role in the establishment of global neoliberalism as a new form of global Empire. These discourses have been systematically strengthened by the popular narrative of the superhero, which has served as the purest, most resilient embodiment of this concept.

Globalization and Convergence Culture

Superheroes are frequently associated primarily with comic books and the fan cultures that surround them. But for a Hollywood summer blockbuster to recoup its high production and marketing costs, it is abundantly clear that movies based on comic book superhero characters must find their primary audience outside this limited group of avid fans. However, with the growth of convergence culture and the increasingly vocal presence of global fan groups via the internet, film studios have learned that the success of contemporary film adaptations of these properties has indeed become dependent in part on the approval of these smaller fan communities. And after the disappointing financial returns and fan communities' lukewarm reception of the costly, heavily promoted *Hulk* (dir. Ang Lee, 2003), producers have attempted to appease these groups by applying new strategies, like exclusive previews of upcoming projects and celebrity attendance at comic book and science fiction conventions. As Marvel president Avi Arad put it in an article about San Diego comics' convention Comic-Con: "These fans love their movies and heroes like no other ... And they're very savvy with the computers. Word about your product gets out very quickly. If you can make a good impression here, your movie has hope" (Bowles n. pag.).

Henry Jenkins confirms that fan culture has indeed developed into an audience group whose tastes and preferences are taken into account to some degree by the producers of films based on their beloved characters and narratives. He proposes that the development of the internet and other new media from the late 1990s onward has changed the media landscape, shifting the power balance away from the large media conglomerates and closer to said fan communities. According to Jenkins, these fans "reject the idea of a definitive version produced, authorized and regulated by some media conglomerate. Instead, fans envision a world where all of us can participate in the creation and circulation of central cultural myths" (267). Whether Jenkins' optimistic view holds entirely true or not, it is clearly the case that large shifts have occurred in the production, distribution, and consumption of popular media texts.

These shifts point to an increased complexity in the ways in which popular culture operates. Catering simultaneously to many different audiences and establishing numerous, increasingly intricate connections to a wide variety of other texts, the films that make up the superhero genre provide a good example of neoliberal convergence culture. One important way in which the superhero movie functions is through its embeddedness in the paradigm of postclassical Hollywood cinema, which relies heavily on pre-sold franchise properties and "the replication and combination of previously successful narratives" (Maltby 37). In the "New Hollywood," three elements may be considered central to an understanding of contemporary American commercial filmmaking: "first, a *new generation of directors* (sometimes called the 'Movie Brats'), second, *new marketing strategies* (centered on the blockbuster as a distribution and exhibition concept), and third, *new media ownership and management styles* in the film industry" (Elsaesser 1998: 191). Of these three central elements, the second, also known as "High Concept" filmmaking, should be considered the most crucial. In short, the New Hollywood's most distinctive feature is its marketability as a branded, recognizable commodity, which helps explain why the superhero, as a distinctive commercial icon and brand name with proven mass appeal, has managed to fit so comfortably into the mold of postclassical Hollywood in the digital age.

This aspect also connects the superhero as a branded commodity to the neoliberal context in which this movie genre took flight from the 1980s onward. Associated for many years very specifically with American national and cultural identity, the superhero has in the past several decades become a global brand. Even as most superheroes are still recognizable as American cultural products, they consistently meet with global commercial success, and typically produce more revenue outside the United States than they do nationally. An illustrative example is the film *Captain America: The First Avenger* (dir. Joe Johnston, 2011), in which an obvious attempt was made to appeal to international audiences by including a multi-national and multi-ethnic support team for the ostentatiously nationalistic protagonist. The film also played down the character's blatant chauvinism with abundant irony and self-reflexivity, thus opening up a space for non-American audiences to engage with the character as a global brand.

This does not mean however that the films or characters no longer represent American geopolitical interests. Instead, one should see this re-engineering of superhero characters in the light of globalization and the forms of "flexible accumulation" that typify neoliberalism and cultures of postmodernity. Instead of representing American neoliberal policies in terms of the iconography of the nation state, the 21st-century superhero is instead presented as a benevolent peacekeeper who stands for supposedly universal interests. In the same way that "the ideology of the world market has always been the anti-foundational and anti-essentialist discourse par excellence" (Hardt and Negri 150), the superhero is increasingly removed from discourses of pure nationalism and comes to represent a universalized ideal in the context of global capitalism.

What has remained more or less unchanged however is the superhero's relation to issues of gender. Although attempts have been made to develop female superhero characters like Elektra and Catwoman, none of these films has even come close to the success of masculine superhero figures. Occasional counterexamples notwithstanding, the superhero's body as a rule is clearly, one might say excessively gendered in ways that connect to other forms of American popular mythologies: "Just as the cowboy served as a masculine source for (racialized) order on the Western frontier, protecting a feminized 'civilization' in regions beyond the reach of the state, superheroes serve as a masculine barrier between the vulnerable, feminized urban population and the chaotic savagery of criminals and supervillains" (Dittmer ch. 2). The patriarchal power embodied by the superhero therefore also extends to America's geopolitical presence as a "masculine" force on the world stage.

From Rambo to Batman

This investment in discourses of masculinity and geopolitics points towards their genealogical relationship to the action movies of the 1980s, when the rise of American neoliberal deregulation and aggressive foreign policy was accompanied by similarly macho movie icons. In the popular action films that became iconic for both the politics and the film culture of the United States in the 1980s, actors like Sylvester Stallone, Arnold Schwarzenegger, Mel Gibson, and Jean-Claude van Damme exemplified the "hard-bodied" image of masculinity that functioned as symbolic embodiments of the Reagan Doctrine. These films about indestructible white male action heroes "provided a narrative structure and a visual pleasure through which consumers actively responded to and constructed a U.S. popular culture" (Jeffords 12). And although the action hero as a Hollywood cinema trope is hardly unique to any historical or political era, we do see that such figures take shape historically in specific ways that "indicate something about what kinds of stories mainstream audiences ... find *pleasurable*" (22) at a specific juncture in cultural and political history.

The immense popularity of the superhero as a popular fantasy in the neoliberal age similarly illustrates what audiences find pleasurable at this point in time. Fantasy in this sense should not be understood in its popular definition, as an individual wish-fulfillment scenario, but rather as "a fundamental mechanism that organizes our desire so as to foreclose the blind repetition of drive" (Williams 211). Genres of popular fantasy such as the superhero movie genre therefore provide symbolic representations of structures and values that help us "make sense" of lived reality, while avoiding any direct confrontation with the traumatic Real. The specific popular fantasies articulated by these ubiquitous cultural commodities can therefore teach us a great deal about what global audiences have been taught to find pleasurable and –perhaps—why.

While the figure of the superhero is often associated automatically with the comic book medium, the superhero movie as a contemporary phenomenon in convergence culture is simultaneously distinct from it and historically specific. The point has often been made that comic book authors have no budget constraints to limit the scope of their fantastical, action-packed storylines, whereas film versions had traditionally been burdened by the huge expense of mounting photographic special effects through techniques like stop-motion animation, model work, and optical compositing. With the development of digital cinema throughout the 1990s, the production of photorealistic visual effects on a previously unimaginable scale soon became not only feasible, but also increasingly affordable. By the time that *Spider-Man* was released in 2002, its "computer-generated special effects produced jaw-dropping scenes of web-swinging that would have been impossible to capture several years earlier" (Wright 292). This newfound ability to create "realistic" renderings of comic book fantasies became a crucial aspect of the superhero movie's success as a genre, with each new release accompanied by promotional efforts that emphasized the technological breakthroughs that had facilitated the creation of these state-of-the-art visual effects.

At this level as well, the superhero film functions as the archetypal embodiment of the fetishized commodity. The vast expense represented by the spectacular visual effects functions as a selling point in and of itself, with both critics and audiences celebrating the excessive production costs of such blockbusters by enthusiastically confirming that "the money is up there on the screen" – to quote a commonly used phrase. Increasingly, this type of blockbuster represents the universal attraction of Capital as it takes visible form on the cinema screen, ostentatiously demonstrating its spectacular nature, its seemingly universal attractiveness, and its global reach. As the workings of Capital become ever more virtual and neoliberal industry is increasingly driven by offshoring and outsourcing labor, there appears to be some comfort in finding these visible traces of the once-mighty American economy represented even in this spectral form (Hollywood film production at this point operating as one of the country's few remaining industries involving actual forms of labor).

But even as they give spectacular form to a nostalgic sense of American cultural, industrial, and technological supremacy, today's superhero movies simultaneously disrupt this process by incorporating those very forms of virtuality. One of the consequences of this ontological shift was a paradoxical step away from the hard-bodied action heroes that had preceded these cinematic men in tights. For whereas the 1980s action film tended to place a strong emphasis on the physicality of the male body and its "physical prowess," played by actors that underwent "extensive body-building for the part" (Jeffords 28), the super-heroes' bodies are usually not only hidden beneath the body armor of their elaborate costumes, but are even replaced entirely by digitally created avatars in most of the crucial action scenes. When the camera follows Spider-Man in dizzying unbroken shots as he swings through the streets of Manhattan, the audience realizes that this is not a death-defying act undertaken by star Tobey Maguire or any of his stunt doubles, but that it is an uncanny moment of digital trickery. And although the shot may look photorealistic, it is continuously flaunting its own "virtuality" by offering up movements and perspectives that would be impossible for any physical camera to register.

Not only does this notion of a "different reality" intersect with many scholarly definitions of typically postmodernist

Spider-Man appears at Ground Zero after the 9/11 attacks (Straczynski, n. pag.).

concerns in literature, but also with the world of superhero narratives. The notion of an alternate reality that is similar to our conceptions of the real world in some ways but crucially different in others has been a mainstay of the genre from its very beginnings. Bradford Wright's cultural history *Comic Book Nation* traces how these texts have continuously reflected shifting cultural, political and social values, with the Marvel series perhaps offering the most complex formulations of a truly parallel universe. Comic book examples of this type of alternate reality range from the 1978 *Superman* issue in which he takes on Muhammad Ali in the boxing ring, to Marvel's superheroes and supervillains appearing together at Ground Zero right after the attacks of 9/11 in a special issue of *The Amazing Spider-Man*.

Such examples of historical figures or events making appearances in the fictional alternate universe of a comic book publisher's otherwise isolated narrative world has been described in terms of structural continuity: "structural continuity … embraces those elements of the real world which are contained within the fictional world of the superheroes, and (for the truly committed) actions which are not recorded in any specific text, but inescapably implied by continuity" (Reynolds 41). Paradoxically, the effect of these occasional irruptions of history into this otherwise unhistorical narrative continuity is not so much to make the world of the superheroes *more* real than it is to make the real world less so: "while this process does not exactly abolish history from superhero comics, it does divorce the superheroes' lives from their historical context" (44). Reynolds' description of superhero narratives as a modern form of mythmaking thereby effectively removes itself and its readers from the flow of time.

These parallel notions of alternate reality at the narrative level and the ontology of digital cinema at the representational level have fed back into each other in the postclassical blockbuster, with its strong emphasis on the popular fantasy genre. Rather than situating fictional narratives within the context of a particular historical period and location, these genres instead represent entire alternate realities that either exist side-by-side with a recognizably contemporary context (e.g. the Harry Potter series), or develop fantastical realms that are presented as existing entirely separate from human history (e.g. the *Star Wars* and *The Lord of the Rings* franchises). Superhero narratives straddle these two categories uncomfortably, creating an alternate world that in many ways follows the familiar trajectory of human history, while in others presenting its stories as entirely fantastical and explicitly unhistorical.

This complex intertwining of two different and contradictory modes of reference has ideological repercussions for the way these texts are decoded by audiences. As Fredric Jameson observed so memorably in his analysis of this type of genre and its ideological subtext, such fantasy "does not involve the substitution of some more ideal realm for ordinary reality ... but rather a process of *transforming* ordinary reality" (1981: 97). In other words: fantastical narratives such as the superhero genre offer models for interpreting our own world and its history that serve to systematically de-historicize the events to which they refer. The genre provides metaphorical representations of historical conflicts as part of a battle that takes classical narrative categories as its basic components and presents catastrophe as an attractive form of spectacle to be safely consumed by passive spectators.

My analysis of the relationship between the contemporary superhero narrative and neoliberal capitalism is organized into five chapters, each of which addresses a concept that connects the superhero figure to discourses of neoliberal capitalism. Each of these chapters draws on elaborate case studies of popular 21st-century superhero franchises that have established and defined the genre in crucial ways. The first chapter thus elaborates how the crucial importance of the establishment of historical continuity can be identified on the one hand in the neoconservative cultures that have filled the ideological vacuum of neoliberal practices, and on the other in a popular film franchise like that of the Superman movies.

In the same way, the second chapter describes how the trauma narrative has taken up a central position in post-9/11 consumerism and the form of disaster capitalism that has taken shape in the past ten years. This emphasis on cultural trauma has in many ways depoliticized the debates surrounding terrorism, while supplying the United States (and even the affluent West more broadly) with a privileged position of heroic victimization. My discussion of the Batman films and the differences that exist between the 1990s movie cycle and the post-9/11 "reboot" of the franchise foregrounds the notion of trauma as a mobilizing element in heroic metanarratives.

The third central theme I develop both in relation to superhero movies and post-9/11 neoliberalism is that of the "Postmetropolis": the spectral city of filmic fantasy that is both a spectacular attraction and a commodity in its own right. In this chapter, I relate developments in the privatization of city spaces, like the "Disneyfication" of Times Square in New York, to the representation of a specific kind of nostalgia in the popular Spider-Man films. While these films, along with many other popular superhero metropolises, represent a utopian fantasy of a specifically urban environment, this section ends with an analysis of the way in which articulations of dystopia reflect these fantasies' distorted mirror image in *The Dark Knight*.

Since the relationship between the superhero and the cities he patrols revolves around notions of surveillance and control, the fourth chapter develops this concept further. Branching out from Foucault's original work on the normative force of institutionalized surveillance in modern society, I extend this argument in order to discuss more fruitfully the relationship between discourses of surveillance and the workings of popular culture.

My analysis of superhero figures Batman and Iron Man focuses on their cyborg-like incorporation of high-tech surveillance apparatus in their costumes, which transforms them into a particular fantasy of militarized agency. A discussion of the more alternative type of superhero represented in the Hellboy films finally examines to what extent it is possible to operate within the superhero blockbuster paradigm while offering some degree of resistance to these archetypes.

The fifth and, fittingly, last theme to be elaborated is that of apocalyptic narratives and the post-historical aspects of neoliberal capitalism and postmodern theory. Beginning with a closer look at the broad history of the monster movie and its dialectical structure, the chapter draws heavily on Lacanian concepts to theorize the process of pleasurable identification so frequently provided by the genre of popular fantasy. The contradictory way in which the disaster movie has operated in relation to historical developments in capitalism offers many points of similarity with the neoliberal superhero movie. Many of the themes discussed in earlier chapters then converge in my discussion of the television series *Heroes*, which offers an apocalyptic fantasy of traumatized superheroes saving the city of New York from a 9/11-like catastrophe.

I

Superheroes, Historical Continuity, and the Origin Story

> In modern society, many different senses of time get pinned together. Cyclical and repetitive motions ... provide a sense of security in a world where the general thrust of progress appears to be ever onwards and upwards into the firmament of the unknown ... And in moments of despair or exaltation, who among us can refrain from invoking the time of fate, of myth, of the Gods? (Harvey 1990: 202)

In the neoliberal age of "flexible accumulation," our experience of time and space seems to have challenged our sense of temporal and even spatial continuity. As the hegemony of capitalism today "resembles Marx's abstract or 'pure' model of the capitalist mode of production much *more closely* than did the capitalism that actually existed during Marx's own lifetime" (Freedman 9), the intensification of Marx's famous "annihilation of space by time" has substantially disrupted traditional notions of historical continuity. Without any gods left to appeal to, the postmodern myths of superheroes offer re-articulations of religious myths, but from the explicit framework of secularized popular culture. The massive popularity of the contemporary superhero movie therefore resides to some extent in the fact that these films offer mythical narratives about defining one's origins.

Herein lies one of the key differences between on the one hand the superhero as a character in comic books, with its endlessly convoluted chronology (referred to by fans with the contradictory term "continuity"), and on the other hand the mainstream superhero movies, which must continuously re-establish points of origin for cultural icons who are familiar characters, but who must also be reinvented over and over again for new movie audiences. The emphasis on the origin story as an integral component in the superhero movie therefore performs not only a stable narrative component, but can help explain the appeal of these narratives and the myths of origination they provide.

Like any other commodity that circulates in a global marketplace, the superhero brand must provide a combination of the familiar and the new in order to remain fashionable and thereby profitable. While there is obviously nothing new about the importance of profitable commodities in capitalism, the ways in which value is created and circulated has changed in the globalized and deregulated age of neoliberalism. This period has seen an intensification of the cultures of flexible accumulation that allow for an unprecedented concentration of power and wealth among the global élite (Harvey 1990: 303-306). According to neoliberal theory, this system will ultimately have a beneficial, even utopian effect on all of humanity:

> Neoliberalism is in the first instance a theory of political economic practices that proposes that human well-being can best be advanced by liberating individual entrepreneurial freedoms and skills within an institutional framework characterized by strong private property rights, free markets, and free trade. (Harvey 2005: 2)

This theory of neoliberal benefits has become so widespread that it is now "hegemonic as a mode of discourse," even to the point "where it has become incorporated into the common-sense way many of us interpret, live in, and understand the world" (3). Within this economic context, where commodities can circulate freely on a global scale, the brand identity of the superhero offers a unique combination of just such universal familiarity while also remaining extremely adaptable to radical reinventions.

Consider the most successful superhero franchise in this

century's cycle of films: each of the three films in Sam Raimi's *Spider-Man* series dealt with the character's origin story in fundamental ways, after which point this particular cycle of films was considered to have exhausted itself, and the franchise underwent a "reboot" in order to start afresh with a new, subtly different origin tale. The *X-Men* films have undergone a similar process, first playing out across three films that have each focused on specific characters' origin stories, after which the franchise started devoting itself to spin-off movies such as *X-Men Origins: Wolverine* (dir. Gavin Hood, 2009), and prequels that go even further back into the cycle's origins, like *X-Men: First Class* (dir. Matthew Vaughn, 2011) and its inevitable sequels. Rather than the shadow that lurks in the background, as it does in the comic books, the origin story has been placed at the very core of the contemporary superhero movie's success and its longevity at the box office.

One reason for this is a practical one: most mainstream audiences are not familiar with the complex and often contradictory narrative trajectories that inform the most successful comic book superheroes. Also, only very few blockbuster film cycles ever run beyond two or three successful sequels that carry on from the original film's basic premise and cast of characters. Two kinds of audience can be identified as these films' primary target: the mass audience, which makes up the vast majority, may be drawn in by a broad cultural familiarity with a superhero's iconic status, and a curiosity about what kind of style and narrative have been used to rejuvenate the character for a contemporary context; the fans, who make up a small but crucial minority, will be drawn in by the fact that "their" character has been re-purposed for a mainstream audience, and will want to experience to what extent the movie version remains "true" to their own preferred style and content.

Given the prominence of origin stories in the superhero movie, this aspect of its formula is worth investigating further, as it connects directly to a postmodern culture in which myths of origination on the one hand and of apocalypse on the other can serve to impart a sense of order to an unstable, decentered world. This point of inquiry is all the more relevant because the origin story in the superhero movie is most commonly organized around father figures, Oedipal trajectories, and patriarchal genealogies. Superheroes in these films undergo an obsessive quest for re-establishing stable points of origin in semi-mythical father figures associated with omnipotent forms of power and omniscient forms of knowledge. This motif points towards a reactionary desire for stable signification in an age of increasing instability, ephemerality, and "flexible accumulation." Meanwhile, the particular types of crisis the superhero must overcome in these origin stories are most typically derived from the specific fears and anxieties of the age of global terrorism, postmodern finance, and disaster capitalism.

The deeply unpredictable nature of neoliberal capitalism has created a cultural environment that emphasizes the short term amidst a culture of perpetual crisis. This has radically increased the sense of ephemerality that has affected all aspects of postmodern theory and the cultural practices of late capitalism. The terrorist attacks of 11 September 2001 played a crucial role in the intensification of these processes and discourses, bringing into sudden focus many of the cultural and economic anxieties that had been developing from the 1970s onwards. The establishment of narratives that suggested continuity and tradition became a prime concern, as "shoring up national identities in uncertain times requires a sense of discursive stability even as the details of the narratives shift to maintain currency" (Dittmer ch. 5). This discursive stability depends not only on the "common-sense truths" that structure our daily lives, but also on the symbolic myths and popular fictions that strengthen such discourses.

In this chapter, I will first introduce the way in which the terrorist attacks of 9/11 offered an opportunity within American

24

culture to (re-)articulate a very specific type of origin story that suited its own purposes at this time. Responses to the attacks tended to emphasize narratives of mythical American exceptionalism, while the notion of heroic victimization took shape as a "common-sense" response. I will then proceed to look at the way in which Superman films, both from before and after 9/11, provide helpful mythical narratives whose patriarchal structures help establish cultural notions of historical continuity and predestination that help sustain the neoconservative values of neoliberal capitalism.

Ruptures and Points of Origin:
The Heroic Victimization of 9/11

"We're going to try and do something." That was the message sent by some very American heroes with names like Sandra Bradshaw, Jeremy Glick, Mark Bingham, Todd Beamer, and Thomas Bennett. They found themselves aboard the hijacked flight 93 that went down in Somerset County, PA on September 11, 2001. They witnessed the brutality on board and somehow summoned the strength to warn us and take action. United they stood, and likely saved our world from an even darker day of perhaps even more unthinkable horror. Since that day, millions of us everywhere of all ages, races, creeds, have asked ourselves "What are we to do?" In their heroic undying spirit, we all feel the need to do something, however small, symbolic, to honor those remarkable heroes among us, those who have fallen and those still standing, united. Those of us here tonight are not heroes. We are not healers, nor protectors of this great nation. We are merely artists and entertainers, here to raise spirits, and, we hope, a great deal of money. We appear tonight as a simple show of unity to honor the real heroes and to do whatever we can to ensure that all their families are supported by our larger American family. This is a moment to pause and reflect, to heal and to rededicate ourselves to the American spirit of one nation indivisible.

The above words were spoken on television by actor Tom Hanks on the evening of September 21, 2001. It was the first of many short speeches delivered by a host of Hollywood stars during a telethon organized to raise money for the American victims of the attacks of 9/11. Entitled *America: A Tribute to Heroes*, the two-hour program was broadcast live and without commercial interruptions on over 320 national broadcast and cable networks, and picked up that same day by broadcast networks in 210 other countries and innumerable radio stations (Spigel 134). Famous actors reading out eulogies alternated with popular musicians ranging from Stevie Wonder to Céline Dion, all performing suitably mournful and patriotic selections from their best-known work.

Coming just ten days after the terrorist attacks that would become a defining moment in 21st-century cultural and political history, the tone during this star-studded media event was relatively understated and "respectful," its organizers deliberately avoiding the garish style commonly associated with this type of fundraiser. It was broadcast without commercial interruptions, a choice that functions along with its cross-media saturation as an indication of the event's importance. Like the general American media response in the first weeks directly following 9/11, the telethon was therefore presented to viewers in terms of its exceptional nature: "the everydayness of television itself was suddenly disrupted by news of something 'alien' to the usual patterns of domestic TV viewing" (Spigel 120-1). The way in which the media coverage of 9/11 set itself apart from those normal patterns of news and entertainment strengthened the perception of 9/11 as a singularity, which had already been established by the endless news coverage of the events and their immediate aftermath.

The concept of the singularity as a recurring phenomenon in American history is known as exceptionalism, or "the idea that the United States is a chosen nation, a country whose history and unique mission in the world defy comparison" (Vågnes 62). This paradigm clearly informs the telethon speech quoted above, with its references to "very American heroes," "larger American family," and "one nation indivisible," while continuously defining the ways in which 9/11 was presented as a narrative without precedent. Media commentators and politicians endlessly repeated the notion that 9/11 was a historical singularity, "arguing that the attacks had hurled Americans into a new world, a new era. The mantra was 'this changes everything'" (Rozario 180). This emphasis on exceptionalism has a well-documented tradition in American cultural history, where it has informed and shaped the national response to every major event in the nation's short history. The concept therefore is implicitly connected to a larger myth of cultural heritage that functions as an origin story for American national and cultural identity.

It is therefore worthwhile to analyze the 9/11 telethon's opening words in more detail, as a closer reading of this short text can help understand how the central ideas associated with the attacks were immediately connected to preexisting mythical structures that serve as nationalist origin stories. The most noticeable aspect of the broadcast is that its central concept—also clearly indicated by the telethon's title—is that of "the hero." As in this opening speech, a great deal of cultural and political discourse surrounding 9/11 has concerned itself explicitly with the canonization of these new hero figures that were suddenly recognized in firemen, policemen and rescue workers. To the point of hyperbole, the aesthetics of comic books and Hollywood action blockbusters were used to enshrine the new "real heroes" as equal to, or perhaps even greater than, the fictional figures that had previously been primarily associated with that term. A sudden proliferation of comic books and special commemorative publications appeared shortly after the attacks, each of which contributed to this canonization of policemen and firemen as the "real heroes" of 9/11.

Superman looks up admiringly at the "real heroes" of 9/11 on the cover of this special fundraising issue.

After so many years of exposure to eerily similar scenarios in untold numbers of Hollywood action films, representations of 9/11 came to suggest that America had "suddenly encountered an Evil which fits the most naive Hollywood image: a secret organization of fanatics who fully intend, and plan in detail, a terrorist attack whose aim is to kill thousands of random civilians" (Žižek 2004: 75). Rather than experiencing the attacks as a sudden resurgence of the Real in an environment that had become increasingly virtual, reality instead came to be defined on the basis of fictional tropes.

Media representations of 9/11 therefore seem to bear out Lyotard's perspective on the cultural shift evident in the postmodern condition, for not only are "the grand narratives of national unity that sprang up after 9/11 ... more performative than sincere" (Spigel 138): the news coverage that dominated the American networks after the attacks also focused mostly on individual tales of personal tragedy. This reduction of large-scale events to the level of mini- or even micro-narratives further illustrates Lyotard's point of view, as the focus moved almost immediately from the larger geopolitical context of the events to individuals' experiences of the attacks. Epitomized by the barrage of personal memories and intimate revelations recounted in the 9/11 telethon, the repeated use of this kind of micro-narrative creates an instant and irrefutable logic behind the events, because "narrative knowledge does not give priority to the question of its own legitimation and … certifies itself in the pragmatics of its own transmission without having recourse to argumentation and proof" (Lyotard 27). The reduction of historical meaning to familiar narrative categories therefore has the advantage of not only being easily digestible, but also of providing familiar coordinates that establish the difference between good and evil, right and wrong, hero and villain, victim and attacker.

An historical moment that could have served any number of purposes, depending on the terms in which political and cultural discourse would define it, was thereby immediately defined by a set of concepts that would ensure continued passivity as a result. This was "a moment to pause and reflect, to heal and rededicate ourselves," not a time to question and challenge the assumptions about the way these events were represented. This approach perfectly complemented the other media depictions of the attacks, as "the saturation of everyday life with uniform images of the second plane crash, the firebomb, and the towers' collapse was transformed itself into the uncontested meaning of the event, foreclosing on historical awareness and seeming to preempt any questioning impulses that might have placed the attacks in a broader critical perspective" (Heller 7). Rather than understanding this approach in terms of any conspiracy theory masterminded by an evil political administration, it may be more fruitful to see this response again as part of a pervasive trend in American culture that emphasizes the country's nationalist mythology of exceptionalism.

Following this generally well-received telethon broadcast, other fund-raising projects soon sprang up across numerous media, all emphasizing a similar perspective on these core concepts: Marvel Comics' special commemorative issue of original work by a who's-who of major-league comics authorship was titled *Heroes: The World's Greatest Super Hero Creators Honor the World's Greatest Heroes – 9-11-2001*, depicting members of the police force and fire department via the aesthetics and iconography of superhero comics; online auction site eBay was flooded with 9/11 memorabilia, like commemorative casino chips picturing a bald eagle and captions like "September 11, 2001 – In Honor of Our American Heroes"; and *World Trade Center* (dir. Oliver Stone, 2006), the only Hollywood film to focus explicitly on the attack on the eponymous towers, devoted its running time to the heroic survival of its two protagonists trapped under the rubble at Ground Zero. What such representations of 9/11 tend to emphasize are recurrent narratives of heroism, continuity, and

national(ist) identity: "what *World Trade Center* presents us with … is the impossible promise that we can all somehow survive *even this*" (Canavan 2011: 128).

The superheroic portrayal of a fireman on the cover of a commemorative comic book tribute.

All of these examples, as diverse as their media, authors, and audiences might be, continuously re-emphasize two major points regarding the events of 9/11: first, that the United States as a nation had been the innocent victim of these attacks; and second, that in spite of this traumatic victimization, its survivors had been instantly identified as transcendent, mythical heroes. This tendency of popular culture to focus so specifically on a combination of American heroism and victimization from late 2001 onwards is strong and widespread enough to constitute a Foucauldian discursive formation that extends far beyond the borders of texts that deal explicitly with the events of 9/11. According to Foucault, such discursive formations come into existence whenever "between objects, types of statement, concepts, or thematic choices, one can define a regularity (an order, correlations, positions and functionings, transformations)" (2002: 41).

One of the best-known applications of this concept is Edward Said's definition of Orientalism as a form of Foucauldian discourse: the concept that "without examining Orientalism as a discourse one cannot possibly understand the enormously systematic discipline by which European culture was able to manage—and even produce—the Orient" (2004: 3). Said's emphasis on the discursive formation's systematic nature is crucial here: it not only makes it possible to speak of a particular topic, but it also limits what can be said about it, thus constituting the speaker within a specific range of expression. These rules, which Foucault has defined as "conditions of existence (but also of coexistence, maintenance, modification, and disappearance) in a given discursive formation" (2002: 42), are easy to identify in the case of the discourses surrounding the events of 9/11, which have centered so strongly on a group of concepts and contradictions that together form a cohesive group of statements.

One particularly telling example of how swiftly 9/11 was transformed from a collection of historical events into a discursive formation with a clearly identifiable political-ideological agenda is the film release of *Black Hawk Down* (dir. Ridley Scott, 2001). Many other action films saw their release indefinitely postponed in the aftermath of the terrorist attacks, on the grounds that Hollywood's high-gloss brand of destructive fantasy was suddenly deemed inappropriate or even offensive. But the release of this war film, originally scheduled for late spring 2002, was instead "rushed into theaters in December 2001" in order to capitalize on prevailing public sentiment in America as the War on Terror began to take shape in the wake of 9/11 (Markovitz 9).

Since the film's subject matter is the embarrassing military defeat suffered by American elite troops in Somalia in 1993, one might wonder in what sense the release of a big-budget action film about these events would be any less insensitive in the traumatized cultural climate of late 2001. But a brief analysis of the film, as well as its immense commercial success, does seem to bear out the studio's highly profitable decision. For unlike the much more balanced account found in the book on which the film was based, Ridley Scott's immaculately produced movie jettisons all but the most basic explanation of the reasons behind the armed conflict pictured in the film. Instead, the movie is devoted entirely to the American soldiers' subjective experiences in the thick of the battle. With political and military policy conveniently reduced to the briefest of text captions that bookend the film's undeniably exciting barrage of gunfire and bloodshed, the film's actual import is summed up by main character Scott Eversmann (played by Josh Hartnett) in the film's closing scene:

> I was talking to Blackburn the other day, and he asked me "What changed? Why are we going home?" and I said "Nothing." That's not true either; I think everything's changed. *I know I've changed.* You know a friend of mine asked me before I got here; it's when we were all shipping out. He asked me "Why are you going to fight somebody else's war? What, do you think you're heroes?" I didn't know what to say at the time, but if he'd ask me again I'd say no. I'd say there's no way in hell. *Nobody asks to be a hero.* [pause] *It just sometimes turns out that way.* (emphasis added)

Either unable or unwilling to comprehend the complex social, political, and economic reasons behind American military policy and his own role in this specific intervention, the character defines the experience (and therefore the film's perspective on the entire narrative) as something that has no meaning beyond its effects upon the individual: the only thing that has been changed by the experience is himself. Therefore, the characters who died in the film were the victims of unfathomable forces beyond anyone's control, allowing the events to leave in their wake only two kinds of subjects: victims and heroes. By focusing exclusively on the soldiers' individual experiences of these events, they are simultaneously de-historicized and de-politicized, leading to an evacuation of meaning and context. The enemy responsible for the American bloodshed on the battlefield is defined only by his otherness, strongly informed by Orientalist stereotypes like religious fundamentalism—assassins on the street screaming out "Allah-u Akbar!"—and non-Western ethnicity—only one of the American soldiers is African-American, while the Somalis, most of whom are seen only from a distance, have dark skin that functions as a strong visual contrast to the Caucasian American soldiers. Therefore, traumatic military conflict from the American point of view is presented as unavoidable, in which Americans are both innocent victims and heroic protagonists, for reasons that remain incomprehensible, and ultimately even irrelevant.

These examples seem to bear out the most pessimistically-minded postmodern theorists, such as Fredric Jameson and Jean Baudrillard, and their central thesis that postmodern (popular) culture serves first and foremost to sever the public's active connection with history by offering up continuous representations of events that are deliberately made unhistorical. These simulations, or, indeed, simulacra, "endow present reality and the openness of present history with the spell and distance of a glossy mirage" (Jameson 1991: 21). These words apply equally to the way in which the images of the 9/11 attacks were so quickly sensationalized and commodified in the media. The sublime imagery of the fireball erupting out of the south tower, the amateur footage of the airplane striking the building, and the videos of panic-stricken pedestrians fleeing a billowing cloud of smoke in downtown Manhattan had a built-in appeal to audiences for whom their similarity to Hollywood blockbusters has been widely quoted: the experience of seeing the attacks (for all but a few, on television) was "famously described by eyewitnesses, television commentators and viewers across the country in terms of its filmic qualities" (Rozario 6). This cinematic   quality strengthened the connection between postmodern film culture and the events of 9/11 that similarly informed the redefinition of "heroes" and "villains" discussed previously.

The spectacular, film-like nature of the 9/11 attacks in news photography.

The spectacular nature of the attacks therefore helps explain the exceptional impact those images had on contemporary culture and history. In his 1967 collection of theses *The Society of the Spectacle*, Guy Debord defined postmodernity and late capitalism in terms of precisely this spectacular nature: "the spectacle is capital accumulated to the point where it becomes image" (24). He argued that the spectacle in its postmodern incarnation "erases the dividing line between self and world, in that the self, under siege by the presence/absence of the world, is eventually overwhelmed" (153). With the continuing development of late capitalism, Debord's manifesto has only gained in relevance, as imagery of 9/11 epitomized his thesis that the spectacle has come to form "the very heart of society's real unreality" (13). This Debordian perspective on the spectacular image as a free-floating commodity, separated from its connection to anything it represents besides abstract capital, has been embraced by many in the ongoing debate on 9/11 and postmodernism. In the post-Cold

War age of intensified neoliberalism and global capitalism, these Debordian concepts continue to apply, as "the need to accelerate turnover time has led to a shift of emphasis from the production of goods (most of which ... have a substantial lifetime) to the production of events (such as spectacles that have an almost instantaneous turnover time)" (Harvey 1990: 157).

Contemporary cultural theorists such as Jameson, Baudrillard, and Žižek have developed this notion further in some of the most influential work on 9/11 and its significance to contemporary Western culture. Although there are important differences between their perspectives on 9/11, they do have in common their shared emphasis on the instant process of commodification that took this "effect of the Real" (Žižek 2002: 10) and instantly transformed it into a form of "collective delirium" (Jameson 2002a: 298). Their reading of 9/11 thereby leads us to a compelling paradox. For on the one hand, the event created the illusion of historicity and periodization with the introduction of the term "post-9/11" and the ubiquity of the phrase "this changes everything." This notion, which has become a fundamental element of 9/11 discourse, is as much a mythico-narrative construct as that of American exceptionalism, because as Jameson has pointed out, "it is important to remember that historical events are never really punctual ... but extend into a before and an after of historical time that only gradually unfold, to disclose the full dimensions of the historicity of the event" (ibid. 301). On the other hand, 9/11 discourse has systematically sealed off any true sense of historical awareness or agency, as its status as familiar spectacle forced us to experience it "as a nightmarish unreal spectre" to be repeated endlessly (Žižek 2002: 19).

Superheroes and Postmodern Theory

In his novel *The Amazing Adventures of Kavalier & Clay* (2000), author Michael Chabon develops an alternate history of the Golden

Age of comic books, in which he emphasizes the connection between the Jewish roots of the first authors of superhero comic books and the fantasies of agency and empowerment that their omnipotent protagonists embody. Chabon's novel relates this desire to engage with fantasy figures of cultural and physical empowerment to the specific historical moment of Nazi Germany and the Holocaust. But his narrative also offers more general ways of thinking about the enduring popularity of superhero figures in the context of late modernity, especially when we connect this desire to contemporary theories of postmodernism.

Fredric Jameson had defined postmodernism as a cultural dominant connected to developments in capitalism that ultimately penetrate every aspect of contemporary life, from literature and film to architecture and fine art. It produces a form of cultural logic that may have become increasingly ubiquitous in the age of global capitalism, but which also leaves room for "coexistence with other resistant and heterogeneous forces which it has a vocation to subdue and incorporate" (1991: 159). This decentered quality of the postmodern condition is something Jameson understands as a cultural movement that reflects the developing logic of late capitalism, in which the normative character of modernism has been eroded to the point where it has become little more than a Lyotardian language game, or another failed Grand Narrative. The totalizing force of social and cultural reification under this new cultural dominant therefore leads him to rethink the concept of the public sphere, and its new ways of producing subjectivity:

> The emergence of a new realm of image reality that is both fictional (narrative) and factual (even the characters in the serials are grasped as real 'named' stars with external histories to read about), and which now—like the former classical 'sphere of culture'—becomes semiautonomous and *floats above reality*. (277, emphasis added)

This separation between postmodern subjective experience and the historical reality that defines it is reflected in a sense of cultural alienation crucially different from the kind associated with high modernism. This new form of alienation is no longer about the individual feeling displaced within a mechanized, increasingly fast-paced social sphere, but is now conceptualized as a more fundamental loss of any sense of identity, in which "present reality has been transformed into a simulacrum by the process of wrapping, or quotation" (118). Jameson locates the reason for this cultural development in the basic structures of late capitalist society, "where exchange value has been generalized to the point at which the very memory of use value is effaced" (18). This erosion of use value is another way of understanding the development from modernism to postmodernism as one in which normative stability is lost, and where temporality is supplanted by the "hyperspace" that defines postmodernity.

Both the cause and the effect of this Jamesonian interpretation of postmodernism are relevant to understanding the pervasive popularity of the superhero as a particularly enduring cultural artifact in this very period of late capitalism. The inescapable logic of commodification, in which everything is transformed into a branded product with a defining and quantifiable market value, is instantly recognizable in the branded nature of the superhero. Not only does the range of diversely branded superhero figures and narratives directly reflect the competitive nature of the commodity-based market, but it also serves as an example of Theodor Adorno's well-known concept of pseudo-individualization: a range of mass-produced commodities, the basic identical nature of which is disguised by the emphasis on smaller-scale differences that are interpellate distinct audiences.

This form of cultural logic is most clearly visible in the ways in which fan culture has developed along lines of strict allegiance to specific branded commodities, which are then paradoxically used as tools for social and personal identity formation. For example, superhero fan culture tends to define itself in terms of its allegiance to individual characters, which are often perceived as representing radically different identities and even world-views. For many fans, Superman represents not only an ideal of transcendent moral and physical perfection, but also a harmonious and ordered universe with clear distinctions between right and wrong. Batman on the other hand is commonly seen as an example of immanence rather than transcendence, while the characters that make up his narrative continuity are often described in terms of their ambiguity, and the absence of absolute moral certainties.

But these oft-repeated differences between archetypal characters like Superman and Batman can be better understood in terms of their basic similarities than their superficial differences. For rather than truly representing philosophies or ideologies that are in any way oppositional, they both exist in the material sense primarily as commodities in a marketplace where each brand must stand out clearly from the other in order to maintain its commodity value. The individual characteristics of either of these branded characters are therefore "no more than the generality's power to stamp the accidental detail so firmly that it is accepted as such" (Horkheimer and Adorno 94). In the context of superhero figures and the fan cultures surrounding them, this "accidental detail" can be interpreted as the iconic features that distinguish superheroes from each other visually and thematically, which is also what has made them so readily identifiable as branded commodities with serialized multimedia franchises.

The other central aspect of Jamesonian postmodernism is that of "a new depthlessness" that has led to a "weakening of historicity" (Jameson 1991: 6). The resulting gap between the variously decentered forms of postmodern subjectivity and the individual subject's ability to relate to what Jameson describes as "real history" has led to a new relation between the imagined self and the subject's lived experience:

> The postmodern must be characterized as a situation in which the survival, the residue, the holdover, the archaic, has finally been swept away without a trace. In the postmodern, then, the past itself has disappeared (along with the well-known 'sense of the past' or historicity and collective memory). (ibid. 309)

This lack of historical bearings can be related to Baudrillard's theory of the hyperreal, which defines postmodern life as a form of simulation; to Lyotard's description of the collapse of the metanarratives, with a strong focus on the dissolution of ideology in its modernist sense; or to what Žižek sums up as "the virtualization of our daily lives" (2002: 19), which again emphasizes the unreal quality of contemporary Western existence. What these articulations of postmodern theory all share therefore is a perspective that foregrounds the highly discursive nature of contemporary life, and the resulting crisis of human agency.

Postmodernity and the Crisis of Agency

The subject's crisis of agency is linked specifically to the onset of modernization, and is already evident in the high modernism of the early 20th century. In this sense, postmodernism should be understood not so much as the opposite of modernism, but rather as its logical successor and dialectical counterpart. Jameson has done the most extensive work in relating the terms "modernism," "modernization," and "modernity" to each other in all of their complexity, and proposes that "modernism is characterized by a situation of incomplete *modernization*," which leads us to arrive at the conclusion that "postmodernism is *more* modern than modernism itself" (1991: 310). What we recognize as being typically postmodern is therefore characterized by the way the object in question embodies aspects of a previous modernity, but more—and therefore differently—so.

This type of postmodern theory is based on a Marxian periodizing hypothesis that sees the superstructure following and reflecting a base that is defined by the historical and material development of capitalism. Jameson's dialectical perspective on modernity, which he defines as a narrative category rather than a philosophical or historical one (2002b: 40-41), helps us understand the seemingly contradictory relationship between the cultural dominants of modernity and their ambiguous relationship to historical moments we have come to associate with rupture. Since "any theory of modernity must both affirm its absolute novelty as a break and at one and the same time its integration into a context from which it can be posited as breaking" (57), the use of a term like "postmodernism" is revealed as a discursive construct that enables cultural narratives of simultaneous rupture and continuity.

Any critical understanding of contemporary popular culture from a Marxian point of view must include such contradictions, and will therefore be dialectical in its focus on the fact that its object itself is inherently contradictory. An obvious example is the way in which Hollywood films have traditionally provided narratives that offer the triumph of the individual over the system, while simultaneously reaffirming the ideological status quo by leaving intact the very system over which the subject supposedly triumphs. Superman is again a case in point, seemingly embodying utopian ideals of a better future for all mankind, while most Superman narratives fail to engage on any level with social or political realities. Instead, Superman and most other superheroes tend to fight the symptoms of crime and injustice while ignoring the causes: "those criminals necessarily embodying a critique of the system remain ignored while the violent criminals whom [the superhero] fights remain divorced from the social fabric which produces them" (Pearson and Uricchio 205).

This dialectic also functions at another level in the reifying force of popular culture: while subjects are constituted through processes of interpellation, the audience is simultaneously framed through and removed from the character on the screen, who functions as the basis for audience identification while also remaining fundamentally "other." The superhero genre again is a telling example: the superhero character on the screen remains a fetishized, branded commodity rather than a true point of identification, while the viewer is reduced to the role of explicit consumer of this spectacle. Or, to put it in the terms used by Walter Benjamin, the character on the screen remains part of the "cult of the movie star," defined by its fundamental "commodity character," while the "cult of the audience" constitutes viewers as consumers, perpetually distracted by this ongoing process of consumption (33).

There are several reasons why the superhero figure can be seen as an especially striking embodiment of this kind of distinction: not only can the superhero as a generic figure take on numerous "pseudo-individualized" forms as variously branded characters and franchises, but many different actors can play the same character without disturbing the brand. Therefore, whether Superman is portrayed on the screen by George Reeves, Christopher Reeve, Brandon Routh, or an animated cartoon figure, the character retains its basic recognizability, its brand identity merely undergoing a form of commodity diversification. The logic of limited consumer choice seems particularly inescapable in these situations, as consumers are encouraged to voice their preference for a specific version of any of these characters, just as one distinguishes other basically identical commodities from each other on the basis of brands, product lines, and their association with "lifestyle choices."

In his influential analysis of "The Myth of Superman," semiotician and literary theorist Umberto Eco focused on the ideology represented by the Superman character, and how it relates to the crisis of agency associated with industrialization and modernity:

> In an industrial society ... where man becomes a number in the realm of organization which has usurped his decision-making role, he has no means of production and is thus deprived of his power to decide. Individual strength, if not exerted in sports activities, is left abased when confronted with the strength of machines which determine man's very movements. In such a society the positive hero must embody to an unthinkable degree the power demands that the average citizen nurtures but cannot satisfy. (14)

As Eco points out, part of the attraction of the ongoing narrative of Superman in serialized comic books revolves around the notion that any postmodern subject "secretly feeds the hope that one day, from the slough of his actual personality, a superman can spring forth who is capable of redeeming years of mediocre existence" (15). Part of the enduring popularity of these narratives therefore lies in the way they appeal to cultural fantasies of overcoming the crisis of agency that is in so many ways fundamental to late capitalism.

But although superhero narratives have been able to attract audiences with their fantasies of powerful super-humans, the dialectical nature of this dilemma cancels out any actual engagement with it. For the superheroes depicted on the page or on the screen provide fantasies that offer the illusion of momentary escape from the powerless nature of the modern subject, but do so in ways that are defined by their fundamental removal from historical reality, and in forms that are grounded in capitalist processes of passive consumerism. This contradiction is recognizable at the narrative level as well, where characters like Batman, who are made attractive by the rebellious non-conformism of their vigilante behavior, actually do "little to destabilize accepted notions of justice" (Collins 1989: 33). Even characters that are supposedly defined by their ability to break free of existing systems and ideologies are thus continuously made a part of the very systems from which they offer the illusion of escape.

Of Myths, Mythologies, and Superheroes

This ideological function of superhero narratives, which has traditionally re-affirmed the fundamental values of patriarchal capitalism, leads us to examine more closely their status as cultural myths. In recent years, it has become commonplace to refer to characters like Superman and Batman as "modern myths" that may be read as contemporary counterparts to classical figures like Prometheus or Odysseus. This assumption has become widespread not only in the popular press, but also in academic work on superhero narratives: from books like *The Myth of the American Superhero* and *Our Gods Wear Spandex* to the many studies tracing Superman's roots in Jewish identity and Judeo-Christian mythology. It may however be more productive to refine the term "myth" along lines first suggested by Roland Barthes, and to identify the tradition of the superhero figure as a signifying system "that transforms meaning into form" (1972: 131).

In his article on Superman, Eco already voiced specific objections to the classification of superhero figures as mythological archetypes, basing his argument on the formal qualities of these narratives. He makes a clear distinction between "traditional figures of classical and Nordic mythology" and "the figures of messianic religions" on the one hand, and the character of the contemporary superhero on the other (15). For whereas truly mythical figures derived their status from the fact that their stories had taken place irrevocably and incontrovertibly in the past, the narrative of a character like Superman continues to unfold in the present, following the narrative logic of the modern novel:

The "civilization" of the modern novel offers a story in which the reader's main interest is transferred to the unpredictable nature of *what will happen* and, therefore, to the plot invention which now holds our attention. The event has not happened *before* the story; it happens *while* it is being told, and usually even the author does not know what will take place. (15)

The result of this is the absence—once again—of a normative structure: a narrative yardstick by which behavior can be measured reliably. In Eco's analysis, the perpetual unfolding of the narrative keeps superhero continuities in a kind of historical limbo, where details about basic temporality—questions about past, present, and future— remain consistently blurry. This lack of historical moorings ultimately establishes what he describes as "a paternalistic pedagogy, which requires the hidden persuasion that the subject is not responsible for his past, nor master of his future" (19).

This de-politicizing, de-historicizing force that Eco relates to the narrative structure of the Superman comic books closely resembles the Barthesian definition of myth. In his elaborate discussion of the semiological system of cultural mythologies, Barthes focuses on the way in which signs can present themselves as natural, thereby camouflaging their political and ideological nature:

In passing from history to nature, myth acts economically: it abolishes the complexity of human acts, it gives them the simplicity of essences, it does away with all dialectics, with any going back beyond what is immediately visible, it organizes a world which is without contradictions because it is without depth, a world wide open and wallowing in the evident, it establishes a blissful clarity: *things appear to mean something by themselves.* (1972: 143, emphasis added)

This definition fits the way in which superhero narratives provide systems whose function it is "to empty reality" and thereby to create representations that operate as depoliticized speech. By showing a diegetic world that appears internally coherent, "a world wide open and wallowing in the evident," these texts suggest that the same logic applies to real-world ideology (ibid.). In the same way that the neoliberal perspective has become hegemonic and now largely regulates the way we experience "reality," myth serves to naturalize all ideological forms: "it purifies them, it makes them innocent, it gives them a natural and eternal justification, it gives them a clarity which is not that of an explanation but that of a statement of fact" (ibid.).

I find it important to emphasize this Barthesian definition of "mythologies," especially when considering the increasing tendency to describe superhero narratives and other forms of popular fantasy as contemporary forms of myth, thus attributing very specific kinds of universal truth and legitimacy to these texts. Although the structuralist paradigm of Barthes' early period may not seem to connect with cultures of postmodernity that are increasingly both experienced and theorized as being decentered, the erosion of the boundaries between high and low culture has fostered a less critical attitude towards popular texts. With alarming frequency, "serious" superhero movies are now often interpreted as social and/or political allegories, and discussed in full earnestness in terms of "what they teach us" about ourselves. Barthes' emphatic foregrounding of the ideological overdetermination of meaning in popular culture offers a much more helpful way to unpack the political implications of this type of fantasy fiction. The emphasis can now be placed squarely on how language and other signifying systems present as natural that which is socially, ideologically, and politically determined, and how these discursive representational systems ultimately embody a form of normative social power.

In the specific case of superhero narratives, this erosion can be witnessed in the wave of "graphic novels" that appeared in the mid-1980s. Authored by figures such as Alan Moore and Frank Miller, DC Comics published a selection of superhero narratives that were aimed at a more highbrow, adult readership than traditional superhero comic books, and which were re-published to great acclaim as single-volume narratives with a more explicitly "literary" appeal. Although this industry move was a strategic development intended to expand the medium's market, and therefore its profitability, one of the results was a renegotiation of the comic book's relative position within the cultural hierarchy. Comics such as *Watchmen* (1986) and *Batman: The Dark Knight Returns* (1986) "expanded the literary possibilities of the superhero genre" by introducing themes, styles and motifs previously associated with "high" literature (Wright 271): familiar characters like Batman were reframed in a more ambiguous context, and their new narratives tended to emphasize the political, moral, and philosophical issues that were previously only rarely made explicit in the superhero genre.

But although this successful group of texts remains most celebrated for its socio-political perspective on the superhero genre, its historical influence on the later development of the medium is again indicative of the decentered nature of postmodern discourse. The introduction of the term "graphic novel" in the late 1980s did not result in a new, stable category of literature. Instead, usage of this term quickly broke off into various definitions that were as arbitrary as they were contradictory. One influential aspect of these texts was that they included more graphic violence than traditional comic books, leading to a trend in comics publishing towards more violent and graphic subject matter, the more explicit sex and violence adding somewhat different associations to the term *graphic*. For publishers, the publicity generated by these texts paved the way to new distribution formats, as collections of previously published installments of superhero comics could now also be re-packaged and marketed as "graphic novels." For other audience groups, the term referred to the developing subgenre of mainstream comic books that were presented in terms of their literary ambitions, and which included a diverse collection of texts ranging from Art Spiegelman's *Maus* (1986-1991) to Neil Gaiman's *The Sandman* series (1989-1996). The introduction of this new term to the vocabulary of comic book culture thus merely increased the level of fragmentation that typified the emerging neoliberalism of its decade.

But despite this apparent fracturing of stable signification, Jameson helpfully points out that "a system that constitutively produces differences remains a system" (1991: 343). What this statement indicates is not that all meaning is lost in postmodernity, or that texts and utterances can no longer be understood as part of a larger system that constitutes subjects in terms of power. It does however mean that our analysis requires a shift of perspective from the classical, normative oppositions to a field of competing discourses in which truth is no longer a matter of objective fact, but of a majority opinion ultimately (if fleetingly) deciding which discourse wins out over others. The process through which subject formation takes place is therefore no longer defined in terms of a simple binary opposition of dominant ideology occupying a position of hegemony, but as a more complex field of multiple competing discourses of power and meaning.

Within this competing field of discourses, those cultural and political statements assigning very specific narrative categories to recent history have been dominant in contemporary American discourse. As cultures and practices of neoliberalism have intensified over the past two decades, the post-9/11 years have seen a strong emphasis on new forms of myth-making emerge alongside anxieties concerning disaster capitalism and global terrorism. Both the desire to reestablish a sense of traditional order and the fears associated with contemporary crises are evident in the contemporary superhero film.

Superman and Patriarchal Predestination: "The Son Becomes the Father"

Few superheroes have consistently embodied aspects of American identity as long or as successfully as Superman. As the first major figure in popular fiction to combine familiar figures from pulp fiction with superhuman abilities that made him virtually indestructible, he was also the first of the Golden Age comics icons to cross over into other media: from the 1940s Max Fleischer cartoons to post-war B-movies, and from radio serials to the popular 1950s television show. A recurring icon throughout twentieth-century popular iconography, the character's appearance in *Superman* (dir. Richard Donner, 1978) and its three sequels would not only help define postclassical blockbuster cinema as a commodity, but also came to function as a de facto template for most subsequent superhero movies.

It is relevant to note that this first true A-list superhero film franchise, made up of four films that appeared from 1978 to 1987, was so lucrative during the Reagan era. Like so many other popular films from this decade, the series displayed a strong tendency towards nostalgia from its very start. Throughout the films, we see jaded, cynical reporter Lois Lane being won over by Superman and his alter ego Clark Kent as the embodiment of the traditional values of a more innocent, less complicated age. Like *Back to the Future* (dir. Robert Zemeckis, 1985), *Happy Days* (ABC, 1974-84), and many other popular films and TV shows from the early 1980s, this film seeks the answers to the post-Watergate, post-Vietnam sense of American cultural malaise in the romanticized patriarchal values of the 1950s. These films fully embrace Jameson's "nostalgia mode" as they de-historicize the postmodern present by continuously referring back to a glorified past that never truly existed in the first place.

Like *Star Wars* (dir. George Lucas, 1977), *Star Trek: The Motion Picture* (dir. George Wise, 1979), and the other popular fantasy films that ushered in the age of the postclassical blockbuster, *Superman* plays up its cultural nostalgia to the hilt. This is most evident in the way gender roles are represented in these films: while central female characters like Lois Lane and Princess Leia superficially seem to align themselves with second-wave feminism, the narratives they populate are organized to restore the radically neoconservative forms of patriarchal power that accompanied the rise of American neoliberalism. While these two terms may sound antithetical, American discourses of neoliberalism and neoconservatism have in fact maintained and even strengthened each other from the 1970s onward. Since neoliberal theory focuses so exclusively on radical economic policies of deregulation and globalization, it has been consistently accompanied by neoconservative values, both in the US and in other nations.

The basic compatibility of these two movements is established by the fact that "neoconservatives favor corporate power, private enterprise, and the restoration of class power," which makes this cultural movement "entirely consistent with the neoliberal agenda of elite governance, mistrust of democracy, and the maintenance of market freedoms" (Harvey 2005: 82). While neoliberalism established a new set of economic rules for the age of global capitalism, neoconservatism supplied a form of cultural mythology that filled up the system's moral and ethical vacuum:

> The moral values that have now become central to the neoconservatives can best be understood as products of the particular coalition that was built in the 1970s, between elite class and business interests intent on restoring their class power, on the one hand, and an electoral base among the "moral majority" of the disaffected white working class on the other. The moral values centred on cultural nationalism, moral righteousness, Christianity (of a certain

evangelical sort), family values, and right-to-life issues, and on antagonism to the new social movements such as feminism, gay rights, affirmative action, and environmentalism. (84)

One important part of the neoliberal political project therefore involved the introduction of mythical frameworks that naturalize these historically specific cultural values. *Superman* is one of the best examples of such an origin story that revolves around the restoration of patriarchal structures, and has since become a model that has been copied by a wide variety of other texts in the larger genre of popular fantasy.

A similar narrative pattern has been described by Joseph Campbell as the monomyth of the "hero's journey," although his perspective attributes a troubling universality and cultural and aesthetic value to this deeply sexist and arguably proto-colonialist narrative framework. A more critical perspective on this type of trajectory using Lacan's psychoanalytical vocabulary allows us to recognize the recurring tropes and patterns in these popular fantasies, but without attributing to them the neutral-sounding qualities associated with enduring mythical structures. Moreover, the Superman myth —especially in this particular incarnation— reveals itself to be more accurately a dramatization of the "natural" superiority of masculine power and the absolute hegemony of patriarchal genealogies.

The film's prologue wastes no time in establishing Superman's father Jor-El (played by Marlon Brando) as the omnipotent, idealized father figure associated with the embodiment of Lacan's symbolic order. The opening scene, set on the planet Krypton, introduces Jor-El not only as just such a God-like father figure, but as one of this alien society's wisest rulers whose prime concern is carrying out Lacan's "paternal function":

The paternal function concentrates in itself both imaginary and real relations, always more or less inadequate to the symbolic relation that essentially constitutes it. It is in the name of the father that we must recognize the support of this symbolic function which, from the dawn of history, has identified this person with the figure of the law. (Lacan 74)

The figure of the father therefore represents in Lacanian terms a symbolization of knowledge and power that ultimately serves to structure the coordinates of existing reality. Although this realm of the Symbolic ultimately proves to be riddled with gaps and inconsistencies, narrative fiction helps to suture these potentially traumatic flaws by reinforcing the father's role as ultimate Law-Giver. Significantly, *Superman*'s first scene shows Jor-El rendering judgment, his deciding vote imposing the "Law of the Father" on the criminal General Zod and his two followers, whose removal from Krypton's symbolic order figuratively represents the castration associated with patriarchal punishment. Lending further weight to Jor-El's dominant hierarchical position, he is also a scientist whose accurate predictions of his planet's impending demise are —somewhat implausibly— ignored and even contradicted by the other members of the ruling council. Rather than fleeing Krypton with his wife and newborn child, he instead sends his son Kal-El to Earth in a star-shaped space vessel, allowing both the narrative and its central imagery to resonate with an abundance of motifs from Judeo-Christian religious mythology.

During his lengthy journey across the universe, the infant Kal-El is subsequently inscribed by the knowledge of his father, as recordings of the paternal voice teach him scientific knowledge and moral values. This literal and symbolic journey marks the first step of Kal-El's development as a patriarchal subject whose identity is defined in the first instance by the father figure's system of rules, and whose trajectory will follow the familiar Oedipal patterns that structure most forms of popular fantasy. As in *Star Wars* and so many other

Clark Kent contemplates the phallic Kryptonian crystal
left to him by his father in *Superman.*

superhero films, the young protagonist in *Superman* is soon
surrounded by an abundance of father figures, each of whom
must perish in order to open up the space for the hero's Oedipal
trajectory that should supposedly culminate in fully developed
masculinity.

Following the death of foster father "Pa" Kent, Kal-El (who
has now adopted the name Clark Kent) discovers his true identity
by —literally— unearthing his biological father's legacy. His
discovery of this phallus-shaped shard of Kryptonian crystal
leads him to abandon his adopted home in provincial Smallville
and journey to the North Pole, where the crystal automatically
constructs for him his famous Fortress of Solitude. Within this
fortress, Kal-El faces a projected image of his father Jor-El, which
imparts to him the knowledge that will finally allow him to
recognize his true fate and become Superman. It is again significant that this moment of self-recognition is predicated upon the
Law of the Father, whose instructions include not only the
explicit acknowledgment of true patriarchal lineage, but which
also provide a strict set of unbreakable rules. The most emphatic
of these rules concerns the prohibition from intervening in
human history: Superman's explicit imperative is to assist
mankind, but unlike the figures from Judeo-Christian mythology

to which he is so frequently compared, he is forbidden from altering the existing power structures.

This crucial moment in Superman's trajectory towards full masculinity clearly marks Lacan's mirror stage: the moment at which the subject recognizes himself as separate from the world around him, and becomes able to assume his role in the patriarchal symbolic order. This interpretation of the scene is strengthened by the design of the Fortress of Solitude, which seems to be constructed entirely out of reflective glass, and even more by the moment at which Kal-El gazes into the mirror, only to see his own likeness transformed into his father's image. Working within the patriarchal coordinates that structure *Superman* and similar popular fantasy narratives, Kal-El's first step towards masculinity thus arrives through an explicit (mis)recognition of himself as his true father, who must remain simultaneously present and absent to bestow a sense of self upon the story's true subject.

Kal-El sees the face of his father reflected back
at him in the Fortress of Solitude.

The fact that Kal-El literally erects his Fortress of Solitude by casting off the phallic shard of Kryptonian crystal inherited from his father also perfectly illustrates Lacan's differentiation between the phallic *signified* and the phallic *signifier*:

The phallic signified is the part of *jouissance* integrated into the paternal symbolic order (phallus as the symbol of virility, penetrating power, the force of fertility and insemination, etc.); while the phallus as signifier stands for the price the male subject has to pay if he is to assume the "meaning of the phallus," its signified. (Žižek 1999: 453)

Thus, in order to gain access to the *jouissance* of unmediated drive that is symbolized in the superhero films by the protagonist's superhuman powers, Superman in this example must first discard the phallic signified. This points towards one of the reasons why the neoconservative myths of masculinity embodied by these popular symbolic fictions continue to resonate so strongly, as the price the superhero always seems to pay for "virility" and "penetrating power" is precisely the loss of the phallic signifier, thereby indefinitely deferring any sense of actual masculinity. In order to maintain the symbolic fiction of pure patriarchal authority, the male hero must in true fact operate as if he has already been castrated and has suffered the loss of that phallic signifier.

This foundational relationship established in the film between Superman's process of becoming a true subject and the role of his absent, idealized father also illustrates what Žižek describes as the "hidden call for a renewed paternal authority, for a father who would really be a 'true father' and adequately embody his symbolic mandate" (1999: 404). But since the traditional role of patriarchal power has been undermined by the increased fluidity and ephemerality of postmodernism, the father figure can no longer operate completely as the true bearer of symbolic authority. Instead of representing the Freudian Ego Ideal, the father is now perceived as one's *ideal ego* or "imaginary competitor — with the result that subjects never really 'grow up,' that we are dealing today with individuals in their thirties and forties who remain, in terms of their psychic economy, 'immature' adolescents competing with their fathers" (ibid.).

This explains why Superman's Oedipal trajectory must also remain incomplete, as the film's narrative so vividly illustrates. His romance with Lois Lane can never be truly consummated in the Superman mythology because the character's Oedipal development is perpetually thwarted: his father's rule has gone unchallenged, and Lois Lane continues to perceive him (in his disguise as Clark Kent) as a boy she continuously corrects and chastises as if she were his mother. Superman's choice to continue to masquerade as the immature Clark Kent thus illustrates the perverse Oedipal engine of one of the narrative's most consistent dynamics. Only when Superman's unfailing acceptance of the Law of the Father ultimately leads to Lois Lane's death does he finally decide to go against his father's primary law, which forbids him from interfering in the larger course of human history. Superman breaks this prohibition by flying around the world in order to temporarily reverse the flow of time, while the ghostly image of Jor-El's face appears briefly among the clouds, and his words "it is forbidden" echo menacingly on the soundtrack again and again.

The image of Superman's father appears in the clouds
with his repeated patriarchal prohibition.

Superman's relationship towards his father therefore follows the exact trajectory described by Žižek in his use of Lacanian terminology: the father is introduced —nostalgically— as the bearer of the symbolic mandate associated with traditional forms of authority. But in order for the film to reach its climax and the protagonist to embrace his own true form of masculinity, he must be forced to break his father's primary prohibition. The primary Law of the Father is always the prohibition of incest, which is here—in an obvious instance of Freudian displacement—transferred onto an arbitrary rule of non-involvement. But since the father now comes to operate as imaginary competitor, Superman's Oedipal trajectory remains incomplete, and the traditional moment of sexual consummation must again be indefinitely deferred, as must his ascension into maturity.

Superman's origin story as presented in this 1978 film is therefore organized along patriarchal coordinates that reflect the postmodern contradictions surrounding the Law of the Father. It is important to note therefore the specific focus of the 1978 film in relation to previous incarnations of the character. Neither the comic books nor the popular television series of the 1950s had anything resembling this kind of elaborate focus on Superman's relationship with his father and his consistent failure to meet patriarchal standards. Instead, the most popular versions of the character in the past, of the Golden Age comic books and the radio and television series, tended to present Superman as an infallible embodiment of patriarchal power himself: "fatherly, conservative, and trustworthy" (Morrison ch. 4). And although part of the film's appeal for late-1970s audiences obviously did lie in its nostalgic qualities, it was (again, like *Star Wars*) very much the combination of the hyper-nostalgic and the hyper-modern that enabled its blockbuster success: while the old-fashioned heroic adventure story together with the resurrection of the age-old childhood icon of Superman continuously played up Jameson's "nostalgia mode," the use of spectacular visual effects and the incorporation of feminism on the most superficial level made the film resonate strongly with contemporary audiences.

In many ways, *Superman* reflects the rising tide of American cultural and political change that would usher in the Ronald Reagan administration and the government's embrace of neoliberal economic policies alongside neoconservative cultural values throughout the 1980s. Three sequels to the film were released in this decade, as well as occasional spinoff attempts like *Supergirl* (dir. Jeannot Szwarc, 1984), but the elaborate visual effects required for this kind of popular fantasy proved to be prohibitively expensive. In its place, the hyper-masculine action film genre flourished, featuring hard-bodied supermen who are not weighed down by Superman's sensitive, more feminine Clark Kent persona. Only with the development of digital cinema in the late 1990s would the comic book worlds of superhero fantasy narratives become more feasible again, and *Superman* proved to be the most frequently copied template for origin story narratives in the 21st-century superhero movie cycle.

Superman Returns: 9/11 and Narratives of Continuity

Given the resurgence of superheroes in the movies since 2001, Superman's return to the cinema screen was all but inevitable, especially when one considers the intensification of neoconservative cultural values and neoliberal policy that made up the Bush Doctrine in the post-9/11 years. Following several abortive attempts to re-imagine Superman in a radically updated guise, he finally appeared in the 2006 summer blockbuster *Superman Returns*. This franchise reboot proved to be an exercise in nostalgic one-upmanship, as Bryan Singer's picture goes out of its way to recreate the experience of the 1978 film, thereby fashioning itself into the ultimate Buadrillardian simulacrum: an identical copy without a true original. From its opening credits, which provide a spectacular recreation of the earlier film's titles, to its nostalgic representation of the urban environment of Metropolis, this 21st-century blockbuster displays an obsessive longing for the pre-9/11 days of 1950s-inspired Reaganomics.

In a remarkable plot twist, the film updates the Superman chronology with the notion that Superman abandoned earth "five years ago," which works out as the year 2001, at which time Lois Lane published the Pulitzer Prize-winning editorial "Why the World Doesn't Need Superman." Returning at the start of the film from his self-imposed exile, an unusually morose and mournful Superman is immediately struck by a brief series of television images that illustrate a context of increased global conflict. The swift montage of instantly familiar imagery is strangely generic: shots of helicopters firing off missiles in a desert sky, firemen digging in burnt-out ruins, and an Arab woman in Islamic head-dress wailing towards the camera. Superman's expression in response to these images conveys disappointment and incredulity: the global situation has clearly deteriorated dramatically during his absence in the five years since the 9/11 terrorist attacks.

This opens up the question whether Kal-El might once again decide to break his father's prohibition and involve himself with human history by turning his attention from individual instances of criminality to the social and political structures and institutions that produce them. But this scene mainly establishes a general sense that things have gone badly wrong in his absence, and that Earth has reached a point of dramatic worldwide crisis. Nowhere else in the film does this crisis take on a specific form that reflects any of the real-world catastrophes and geopolitical conflicts suggested by this news footage. As in the 1978 *Superman* film, references to contemporary history remain limited to the fashions and technologies that were current at the time of production, while no mention is made of recent terrorist attacks, wars being fought by American troops, or economic crises. Instead, Superman's new global presence is limited to international news reports of his assistance in natural disasters, averted suicides, bank robberies, and so forth. While *Superman Returns* does give its hero an increased global presence, it does so in ways that affirm American imperial sovereignty: what stands behind Superman's interventions around the world "is not just a permanent state of emergency and exception, but a permanent state of emergency and exception justified by *the appeal to essential values of justice*" (Hardt and Negri 18). In other words, Superman now functions as the physical embodiment of the universality associated with American Empire in the age of globalization.

Unlike most other superhero franchise reboots, this new adventure operates not so much as a reinvention of its main character, but instead functions as a combined sequel and update to the first two films in the 1980s Superman film franchise (albeit one that reorganizes the chronology and — obviously — reshuffles characters and events). This unusually complex and even contradictory relationship between this film and its precursors in the previously established franchise illustrates that Eco's observations about the character's ahistorical nature continue to hold true outside of the comic books: the exact chronology of story events from one episode to the next becomes increasingly blurry, for "the narrator picks up the strand of the event again and again as if he had forgotten to say something and wanted to add details to what had already been said" (17).

But although there are no explicit references to contemporary real-world issues in *Superman Returns*, the film does continuously reference the imagery and sets of discourses that are specific to its historical moment. This is made very clear in its first major action set piece, when the once-ubiquitous superhero makes his first public appearance. Superman's return is made known to the world by his spectacular rescue of an airliner that is about to crash into a sold-out baseball stadium. This scene offers up a remarkable rewriting of the 9/11 attacks, organized around the image of an airliner hurtling towards an assembly of innocent Americans. The crucial difference in the film is of course is that Superman is able to use his death- and gravity-defying power to stop the plane at the very last moment before it destroys a site that symbolizes youthful innocence, American cultural identity, and traditions of passive spectatorship. The location also turns this remarkable last-minute rescue operation into a sheer spectacle that is immediately followed by rapturous applause, thereby managing to transform a historical moment of disaster and trauma into a celebration of heroism and visual spectacle.

This rewriting of calamity is typical of the way in which popular culture relating to 9/11 has relegated the events to representations voided of all historical meaning. The specificity of the baseball stadium as the location for this explosive sequence thereby functions at two different levels. Firstly, it embodies the basically spectatorial nature of postmodern culture, with the crowd functioning as surrogates, or even virtual duplicates, for the movie audience watching the spectacle unfold in a movie theater, which is encouraged to mimic the screen audience's thrilled response. Secondly, the choice of a baseball stadium as the site for which the crashing aircraft is headed avoids the potentially traumatic irruption of historical reality within this fantasy film. With baseball embodying a strongly transhistorical sense of "American-ness," the location activates associations of nostalgia that reach into a hazy past defined in terms of "innocence" rather than class, geopolitics, or ideology. As in the earlier example from *Black Hawk Down*, this once again creates an evacuation of historical meaning, in which the experience is defined in terms only of an inexplicable, unforeseeable, and visually spectacular threat. While the sequence therefore does clearly play on the tension and anxiety associated with a specific historical trauma, it is transformed into delighted relief through the use of a superior force that leaves the audience thoroughly impressed, adequately entertained, but essentially powerless.

Narratively similar but tonally different from its 1978 antecedent, the film then proceeds to alternate between elaborately staged action set pieces and the narrative development of the film's two major plots: Superman's troubled relationship with Lois Lane, which has lost some of its former innocence now that she has a husband and child, and villain Lex Luthor's plans to use Kryptonian crystals to create a new continent in the middle of the Atlantic Ocean. These two main plots converge as Luthor captures Lois Lane and her son, and Superman must again find a way to save both the world and the object of his personal affection. As the film builds towards its climax, the creation of Luthor's new continent causes shockwaves that surge through the streets of Manhattan, shattering skyscraper windows as the tall buildings of Metropolis teeter and sway realistically, their occupants and passers-by alike helpless in the face of their predicament.

Generically speaking, this part of the narrative is nothing short of a requirement for the Superman franchise, referring back not just to the original *Action Comics* panels, which were based "more than anything before it ... on the destruction of New York City" (Page 92), but also to the iconic Fleischer brothers animated shorts, which "give one the sense that the city is a fragile vessel, constantly under attack, crashing, breaking, bending" (98). Much of the pleasure of *Superman Returns* results from the film's determination to satisfy these expectations, providing spectacular imagery of Superman dashing around the city in a series of last-minute rescues that update the visual effects while remaining true to the established narrative formula.

But beyond these generic requirements, *Superman Returns* develops a more complex relationship to the 1978 *Superman* that establishes a direct genealogical lineage for this new film. For while the other characters are now played by a new cast of actors, Superman's dead father Jor-El is once again represented by Marlon Brando, seemingly acting from beyond the grave in a series of outtakes from the older film that have been digitally integrated into this new picture. Choices such as these create a deliberate sense of continuity between the two texts, pointing towards a clear point of origin that anchors the 2006 film to a very specific tradition within the fragmented Superman chronology. The character's reverence for the father figure of Jor-El is mirrored not only through the incorporation of the Brando footage within the film, but also extradiegetically by director Bryan Singer's devotion to Richard Donner, composer John Ottman's tribute to predecessor John Williams, and actor Brandon Routh's casting in the film "because he physically resembles Christopher Reeve" (Ebert n. pag.).

This tremendous accumulation of patriarchal tradition is enhanced even further by the ways in which *Superman Returns* explicitly thematizes anxieties surrounding patriarchal lines of heritage as central to its plot. Besides the introduction of Lois's son and the many questions revolving around the identity of his "real" father, Singer's film also positions Lex Luthor as a direct interloper who seeks to supplant Superman in the line of patriarchal succession. The key moment in this plotline arrives when Luthor invades the Fortress of Solitude and plays back the holographic recordings of Jor-El that were intended to impart knowledge to Superman. As the recording is activated, Luthor sees the face of Jor-El reflected in the collection of mirrors all around him, addressing Luthor as "my son." When Jor-El speaks to Luthor, an extreme close-up of actor Kevin Spacey's face communicates surprise and emotion as he says: "He thinks I'm his son." This adds to the ongoing Oedipal narrative a motif of fraternal rivalry, with Luthor playing Cain to Superman's more perfect Abel. And if Superman is represented as the inheritor of a benevolent form of patrician aristocracy, Luthor clearly stands for the destabilizing force of "new money" and speculative capitalism.

As in *Superman*, Luthor's jealous scheme to outwit Superman is based on financial speculation in real estate values: by sinking California into the Pacific Ocean in an attack on America's west coast in 1978, and by creating a new Kryptonian continent off the

Lex Luthor sees the image of Jor-El reflected
back at him in the Fortress of Solitude.

eastern seaboard in the 2006 film, and thus submerging the eastern states. In both cases, Luthor's plot revolves around concepts central to neoliberal capitalism: the manipulation of financial markets, the radical instability of value, and the profitability of disaster capitalism. *Superman Returns* thematizes even more strongly than the earlier film Luthor's desire to supplant not only Superman's hegemony over Earth by radically remapping geographical coordinates, but the fact that he does so in order to usurp his place in the patriarchal order. Luthor's failure is ultimately compounded by the establishment of Superman as the true father of Lois Lane's young son, allowing him to end the film by repeating his own father's words "The son becomes the father. And the father, the son."

This continuous foregrounding of the cyclical nature of patri-archal genealogies is typical of the origin story in the superhero movie, which has responded in numerous ways to the contra-dictory anxieties of postmodern ephemerality and new systems of flexible accumulation. While the fundamental forms of social and economic instability associated with finance capitalism have been developing since the 1970s, they have undergone substantial intensification in the more recent years of globalized neoliberalism. For as David Harvey has suggested, it is exactly "at such times of fragmentation and economic insecurity that the desire for stable values leads to a heightened emphasis upon the authority of basic institutions" (1990: 171). In both Superman films under discussion here, these "basic institutions" are clearly represented in terms of the authority of the father figure and the continuity that is associated with the re-establishment of an unbroken genealogy passed on from father to son. They therefore develop ongoing myths of patriarchal predestination that strengthen neoconservative values in the form of mythical popular fantasies.

While the Superman films so clearly foreground this obsession with undisputed origins in relation to existing power structures, these mythological frameworks are simultaneously brought into collision with specific contemporary anxieties such as global terrorism and disaster capitalism. This collision is most evident towards the end of *Superman Returns*, as the film seeks to consolidate the narrative's mythological qualities with imagery that resonates strongly in its connection to post-9/11 concerns. This strange dissonance between the unavoidable associations with recent history and the Jamesonian "perpetual present" of postmodernism that typifies this sequence in generic terms is one of the most interesting theoretical issues raised by *Superman Returns*: how can this film simultaneously de-historicize while drawing its significance from clear references to historical events?

This paradox comes into sharper focus when Superman confronts Luthor in the middle of the surreal landscape of Luthor's newborn continent, where he discovers that his extraordinary powers have unexpectedly abandoned him. In a scene that has alienated many Superman fans, the superhuman "Man of Steel" is beaten savagely by Luthor's henchmen, strangely noticeable for being the only ethnically diverse group in the film, and finally stabbed in the back by the villainous mastermind himself. He stands up to face his attackers, but teeters and falls powerlessly off the edge of an immense precipice. In what may be the film's most provocative image, a long, unbroken shot shows "flying man" transformed into "falling man."

Few images have been as disturbing a summation of America's sense of helplessness and defeat as those of the people falling or jumping from the towers after the attack, and literary texts such as Jonathan Safran Foer's *Extremely Loud and Incredibly Close* (2005) and Don DeLillo's *Falling Man* (2006) have mobilized this iconic image of national disempowerment as a potent narrative metaphor:

> We are all, DeLillo suggests, in free fall. The plots, myths, institutions we once relied on to provide meaning and purpose are suspended. Our idols have fallen too: "God is the voice that says, 'I am not here.'" (Kauffmann 372)

This motif resonates not only with Superman's literal fall from grace in the above scene, but also with his earlier retirement as one of the planet's idols. If God is indeed the voice that says "I am not here," then *Superman Returns* may be read as an attempt to restore that godlike presence as a stable and reliable point of origin. But not only must Superman experience this fall from

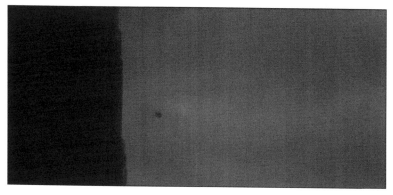

A powerless Superman tumbles down Luthor's cliff
as "flying man" becomes "falling man."

grace along with the American public; he must also somehow once again reverse time—another narrative motif in many 9/11 novels—and change the past in order to rectify the future. And indeed, after his inevitable moment of messianic resurrection, he lifts up the whole of Luthor's new continent into space, and playing on the film's innumerable references to Atlas, Milton, and Christian iconography, saves mankind by bearing the weight of the world for us, before plummeting once more back into the streets of Metropolis.

This sequence obviously offers a rewriting of the events of 9/11 that is different from the airplane sequence that occurred earlier in the film, which played on the imagery associated with the horrifying scale of the attacks, and the inevitability of their consequences. Through the intervention of a superheroic figure, disaster was transformed into victorious celebration, while simultaneously evacuating the moment of all context. The scene with Luthor uses 9/11 imagery to act out the defeat of Superman, as the returned embodiment of "truth, justice, and the American way" is brought to his knees by evil forces whose violence literally pierces his supposedly impenetrable physique, before dropping his body off a precipice. The violent penetration of Superman's body is as shocking, violent, and traumatic in the context of this superhero narrative as the violation of American geopolitical space for which this scene may be read as a clever metaphor. But again, this defeat is subsequently transformed into resurrection and triumph, the film's neoconservative values once again becoming evident in Superman's salvation by Lois Lane and her family. The traumatic wounding of Superman effectively functions to re-unite the traditional family, thus staving off the clear threat of divorce as the family unit is brought together again through the protagonist's heroic sacrifice.

Superman, as the picture suggests, is the pure embodiment of America's mythical exceptionalism, and his messianic return will relieve the country from the burden of the past by transforming the trauma of 9/11 into a narrative of heroic salvation and resurrection. Images of crashing airliners and falling men come to serve the dual narrative purpose of re-establishing a triumphant belief in transcendent American heroism bolstered by neoconservative family values. Kal-El's Oedipal trajectory, established so emphatically in the 1978 film, is continued here, even as its endpoint remains indefinitely deferred: having previously broken his father's prohibition, Superman now takes up his place in the patriarchal order by sacrificing his own desires in the interest of the newly restored family unit of which his biological son (and implied heir) is a part. Jor-El's oft-repeated line "the son becomes the father, and the father becomes the son" is repeated once more at the new film's climax in order to emphasize the cyclical nature of this endlessly repeatable (and sellable) narrative.

Both the traditional patriarchal organization of *Superman Returns* and its emphatic connection to the older film franchise therefore offer up a sense of continuity that is reassuring in times of crisis: "cyclical and repetitive motions ... provide a sense of security in a world where the general thrust of progress appears to be ever onwards and upwards into the firmament of the unknown" (Harvey 1990: 202). This form of symbolic narrative embodies ideology in the Althusserian sense at its clearest: as "a representational structure which allows the individual subject to conceive or imagine his or her lived relationship to transpersonal realities such as the social structure or the collective logic of History" (Jameson 1981: 14-15). By drawing on the iconography and themes of contemporary public and political discourse while situating their narratives in an explicitly fantastical realm, these superhero narratives provide legitimizations of ideological perspectives in ways that are similar to those of romance literature. As Fredric Jameson observed so memorably in his analysis of this type of text and its ideological subtext, this genre "does not involve the substitution of some more ideal realm for ordinary reality ... but rather a process of *transforming* ordinary reality" (ibid. 97). In other words: films like *Superman* and *Superman Returns* offer models for interpreting our own world and its history that serve to systematically de-historicize the events to which they so obviously refer, thereby transforming historical reality into a fantastical work of fiction.

2

Disaster Capitalism
and the Traumatized Superhero

If the superhero movie is defined primarily by its continuous re-establishment of points of origin, as the previous chapter has argued, our second observation must be that these narratives are most commonly associated with notions of trauma. The superhero movies' representations of trauma seem to connect back in complex ways to a number of key historical ruptures, such as the Holocaust, the Vietnam war, and the terrorist attacks of 9/11. The phenomenal success of the superhero movie genre in the intensified neoconservative/neoliberal age of the post-9/11 years therefore begs the question in what way these films' popularity reflects the political and ideological issues that defined American and —increasingly— global policies and debates that have taken shape in the first decade of the 21st century.

The post-Cold War era of the 1990s was experienced by many in the affluent West as a period of relative political and economic stability. Given the crisis-prone nature of neoliberal capitalism, it should however not have come as a surprise that Clinton's "Pax Americana" would be followed in turn by years of chaos and disruption. Crises and catastrophes, David Harvey tirelessly reminds us, function as "the irrational rationalisers of an always unstable capitalism" (2008: 71), and will therefore logically and predictably erupt over and over again as long as the system of capitalism continues to exist. The resulting lack of stability has come to be known in our own time as "disaster capitalism," a term that was popularized by author Naomi Klein in her book *The Shock Doctrine*. In this book, Klein argues that the forceful introduction of neoliberal economic doctrine has generally been accompanied by torture, militarization, and the loss of civil liberties.

This argument connects on the one hand to contemporary critical theory, where radical thinkers such as David Harvey, Slavoj Žižek, Paul Virilio, and Michael Hardt and Antonio Negri have articulated the relationship between capitalism and perpetual states of crisis and global catastrophe. On the other hand, cultural historians have described how capitalist culture has grown increasingly immersed in forms of imagery and popular narrative that articulate this relationship between capitalism and catastrophe. While all of these diverse perspectives demonstrate that there is nothing new about the catastrophic nature of capitalist cultures and economies, they do agree that the form of global capitalism first introduced in the 1970s, and incrementally intensified in subsequent decades, has strongly increased the more volatile aspects of this system.

One of the main effects of the rise of neoliberalism has been the institutionalization of class-based wealth and power, as each new crisis provided political opportunities for the disenfranchisement of the working class and the concentration of monopoly power. With the waves of privatization and the dramatic increase in the outsourcing of traditional government functions from the early 1980s onwards, neoliberalism became a truly global phenomenon in the 1990s, after the end of the Cold War and the dissolution of the Soviet bloc. Increasingly, governments and corporations became interchangeable entities, heralding a new constitutional form described by Philip Bobbitt as "the market state," and by Naomi Klein as "corporatism":

A more accurate term for a system that erases the boundaries between Big Government and Big Business is not liberal, conservative or capitalist but corporatist. Its main characteristics are huge transfers of public wealth to private hands, often accompanied by exploding debt, an ever-widening chasm between the dazzling rich and the disposable poor and an aggressive nationalism that justifies bottomless spending on security ... But because of the obvious drawbacks for the vast majority of the population left outside the bubble, other features of the corporatist state tend to include aggressive surveillance (once again, with government and large corporations trading favors and contracts), mass incarceration, shrinking civil liberties and often, though not always, torture. (18-19)

The corporate benefits of this system have been many: not only do economic, ecological, and terrorist disasters provide opportunities for direct economic profits, but they also have the advantage of keeping populations in a perpetual state of shocked pliability. The traumatizing and disorienting nature of catastrophe has thus facilitated the introduction of many political and economic changes during or directly after such moments of calamity, as they were likely to be met with little resistance by populations that were increasingly reduced to a perpetual state of traumatized passivity.

As I have discussed in the previous chapter, the primary Western catastrophe of the early 21st century came in the form of the terrorist attacks of 11 September 2001, which serve as an example of how such disasters can be seized by political and economic leaders as an opportunity to intensify the cultures and policies of globalized neoliberalism and neoconservatism. The attacks, instantly transformed into a spectacular visual image that emptied out the events of all historical and geopolitical context, became the lightning rod that displaced growing economic anxiety and the looming financial crisis onto a global culture war that would be fought on all possible fronts, including military interventions: "just as the internet had launched the dot-com bubble, 9/11 launched the disaster capitalism bubble" (Klein 377).

The resulting political and cultural polarization built upon a number of Gramsci's "common-sense truths," the first of which was the sense of trauma that was widely experienced as the public's natural response to the attacks. The attacks and their exceptionally homogeneous media representation achieved the impossible: America and, by association, the entirety of the affluent West could now suddenly adopt the role of the victim of history rather than its violent oppressor. In Islamic fundamentalism, America had identified a new and unexpectedly capable "Other" that enabled the emergence of a simplistic set of binary opposites. The identification of this new enemy would further legitimize the American government's neoliberal agenda, even as the War on Terror served mainly to increase the wealth of a small elite: "it has been part of the genius of neoliberal theory to provide a benevolent mask full of wonderful-sounding words like freedom, liberty, choice, and rights, to hide the grim realities of the restoration or reconstitution of naked class power" (Harvey 2005: 119). In other words, the comforting myth of trauma and victimization served to camouflage a series of aggressive neoliberal policies that had the increase of corporate wealth and political power as their primary aim.

This social and political reorientation on the basis of new fears was also articulated via the narratives of popular culture, which — as ever— reflected many of the concerns and anxieties that come to inform the "Zeitgeist." As nebulous a notion as this is, new groups of texts and the developing cultural practices that surround them do have themes in common that are ultimately determined by their underlying economic and political structures, similar to what Jameson describes as the text's "political unconscious." In the case of America's political and cultural responses to the attacks of 9/11, an analysis of representations of trauma and other rhetorical devices that have attempted to legitimize the War on Terror can teach us more about the relationship between neoliberalism and the cultures and narratives that help sustain it.

It has become commonplace to describe how the Bush administration's response to the attacks was economically motivated far more than it was ideological. Quickly adopting the vocabulary of Samuel Huntington's "clash of civilizations," the direct benefits from an American point of view quite obviously involved the swift development of "a booming new industry that breathed new life into the faltering U.S. economy" (Klein 14). Armed geopolitical conflict had previously saved the American economy from a severe economic depression in the 1940s, resulting in the development of the nation's all-powerful military-industrial complex. But the military response to the trauma of 9/11 took on a different shape, as it used this new conflict as an opportunity to intensify the privatization of the military alongside what Paul Virilio has termed the militarization of public space.

Every aspect of the ongoing War on Terror thus came to reflect and adopt the logic of neoliberalism, which includes both its basic "There Is No Alternative" forcefulness and the way in which its flexible definition has "served to maximize its profitability and sustainability as a market—from the definition of the enemy to the rules of engagement to the ever-expanding scale of the battle" (Klein 379). Since this logic inevitably resulted in a hollowing-out of federal institutions, increasingly outsourcing traditional government functions to private companies, its result was not the utopian consumer society envisaged by many in the post-WWII years. Instead, the public witnessed a concentration of wealth among the ruling elite, while private debt, growing unemployment, and waning benefits resulted in an exponential increase in the quickly growing class of the disposable poor.

In short: the attacks of 9/11, as they were presented by American government and corporate-controlled mass media, were experienced by many as a moment of national trauma that allowed America to take on the role of the innocent victim in a new battle between good and evil. The Bush administration, following a strictly neoliberal agenda, took on the role of the reluctant stalwart hero, presenting its for-profit military enterprises as a violent revenge fantasy against an invisible global enemy. The superhero movie genre, one of the most popular and profitable mainstream genres to take shape during this period, gave dramatic form to the new fantasies, fears, and anxieties of this post-9/11 era of traumatized consumerism.

9/11 and the Trauma Narrative

On September 12, 2001, ABCnews.com published "Blow to the Psyche: Americans Will React With Fear, Anger—Danger for Some." According to this article, the destruction of the World Trade Center had already been dubbed an "Attack on America" and journalists were seeking the advice of mental health specialists concerning its effects on America's "psyche." One specialist cited in this article argued that "the trauma of the tragedy will be hard to escape regardless of physical distance from the wreckage in New York or Washington D.C. People who saw it or were part of it will obviously experience some trauma... Trauma is experienced vicariously by those who are some distance away." (Trimarco and Depret 31)

As the above example illustrates, trauma was one of the first public concerns to be explicitly associated with the events of 9/11. The attacks had famously been planned and staged for maximum media saturation, their impact grossly enhanced by the fact that a worldwide audience could watch the situation unfold on live television. This created a sense of immediacy that contributed to the general feeling that everyone watching the images on a television or computer screen was directly involved with the attacks, and therefore similarly affected by them. The resulting sense of widespread cultural trauma thus stood in no proportion to the number of people that had been physically present, or who had friends or relatives among the victims.

The term "trauma" is however often employed somewhat irresponsibly in these contexts, without much attention paid to specific symptoms, while causes are all too easily attributed to the similarly underdeveloped feelings of anxiety associated with terrorist attacks. Countless publications have been based on the simple assumption that the "imagined community" of the American people had been traumatized by the attacks of 9/11, and have then proceeded to read various forms of post-9/11 culture as direct symptoms of this trauma. Groups of literary texts were for instance identified as "9/11 novels," and have been widely interpreted as expressions of this sense of shared national trauma. Similarly, popular genres have been perceived as direct expressions of a wider sense of national grief in response to the attacks.[3]

Trauma theory may therefore be helpful in coming to terms with the relationship between these historical events and the narratives (both fictional and non-fictional) that have been identified as expressions of their traumatic effects. In their work on trauma theory, Cathy Caruth and Shoshana Felman have argued for the establishment of a connection between narrative and psychoanalysis because both are "interested in the complex relation between knowing and not knowing" (Caruth 3). This relationship between fictional narratives and personal memory is developed further by the theory that it is "at the specific point at which knowing and not knowing intersect that the language of literature and psychoanalytic theory of traumatic experience precisely meet" (ibid.). The application of psychoanalytical theory to fictional texts (whether in literature or from other media) is therefore appropriate not only because these texts, like personal memory, are invested in similar epistemological questions, but also and especially because fictional texts play a crucial role in the construction of cultural memory. Following Jameson, we can even make the claim that texts combine with each other to form an archive of cultural memory that provides our only point of access to the "Lacanian Real" of history (Jameson 1981: 20).

This conception of the trauma narrative is evident in the quotation that opened this section, as it strongly emphasizes the way in which the memory of traumatic events extends not only into recollections of the past, but affects our perception of the present and the future as well. The discursive activity of constructing a coherent narrative of the past is therefore an essential dialectical component of identity formation and the establishment of subjectivity. In order to create such a narrative, one necessarily requires more than merely a subjective memory of particular events: individuals must rely on interpretative communities and specific forms of mediation that ultimately produce a "common-sense" narrative, providing a shared framework for understanding the events that took place.

The traumatic nature of the events that cause this sensation of temporal and geographical dislocation can be understood through Freud's definition of the term "trauma," which Caruth employs as follows:

> The term trauma is understood as a wound inflicted not upon the body but upon the mind. But what seems to be suggested by Freud in *Beyond the Pleasure Principle* is that the wound of the mind – the breach in the mind's experience of time, self, and the world – is not, like the wound of the body, a simple and healable event, but rather an event that … is experienced too soon, too unexpectedly, to be fully known and is therefore not available to consciousness until it imposes itself again, repeatedly, in the nightmares and repetitive actions of the survivor. (3-4)

This definition of trauma as something experienced "too unexpectedly to be fully known" coincides with the singularity associated with 9/11, as discussed in more detail in the previous chapter. The continuous depictions and discussions of the attacks as exceptional events without warning or precedent facilitated their wider traumatic impact, along with the marked absence of attempts to produce narratives that could have established a political-historical context for them. For as Caruth argues, the required "rethinking of reference is aimed not at eliminating history but at resituating it in our understanding, that is, at precisely permitting history to arise where immediate under-standing may not" (11).

The importance of introducing historical awareness in coming to terms with traumatic events is especially noteworthy in the context of the earlier discussion of postmodernism: as a cultural dominant that is experienced as Jameson's "perpetual present" (1998: 119) or as what Paul Virilio defines as "monochronic time" (1997: 28). The lack of any historical bearings, not only in postmodernist culture at large, but also specifically as part of 9/11 discourse, strengthened the sense of public trauma that developed into such a strong characteristic of the events' cultural and political aftermath. This feature has become increasingly evident when looking not only at political discourse, but also at contemporary cultural life. My argument in this chapter will therefore be in some way circular: if developments in late capitalism have removed the historical coordinates and Grand Narratives that could help the individual "make sense" of historical trauma, the logical result is that postmodern subjects are deliberately kept in a state of disorientation. The result of this disorientation under neoliberalism is the creation of the "traumatized consumer": the true subject of disaster capitalism, whose conditioned response to each new crisis or catastrophe is expressed through higher levels of consumption, increased degrees of social alienation, and the thorough commodification of trauma through branding and popular narratives.

The contemporary superhero movie offers many instances of precisely this kind of trauma narrative. Just as many superhero movies have foregrounded the establishment of clear origin stories that create a sense of historical continuity, they have simultaneously provided trauma narratives that suggest a connection between traumatic experience and heroic victimization. Many of the post-9/11 films have connected these trauma narratives directly to contemporary themes and images associated with the terrorist attacks and the War on Terror, but the larger themes have been visible in the genre much earlier. Since the superhero archetype associated most strongly with trauma as a defining characteristic is Batman, the case studies in this chapter will draw on a number of different incarnations of this popular character. From the 1989 blockbuster that fully embodied the cultural logic of flexible accumulation to the post-9/11 film franchise, the most popular Batman films have mobilized some of the strongest contradictions in late capitalist culture, driven in each case by the explicit connection between traumatic memory and heroic victimization.

Branding the Batman

The superhero genre underwent a transformation in the public consciousness in the mid-1980s, when a series of comic books was published as part of a cycle that ultimately popularized the term "graphic novel." The popularity of limited series and one-off comic book issues brought increased mainstream attention to the superhero figure, and helped the medium acquire some degree of cultural and literary legitimacy. Much of this attention focused on the redefinition of familiar characters and narratives by new authors such as Alan Moore, Frank Miller, and Grant Morrison, with titles like *The Killing Joke*, *The Dark Knight Returns*, *Batman: Year One*, and *Arkham Asylum* effectively diversifying the appeal of the Batman brand for publisher DC Comics. These bestselling comic books had in common their more literary approach to the character and his mythology, while their varying levels of artistic ambition were embraced by a large readership as a welcome new maturity in superhero comics. But besides increasing the public visibility and commercial success of the Batman brand, these texts connected discourses of (re-)authorship to the generic superhero figure, while simultaneously diversifying the product to make it attractive to multiple audiences.

All of these traits are in evidence in the popular phenomenon *Batman* (dir. Tim Burton, 1989), the film that was released in a successful attempt to capitalize on the growing interest in the Batman comic books. But rather than adopting the more complex, ambiguous worldview of Frank Miller and Alan Moore's graphic novels, Tim Burton's film instead followed the model established by *Superman* a decade earlier, offering a nostalgic superhero tale driven by massive production values, high-profile casting, and ubiquitous marketing. This picture was also emphatically presented as a "franchise reboot" of a superhero narrative: a new film that reorders and reinterprets narrative and aesthetic elements from the ongoing history of a character with more than seventy years of chronology across numerous media. A film such as this has four main groups among its target audience: "'Long term fans of the comic books,' 'Short term fans,' 'Fans of the television series' and 'Audiences who were not fans of Batman in any sense'" (Brooker 279). During pre-production and early test screenings of the 1989 film, it became evident that the group of casual filmgoers was by far the most important group in terms of marketing, and was in fact the only audience of sufficient size to make such a film profitable. It makes more sense that superhero movies are tailored for audiences with the least investment in the comic book character when one realizes that comic books have been little more than a niche market for the past decades, in which time best-selling books only very rarely sell more than 100,000 copies per issue (Wright 293).

Big-budget films based on comic book properties therefore appeal to the largest possible audience by using ubiquitous advertising and product diversification. By the late 1980s, this type of branding and merchandising had developed into the primary force in Hollywood marketing and distribution. The original *Star Wars* franchise (1977-1983) had demonstrated with overwhelming force that the proceeds from ancillary products like toys, T-shirts, and video games could be far more profitable than the films they were organized around. This particular way of transforming a narrative property into a brand that could be successfully deployed across a wide variety of platforms was

bolstered further by the neoliberal turn in the 1980s, as the decade's wave of corporate mergers resulted in the swift vertical and horizontal integration of media and entertainment businesses: "companies upgraded international operations to a privileged position by expanding 'horizontally' to tap emerging markets worldwide, by expanding 'vertically' to form alliances with independent producers to enlarge their rosters, and by 'partnering' with foreign investors to secure new sources of financing" (Balio 58).

The theatrical poster for *Superman* (1978) and its tagline "You'll believe a man can fly."

In this context of corporate mergers and business diversification that was the direct result of neoliberal deregulation, global media companies developed an ever-stronger focus on branded entertainment commodities. The success of Batman as a ubiquitous global brand in 1989 thus represented the pinnacle of the neoliberalism that had dominated government policy throughout the preceding decade in Great Britain and the United States. The introduction and enforcement of neoliberal doctrine is indeed primarily associated with that period's government administrations of Reagan and Thatcher.

But as David Harvey suggests, their electoral victories and government policies should be understood as "a consolidation of what was already under way throughout much of the 1970s" (1990: 166-7). In the same way, the multimedia success of the *Batman* brand in 1989 may be considered a milestone in the sense that it represents an intensification of cultural and economic practices that had also started to take shape in the 1970s. These shifts were further facilitated by the growing neoliberalism of the 1980s, and found a new, heightened form in the cross-platform marketing of the Batman icon.

The theatrical poster for *Batman* (1989) emphasizes the logo over all else.

When comparing this 1989 film with the launch of *Superman* in 1978, some of the differences in the ways these films were marketed are significant. *Superman's* advertising campaign was primarily organized around the tagline "You'll believe a man can fly" in combination with the iconic Superman logo, which was pictured on the poster in embossed silver before a background of a dynamic cloudscape, neatly divided by a beam of red, yellow and blue light disappearing into the background. While the use of the Superman logo/shield guaranteed instant recognizability, the tagline emphasized the groundbreaking special effects, which were universally acclaimed for their spectacular realism, while its wording even suggested the veiled promise of a resurrection of some older belief system. The intertextual nature of the logo thus mobilized the spectator's knowledge of "Superman" as a familiar and fundamentally nostalgic brand, while the marketing campaign remained focused on the new film as a central, unifying text.

Batman's promotional materials on the other hand were much more polysemic, pointing in multiple directions simultaneously. The phenomenally successful marketing campaign was focused entirely on establishing the iconic Batman brand as a valuable property in its own right, rather than merely advertising a single commodity or text. The poster, which was circulated globally in every possible form, famously featured a newly refurbished black-and-gold Batman logo, bearing below it only the text "June 23." The studio's successful attempts to pre-sell the picture by establishing it as a multimedia event rather than a movie premiere had many benefits: the film poster served to publicize not only the film from which it was supposedly derived, but also anything else that featured this copyrighted brand. An identical image for instance was used for the cover of the Prince album featuring pop tracks both drawn from and inspired by the film, and which too was produced and distributed by parent company Time Warner. The track "Batdance," released as the album's first single, therefore came to function not only as a purchasable commodity in its own right, but was also "released before the film to precede it as an advertisement" (Donnelly 143).

The Warner Brothers logo morphing into the Batman sign in *Batman Forever* (1995).

Licensed baseball caps, T-shirts, pajamas, lunch boxes, and any number of other consumer products were distributed and sold on the basis of the unifying image of the gold-and-black Batman logo. Instead of functioning as the central text that unified its promotional materials, the film instead became one of many ancillary products of the ubiquitous logo: only a single instance of an endless number of ways of consuming the Batman brand, as the $1 billion made by *Batman*'s licensed merchandising products in that year accounted for four times the film's box-office earnings (Maltby 24). The governing logic behind the postclassical "event film" therefore became identical to that of a global corporation like Nike, marketing and selling a potentially infinite number of diversified commodities based on the instant recognizability of a single copyrighted brand. Wearing clothing or purchasing products that bore the yellow-on-black Batman logo had come to signify not so much one's fandom of the film, or even any particular appreciation of the new film's specific articulation of the character, but became instead "a mere gesture of participation in a particular cultural moment" (Pearson and Uricchio 183).

The degree to which the Batman film franchise came to be overshadowed by its corporate logo is illustrated by the opening of the third film in the series, *Batman Forever* (dir. Joel Schumacher, 1995). The movie begins, like all others distributed by Time Warner, with the image of the Warner Brothers logo, which subsequently morphs into the Batman logo, using computer technology that was a relative novelty at the time. This unusual moment, which was repeated in the next film in the Batman cycle, demonstrates an ostentatiously excessive degree of branding, illustrating how strongly the Batman logo had become synonymous with the corporate brand of its parent company. Similarly, the teaser trailer for the fourth film in the series, *Batman & Robin* (dir. Joel Schumacher, 1998), was devoted entirely to the introduction of a new logo that added a second, slimmer bat-shaped silhouette to the already world-famous Batman brand. Decisions like these made the film itself, its cast, and its plot even more of an afterthought to the marketing of a single copyrighted brand than before.

As blatant as these branded images of corporate-owned enter-tainment are, the neoliberal model of business integration and image marketing is also a core element in the films' narratives. The conflict between Batman and the Joker that provides the main plot for the 1989 film is presented first and foremost as a struggle over which one of them gains control of the mass media. Bruce Wayne is introduced in his mansion in an environment that most resembles a television studio, suggesting that he is as much a media mogul as a reclusive billionaire. Over and over in the film, we see both Batman and the Joker "watching television and manipulating images," reminding us that "the struggle between them is in large part a televisual one" (Collins 1991: 167). This reflects the film's hyperconsciousness, displaying an explicit awareness of its own status as a media product that relies on various forms of mass audience manipulation and media saturation. The film's self-reflexive play with the characters' many previous incarnations and traditions similarly foregrounds its emphasis on branding and convergence culture over narrative content.

The relationship that exists between these excessively branded films and their political and historical context is therefore primarily one of directly replicating the governing economic logic of the time: the form of "flexible accumulation" embodied by the cross-media diversification of the Batman brand accurately reflects the dominant paradigm that defined Western economic models of the period (Harvey 1990). The post-Cold War era was able to indulge once again in mythical archetypes organized around Manichean narrative structures: in *Batman*, the hero and villain represented uncomplicated icons of good and evil who not only balanced each other out in the story, but who were ultimately revealed to be responsible for each other's existence. The Joker is a psychopathic gangster, disfigured by having fallen into a vat of chemicals, whose preening, hammy performance relates back in equal measure to the character's garish comics and television incarnations as it does to actor Jack Nicholson's extra-diegetic celebrity persona. Bruce Wayne's childhood experience of losing his parents during a random back-alley mugging remains the primary origin story for the Batman character, but other than irrationally (or, more accurately: insanely) motivating his desire to fight crime, the trauma seems to have had little discernable effect on his character.

This is not unusual within the Batman comic book continuity: from *Detective* issue #33 onwards, where this origin story made its first appearance in November 1939, these formative events have usually tended to be presented with little fanfare (Brooker 54). In Tim Burton's film, Batman/Bruce Wayne views the murder of his parents primarily as a mystery to be solved, which the plot then proceeds to untangle by building towards the revelation that his arch-nemesis the Joker had been personally responsible for the crime. Instead of establishing any kind of explicit connections to the world outside the text, *Batman* instead presents a hermetically sealed world that is deliberately removed from historical context and psychological verisimilitude. Like *Superman* before it, the film plays on the audience's familiarity with discourses on the character that were dominant at the time of its release. Rather than offering an adaptation of the "original" source material, the film should be understood instead as "the adaptation of late-1980s discourses around the comic book Batman into the medium of cinema: firstly the notion of Batman as 'dark,' 'adult,' 'serious' and defined against the TV show, and secondly, the notion of creative freedom around authorship, of a new creator 'doing different' with the character" (Brooker 290).

The successful 1989-1997 Batman film franchise thus revolved around the economic model of ubiquitous branding and cross-platform diversification that defined this quickly developing age of neoliberalism and flexible accumulation. Powerful multimedia corporation Time Warner had capitalized upon one of its most long-standing brand names, and as a result, *"Batman* now belonged to a multi-national conglomeration and the global audience who bought the tickets and the merchandise, rather than to the dedicated comic readers and the community of writers, artists and editors who had themselves emerged from the ranks of fandom" (293). Its relationship to its moment in history resides both in its plot's emphasis on the media war undertaken by Batman and the Joker as well as in the way the films' production, marketing and distribution practices offer one of the clearest examples of the product diversification and economic deregulation provided by neoliberalism.

Batman Begins: Capitalist Heroes and the Clash of Civilizations

Batman Begins (dir. Christopher Nolan, 2005) offers a 21st-century retooling of an indestructible Golden Age superhero that is similar in many ways to that of *Superman Returns*, as discussed in the previous chapter. But like the title indicates, this superhero's return comes with a different kind of twist. For rather than the moderately revisionist continuation of an existing chronology and an established film franchise, Nolan's film presents itself as a new origin story or "franchise reboot": it reinvents an iconic character for a contemporary audience by re-sorting, re-shifting, and re-defining narrative and visual elements that make up the character's long and contradictory history. Like the 1989 film before it, *Batman Begins* plays up aspects of the character's mythology that are perceived by a contemporary audience as "authentic," and which re-define the brand's appeal in sharp contrast to an earlier, less popular incarnation.

The economic motivations behind the 21st-century film series devoted to the character are most likely identical to the main considerations that ultimately spawned the 1989 film and its sequels: once again, a set of discourses had emerged that made a superhero character a potentially profitable investment in mass culture. Whereas the 1980s had provided fertile ground for a big-budget Batman film thanks to developments in the comic book industry and deregulated media corporations, superheroes had re-emerged as a popular asset in Hollywood cinema. Not only do these entertainment franchises offer unique commercial opportunities for media corporations on a global scale, but they also thematize concerns that are central to post-9/11 disaster capitalism. Like many of the other films in this cycle, Nolan's film clearly draws on themes and images associated with 9/11 and its aftermath. But unlike the Spider-Man films (discussed in more detail in the next chapter), *Batman Begins* tends to avoid the garish forms of nostalgia that had been most common in the superhero movie genre since *Superman*, and focuses instead on a sustained investigation of trauma and its defining role in the post-9/11 superhero narrative.

In contrast to the Superman and Batman movie series of the 1980s and 1990s, the style of these new superhero movies was no longer based primarily on the nostalgic appeal of one-dimensional comic book characters on the big screen. These new films instead emphasized the protagonists' troubled psychological states, combining the attraction of innovative digital effects with a new focus on the characters' status as "troubled hero." The most popular post-9/11 superhero movies have tended to add psychological depth to their comic book protagonists, as they "dwell in detail over the uncertainties, weaknesses, doubts, fears and anxieties of the supernatural hero, his struggle with his inner demons, his confrontation with his own dark side, and so forth" (Žižek 2009: 43).

Hulk (dir. Ang Lee, 2003) is perhaps the strongest example of the way in which psychological complexity was added into the established formula of cartoonish action heroes engaging in spectacular battles with supervillains. Through a complex structure of montage, split-screen, and flashbacks, *Hulk* continuously foregrounds the emotional struggles of its scientist-hero

Bruce Banner and his fragmented sense of self. His superpowers, as with most other Marvel superheroes in films such as *Blade* (dir. Stephen Norrington, 1998), *X-Men* (dir. Bryan Singer, 2000) and *Spider-Man* (dir. Sam Raimi, 2002), are presented as a burden as much as they are a blessing, thus transforming the superhero from an uncomplicated embodiment of nostalgic American values into a figure who is as much a victim as he is a hero.

This duality is systematically related back to moments of trauma, many of which are clearly located in childhood or early adolescence: in *Blade*, the death of the hero's mother during childbirth; in *X-Men*, Magneto's separation from his parents in a Nazi concentration camp during World War II; in *Spider-Man*, the death of Uncle Ben as a result of Peter Parker's own callousness; and in *Hulk*, the death of Bruce Banner's mother and the disappearance of his father after a nuclear experiment gone wrong. As I have described in the previous chapter, these origin stories continuously revolve around obvious Oedipal concepts, with plots that seek to restore a lost connection with authentic patriarchal power. But unlike the earlier superhero franchises, the new "troubled superhero" of the post-9/11 era consistently suffers through the psychological consequences of traumatic experience.

The addition of this form of psychological depth to the superhero formula made the genre accessible to a new, more upscale audience by its association with critically acclaimed directors. Like Tim Burton's *Batman*, as well as with many other high-profile superhero films from *X-Men* onwards, the 2005 reboot of the Batman franchise builds on this concept of authorial intervention. Much of the publicity surrounding the film emphasized director Christopher Nolan's "vision," and the ways in which this new film would re-establish the character's mythology by presenting a version that was once again radically different from the earlier movies. Rather than the ubiquitous branding and endless cross-media merchandising opportunities that defined the previous series of films, this new incarnation drew on the aspects of the franchise that fans had found the most "authentic" at least from the 1980s onward—dark, violent, serious—and developed a campaign that maximized the film's legitimacy to these fans while also appealing directly to audiences that were only passingly familiar with this particular superhero.

Batman Begins focuses more directly than any previous film version on issues of childhood trauma in relation to identity, placing an unusually strong emphasis on the formative aspects of traumatic experiences. The first part of the film is dominated by flashbacks to Bruce Wayne's multiple childhood traumas, which serve to fragment the larger narrative as sudden flashes of traumatic memory repeatedly impose themselves on Wayne's adult point of view. This style, familiar to many viewers from director Nolan's previous arthouse successes like *Following* (1998) and *Memento* (2000), gives *Batman Begins* a decidedly more highbrow appeal than most other comic book movies, especially since the film's depiction of Gotham City is more classically realistic and its characters are more psychologically rounded.

The seriousness of the new Batman film informed all aspects of the publicity campaign: the bat-logo for instance was given a radical redesign, as the glossily embossed 1989 version was transformed into a slimmer, distressed-looking insignia that communicates the film's more "realistic" approach, but without losing the brand's iconic recognizability. Similarly, the film's teaser trailer placed the thematic emphasis firmly on Wayne's psychological journey. As we see images of visually impressive remote locations, actor Liam Neeson's voice intones: "You've traveled the world. Now you must journey inwards. What you really fear... is inside you." A montage of shots then shows actor Christian Bale undergoing various forms of martial arts training, interrupted again by brief shots of childhood memories, while Ducard tells Wayne: "Your parents' death was not your fault," thus establishing this burden of traumatic guilt from the very start. By combining an acclaimed director's artistic credibility with an emphasis on more "mature" themes of psychological trauma, this new approach was designed to expand the franchise's audience to include groups without a prior attachment to the genre.

In the film proper, Wayne's originary childhood trauma culminates in a portrayal of the young adult Wayne as a subject who suffers considerably under the weight of this experience. The impact of his psychological wound is communicated not only by Christian Bale's brooding, mostly humorless performance, but also by the development of the plot in this new origin story. The first part of the film shows Wayne in self-imposed exile in an unidentified mountainous region in Asia. While there, seeking an outlet for his grief, Wayne is approached by Henri Ducard (played by Liam Neeson), who entices him to join a secret society called the League of Shadows. Ducard has little trouble convincing Wayne to support his organization:

> *Bruce Wayne*: What makes you think I need a path?
> *Henri Ducard*: A vigilante is just a man lost in the scramble for his own gratification. He can be destroyed, or locked up; but if you make yourself more than just a man, if you devote yourself to an ideal, and if they can't stop you, you become something else entirely.

This exchange is crucial to the post-9/11 rewriting of Batman's origin story in the more explicit terms of trauma as a mobilizing force. The film's opening scenes had emphasized two moments of childhood trauma as crucial to Batman's later identity: first, the young Bruce Wayne's experience of falling down a well, where he is frightened by a multitude of bats; and second, the murder of his parents after his fear of bats causes them to leave an opera performance prematurely. This new version thus transforms this familiar comic book crime from a random act of violence into a moment from which Bruce Wayne's guilt is allowed to flourish, while also placing additional emphasis on the Oedipal aspects of the core narrative.

Wayne's failure to avenge his parents and the ongoing trauma of their deaths causes him to feel a strong disconnect from Gotham City, which is presented here as a former utopia that has developed into a crime-ridden, despairing urban environment. But in Wayne's case, he learns from Ducard that he can use his traumatic experience as a way to break free of his feelings of immobilization: his parents' murder motivates him to fight crime, while his traumatic fear of bats provides him with the symbolic status that will make him "more than just a man." While this stronger emphasis on Batman as a more complex character can be seen as the authorial involvement of a new director, it clearly also connects to wider post-9/11 discourses of American trauma and heroic victimization, just as the Superman reboot that followed a year later would give its superhero an unusual burden of guilt and parental abandonment anxieties.

But unlike *Superman Returns* and its repeated stagings of familiar catastrophes with triumphant heroic endings, *Batman Begins* provides a different kind of avenue into 9/11 discourse and iconography. In the 1990s cycle of Batman films, the superhero was portrayed as a figure who fought crime in league with the police force as a masked vigilante. In these films, the character's motivations and his commitment to justice were never questioned, neither by himself nor by other characters. His actions conformed to the traditional superhero paradigm, in which "the villains are concerned with change and the heroes with the maintenance of the status quo" (Reynolds 51). Thus, in the Batman universe, an eccentric villain like the Joker attempts to change the way the world is organized, while Batman is dedicated to keeping it as it was.

Batman Begins reverses this dynamic by introducing its hero as someone devoted to changing the existing structures of Gotham City. The film compounds its connection to 9/11 discourse by illustrating how trauma can lead to the kind of ideological radicalization associated with Islamic terrorism. The disillusioned and disoriented Bruce Wayne of *Batman Begins* is easily taken in by villain Ra's Al-Ghul's League of Shadows, which provides him with an ideological perspective that seems to suit his personal agenda, along with a paternal authority figure to replace the loss of his actual father. The discovery of Wayne's "true" identity as Batman, to which this origin story must inevitably lead, is thus associated explicitly with the basic trajectory of the trauma narrative. Simultaneously, it serves to re-establish the Law of the Father as a form of symbolic order that is reconstituted by Wayne's induction into Ducard's organization.

Once he joins the League, Wayne receives extensive training in martial arts and new, mystical forms of awareness, derived from the intake of mysterious drugs. This makes him an effective unit in a terrorist organization bent on maintaining order in the world by punishing societies it deems overly decadent and/or corrupt. What makes this training sequence remarkable, and what sets it apart from previous superhero film narratives, is the fact that a clear process of "othering" takes place. As Edward Said had argued, the West has tended to identify itself as separate from the East by using simplistic dichotomies (e.g. scientific vs. mystical, rational vs. irrational, advanced vs. primitive) that justify viewing entire populations as inherently "other" from a Western "us." This kind of thinking has allowed for reductive statements about the nature of terrorism that cast the perpetrators of the 9/11 attacks as "an irrational 'Other' bent on destroying the West" (Norlund 3).

The reinvention of Batman as a character who learned his skills in the Far East also represents a clear departure from Miller's graphic novels and established comic book continuity: *Batman: Year One* includes panels that show Bruce Wayne in training to become Batman, all of which visibly takes place on the grounds of Wayne Manor. This is significant for the fact that as much as Miller's graphic novel represents a revisionist approach to the character's roots, Batman/Bruce Wayne still remained firmly anchored within Gotham City (and therefore within the U.S.), as are the threats from which he must defend the city. *Batman Begins* on the other hand frames the character's beginning from a specifically foreign context, as if the Batman franchise in the age of globalization has been contaminated by the evil associated with the Far East.

This new addition to the Batman origin story is relevant for how it establishes a deliberate connection between a specific representation of villainy and its relationship to the American city. If previous Batman narratives offer dramatizations of urban spaces as environments that foster crime and perversion, *Batman Begins* trumps this interior threat by introducing a far more serious danger from outside. Like the deeply traumatic penetration of Superman's body as a metaphor for the infiltration of American geopolitical space in *Superman Returns*, the new Batman film similarly revolves around fears of contamination and outside invasion. Organized crime in this film's Gotham is introduced as a problem that is endemic to the inherently corrupt postmodern city, but is quickly marginalized and overshadowed by the Orientalist threat that is presented in terms familiar from Samuel Huntington's "Clash of Civilizations" theory.

Huntington's notion, which he first introduced in a *Foreign Affairs* article in 1993 and developed further in his best-selling 1996 book, gained substantial ground as part of the public debate after the attacks of 9/11, which have frequently (and alarmingly) been cited as evidence of Huntington's perspective on contemporary global conflicts:

> It is my hypothesis that the fundamental source of conflict in this new world will not be primarily ideological or primarily economic. *The great divisions among humankind and the dominating source of*

conflict will be cultural. Nation states will remain the most powerful actors in world affairs, but the principal conflicts of global politics will occur between nations and groups of different civilizations. The clash of civilizations will dominate global politics. The fault lines between civilizations will be the battle lines of the future. (Huntington 22, emphasis added)

Huntington's emphasis on cultural difference as the defining force in current and future conflicts has contributed heavily to the post-9/11 perception that Islamism is directly to blame for current perceived threats against Western freedoms. Examples of this kind of discourse are frighteningly easy to find, and extend as far as Martin Amis's notorious suggestion that Islam is to blame for the inconveniences of post-9/11 airplane travel, grumbling that "the age of terror … will also be remembered as the age of boredom" (77).

Batman Begins contributes directly to this offensive and reductive form of discourse by presenting its world along lines of an ideological conflict similar to Huntington's clash of civilizations: the League of Shadows corresponds directly with the terrorist cell structure associated with Al Qaeda and its extremist agenda, while its Orientalist representation in the film builds on cultural stereotypes without connecting its roots to any specific nation-state or ethnicity. A traumatized Bruce Wayne proves susceptible to the temptations of a terrorist group led by Ra's Al-Ghul, who may not be portrayed as a Middle-Eastern Muslim, but whose appearance and attitudes answer to all the classical stereotypes that make him the archetypal Orientalist enemy of Western values. This sect leader, played by Japanese actor Ken Watanabe, is later revealed as an empty figurehead meant to distract from the actual villain: Wayne's charismatic Caucasian mentor Ducard.

Orientalist stereotype Ra's Al-Ghul in *Batman Begins* (2005).

Like *Iron Man* (dir. Jon Favreau, 2008), the television series *24* (20th Century Fox Television, 2001-2010), and many other popular 21st-century narratives, *Batman Begins* trades casually in these familiar Orientalist stereotypes, only to make a last minute about-face that recasts the film's surrogate father figure as the true source of evil. What on the surface would appear to be politically correct efforts to avoid suspicion of racist stereotyping could in fact be regarded as a more troubling type of oblique racism than that of pre-9/11 action movies—from *Into the Night* (dir. John Landis, 1985) to *True Lies* (dir. James Cameron, 1994)— in which the villains were rabid Arab caricatures. For not only do these post-9/11 films put the patronizing stereotypes to unquestioning use in order to establish the antagonist's otherness, but the Orientalist villain's unmasking as a red herring also robs the character of agency in the narrative. This effectively removes the stereotype's narrative power, without dissolving the negative connotations that continue to define it, thereby adding insult to injury.

These connotations come to the fore when Bruce Wayne arrives at the League of Shadows' headquarters, where he undergoes his combat training. These headquarters are set in a temple in a remote Asian mountain range, a type of location loaded with connotations of mysticism and Oriental "otherness." The edifice closely resembles the clichéd enemy headquarters, such as that of terrorist organization Cobra in *G.I. Joe* comics, which are "designed architecturally to resemble a temple hidden in a Himalaya-like region" (Norlund 8). Like the common comic book archetype, Ra's Al-Ghul is also "a terrorist personality [portrayed] as a disingenuous religious leader, suggest[ing] that no terrorist or religious leader is authentically devout" (ibid.). This prejudicial stereotype is further solidified by the presence of oblique religious signifiers such as Buddha figurines on prominent display in the location's interior.

Besides the Eastern iconography that overdetermines the League's costumes and headquarters' set design, the cruelty and mysticism associated with these stereotypes are communicated by the scenes in which Wayne undergoes his training. Ducard, a Caucasian man nonetheless clearly marked as "Other" by his Fu Manchu mustache, first inflicts the kind of pitiless regimen on Wayne that is associated with radical terrorist groups, all the while quietly intoning the League's radical "warrior code." A key moment during this sequence arrives when Wayne must inhale the smoke of a poppy-like blue flower. The effect of this drug is that it makes its user somehow more attuned to his environment, giving one the "hyper-awareness" often associated with superhero characters. As Wayne subsequently undergoes another test, the pulsating, unstable point-of-view shots illustrate Wayne's altered consciousness, while the fact that he passes the test suggests that this mystical ritual is indeed capable of producing preternaturally effective fighters.

All of the elements in this sequence play directly into the Orientalist discourses that associate the East with mysticism, irrational thought, mystery, the unpredictable, seduction, and the prohibited. This allows us to define the West as the Orient's binary opposite: rational, open, transparent, and governed by law. Like so many other Western subjects in the long history of Orientalist discourse, Bruce Wayne is temporarily seduced by the attraction of this form of alterity, which obviously preys upon his feelings of trauma and alienation. But the sect's methods nonetheless prove to be too radical for a political moderate: as soon as Wayne is instructed to execute a thief as the final step of his induction in the League, he refuses to cooperate. Unlike the other members of the League, Wayne demonstrates a deeply ingrained moral code that transcends any attempts at indoctrination, and which allows him to break free from this environment where others clearly could not.

His sudden rejection of the League of Shadows' allows Bruce Wayne to develop his own brand of crime-fighting, which ultimately puts him in conflict with his former mentor's true purpose: a large-scale attack on Gotham City. The League's motivation for this plot sounds remarkably similar to the "they hate our freedoms" rationale that was repeated so frequently in the wake of the 9/11 attacks, with its emphasis on New York City as the pinnacle of decadence. This resonates once more with Huntington's "clash of civilizations" theory, as the film's dialogue plays up the cultural values that motivate the villain's plot:

> Ra's Al-Ghul: Gotham's time has come. Like Constantinople or Rome before it the city has become a breeding ground for suffering and injustice. It is beyond saving and must be allowed to die. This is the most important function of the League of Shadows. It is one we've performed for centuries. Gotham must be destroyed.

The League's plot to destroy Gotham City, Batman's fictitious city of residence since 1941 that "for all intents and purposes is still New York, and more specifically Manhattan" (Brooker 48), ultimately involves an attack that is to culminate in the destruction of Wayne Tower, Gotham's skyline-defining skyscraper and the symbolic and infrastructural heart of the city. The similarity to recent real-world events could hardly be more obvious. Film critic and genre specialist Kim Newman has described the similarity between the film's main narrative and the attacks of 9/11 in his article "Cape Fear," suggesting that Gotham City is attacked in the film "by a fanatic eastern sect with a charismatic but impossible-to-catch figurehead which is bent on crashing a mode of transport into a skyscraper to trigger an explosion of panic that will destroy society" (21).

Although Batman succeeds in thwarting the larger attack on Wayne Tower, derailing the speeding subway train at the last possible moment, some parts of Gotham City still fall victim to the terrorist plot. A vaporized hallucinogen is released throughout the poorest part of the city, transforming the masses on the streets into a mob of zombies that "threaten to consume and destroy Batman" even as he fights to save them (Fisher 2006: par. 20). This sequence reveals a great deal about the superhero's relationship to the public he is supposedly devoted to protecting. On those rare occasions in which an ordinary citizen makes an appearance in the film, it is all too frequently in the threatening form of a monstrous, uncontrollable mob. Rather than offering a renewed sense of social solidarity across class boundaries, as allegedly happened in New York in the direct aftermath of the terrorist attacks, *Batman Begins* suggests instead that 9/11 was caused by "the crisis of *excessive social solidarity*, the arrogance of masses *not being sufficiently terrified of their shepherds*" (China Miéville, qtd. in Fisher 2006: par. 19).

As in *Superman Returns*, the superhero figure in *Batman Begins* takes on the role of the martyr who suffers for our sins, remaining fundamentally alienated from the ordinary people whose well-being he safeguards. While Superman rescues admiring and helpless citizens as the embodiment of mythico-religious ideals, Batman takes on a more troubling role of enlightened despot whose "inheritance and obsession both stem from an attempt to defend property ... against violation" (Pearson and Uricchio 203). Batman's originary trauma, resulting in his dual status as innocent victim and terrifying avenger, is perhaps easier for many to relate to again from a post-9/11 context, in which American real-world superpower has taken on a remarkably similar role. Like Batman's struggle, the obligation to fight a Sisyphean War on Terror is motivated primarily by this sense of trauma, which, like the representations of the 9/11 attacks, is revisited endlessly as a familiar but fundamentally ungraspable moment of historical rupture.

The superhero fantasy of *Batman Begins* thus offers a way of incorporating traumatic historical events in a symbolic way that ultimately rewrites them as a narrative of simultaneous triumph and victimization. The September 11 attacks are metaphorically re-staged as part of a larger plot that places them in the framework of mythical narratives of good versus evil, which in this case revolve around Orientalist stereotypes and prejudices. This confirms the "common-sense" way of understanding the 9/11 attacks and their associated sense of trauma on the basis of familiar patterns and relatable discourses. The reasons for the attack, as summarized in the villain's dialogue cited above, hew quite closely to the usual reductionist answers prevalent in American popular culture and political speeches about how terrorists simply "hate 'freedom and democracy', they irrationally want to 'kill Americans'" (Norlund 4). While *Batman Begins* therefore clearly addresses the cultural fallout of 9/11 and the public wish to indulge in trauma narratives and engage with wish-fulfillment scenarios, it still does so in a way that reaffirms many of the cultural assumptions and preconceptions that maintain and support the mythical narratives of neoliberal capitalism.

The film version of *V for Vendetta* (dir. James McTeigue, 2005) features a similar Batman-type superhero figure as its protagonist, but attempts to develop a different perspective on the relationship between its main character and his dystopian society. Even more than in *Batman Begins*, the masked superhero known only as "V" is presented emphatically as a trauma victim:

his identity has been shattered by the medical experimentation that was performed on him by scientists working for a totalitarian government in a near-future fascist Britain. Like *Superman Returns* and *Batman Begins*, this film engages centrally with narratives and imagery surrounding 9/11, but it does so in a way that foregrounds political processes that the other films ignore or even deliberately avoid. In doing so, the film raises the question whether a Hollywood action blockbuster operating in this genre can indeed provide a more productive engagement with politics, as the film's radical source material would suggest.

V for Vendetta: Apolitical Radicalism and Infantile Citizenship

V for Vendetta, which was distributed globally by Time Warner, is based on the comic book by writer Alan Moore and artist David Lloyd, but has an unusual relationship with its source material. When the film was released, author Alan Moore demanded that his name be removed from the credits, stating that in his opinion the story had been "turned into a Bush-era parable by people too timid to set a political satire in their own country" (Moore 2006: n. pag.). The differences between the comic book, which was first published as a single volume in 1989, and the commercially successful film from 2005 are revealing: not so much as an indication of whether the film is a faithful adaptation of the source material, but as an illustration of the contradictory ideological values that inform mass-market entertainment.

In both the comic book and the film, superhero character V makes his dramatic entrance with his rescue of Evey, the film's secondary protagonist and the primary focus for audience identification. This scene, in which an innocent young woman is rescued from hoodlums by a mysterious masked savior, conforms to one of the most familiar tropes in the superhero narrative, even to the extent that it has become a genre cliché. What is unusual however is that the goons molesting Evey are in this case government agents, and that the masked vigilante reveals himself as a radical rebel against the state. As soon as V has vanquished Evey's attackers, he takes her up to the rooftop of a nearby building to witness his spectacular demolition of the Old Bailey in London, symbolizing his disdain for this dystopian society's system of justice.

Not only does this crucial early moment set the scene for Evey's subsequent indoctrination by V, it also establishes the superhero's persona as a witty, physically powerful, and unusually articulate character whose actions are unambiguously justified, and whose first terrorist act is a spectacular fireworks display without any human casualties. When a still-skeptical Evey questions the legitimacy of his actions, V heavy-handedly explains to her the symbolic nature of his destructive acts:

> V: The building is a symbol, as is the act of destroying it. Symbols are given power by people. Alone, a symbol is meaningless. But with enough people, blowing up a building can change the world.

Besides underlining the political aspects of V's actions, his short speech introduces the topic of democracy and terrorism in a way that is unusual for the genre. For as the film's plot subsequently demonstrates, V's struggle hinges upon gaining the support of the people by undermining the credibility of the mass media, which are forcefully controlled directly by the government, operating in a distinctly Orwellian mode of Stalinist propaganda. Similar to *Batman*, the battle between hero and villain in this superhero narrative is therefore to large extent televisual in nature, as both parties engage in a media war aimed at convincing the audience of their point of view.

But just as the Joker's pirate broadcasts are forthright and unsubtle in representing explicit disruptions of a stable moral order, V's television appearances are equally unambiguous in their heroic and "authentic" nature. Although this struggle is clearly asymmetrical in nature, the audience is immediately made complicit by the fact that V's pirate broadcasts are truthful and legitimate, while the government-controlled programming represents a villainous "process of deformation," as images and narratives are distorted and manipulated to serve the fascist ruling party's interests (Collins 1991: 167). Interestingly, *V for Vendetta* thereby reverses the traditional structure of the superhero narrative, in which the protagonist supports the status quo, while the villain's acts of sabotage attempt to disturb the balance of power.

In this instance particularly, the difference with the comic book is revealing. Peter Y. Paik explains it best in his analysis of the film's failure as a politically productive text:

> The situation that prevails in the fascist Britain of the comic is unremittingly brutal and desperate, far bleaker by any measure than the one shown in the film ... Crushed by the agony of their losses and consumed by the arduous struggle to survive in a dangerous and poisoned environment, the traumatized subjects of this postapocalyptic totalitarian dystopia elected to deafen themselves to the voice of conscience in order to secure the practical necessities of life ... The film is by contrast wholly devoid of any trace of such overwhelming and pervasive despair. The totalitarian society it depicts is a flimsy and superficial construction, an incoherent and self-refuting nightmare lacking in any plausible historical exigency. (156-7)

The comic book thus portrays a society that may truly be described as traumatized, having suffered many of the worst kinds of military, political, and environmental crises, each of which resonates historically with specific 20th-century catastrophes. The result is a population reduced to mere animal survival, one that has lost the relative luxury of independent thought and social solidarity.

On the one hand, this does make the fascist dictatorship's strong hold over the population in the film adaptation rather implausible, a Britain that "is essentially a prosperous, technologically advanced nation that merely happens to have a fascist government" (Paik 157). But the way in which the film presents the country's inhabitants as gullible, easily-controlled subjects makes more sense if we view it in the context of neoliberal consumerism and disaster capitalism. The film presents the population as a basically benign but easily manipulated mass, which remains unaware of its lack of civil liberties until a heroic rebel breaks the spell of mass media indoctrination. It therefore also absolves the public from any complicity with the film's fascist regime, making them instead the innocent dupes of manipulative mass media and evil, conspiratorial politicians.

This representation of audience manipulation flatters its viewers by letting them off the hook in its attempt to offer topical satire. Liberal audiences are invited to snigger self-righteously at the film's exaggerated depiction of neoconservative television pundits associated with news broadcasters like Fox News. But by presenting a society in which mass media are controlled entirely by a single evil government, the film willfully ignores the social and political realities that ultimately inform and sustain our own mass-media culture. By setting up the naïve, easily fooled population in the film as one that is childishly innocent and bizarrely ignorant, it removes itself further from the media-literate audience for which the film is itself intended. The infantile audience in the film, responding naturally and common-sensically to the obvious truth of V's speech, is one that automatically rises up to restore the original democratic/capitalist order that had been upset by the fascist dictatorship. The movie version of *V for Vendetta*, like most superhero narratives, thus offers as a solution to its political crisis the indestructible moral leadership of a single enlightened subject, who also functions as a clearly branded celebrity both inside and outside of the text.

The supernatural infallibility of these hero characters is traditionally juxtaposed by all-too-human alter egos, and in many ways, Evey in the *V for Vendetta* film functions similarly. She is introduced as an ordinary citizen just trying to get by while minding her own business in a less-than-perfect world. She has no involvement with politics, nor is she presented as particularly heroic. But the childhood trauma of the violent abduction of her parents, who come to symbolize the natural order that has been disrupted, is ultimately what makes her not only a suitable candidate for recruitment by a superhero: it even suggests that this is a matter of destiny rather than the accidental recruitment of an ordinary subject. This stands again in stark contrast with the comic book, in which Evey's encounter with V is presented as arbitrary, and her final choice to complete V's revolutionary project is her own decision rather than a matter of predestination. In the film, the happy accident that brings her into contact with V ultimately seems to be cosmically predetermined, her traumatic victimization prefiguring her later alignment with the superhero.

This sense of predestination corresponds perfectly with that of the main characters in *Batman Begins*, as audience surrogate Evey follows a path remarkably similar to that traveled by Bruce Wayne in Nolan's film. If the traditional superhero narrative presents its main character as a functioning schizophrenic who nevertheless has great difficulty consolidating the two aspects of his identity, the film version of *V for Vendetta* works towards the reconstitution of a single subject from two separate characters. Evey grows increasingly intimate with V throughout the narrative, although this intimacy develops into a relationship that is paternal rather than sexual. Like Bruce Wayne, who is also surrounded by "a superfluity of fathers" in *Batman Begins*, Evey is indoctrinated by this "hyperstitional mentor-guru" to change her perception of the world around her and to undergo a form of conditioning that will allow her to follow in her mentor's footsteps (Fisher 2006: par. 3). In both cases, as is so common in the genre, the character's acceptance of this process of explicit subjectification revolves around the authenticity of the father figures in question, as explicit goals, values, and ideological coordinates are established on the basis of their primal authority.

For Bruce Wayne, the father figure he finds in Henri Ducard is quickly revealed as inauthentic, and Wayne rejects him as soon as Ducard blames the death of Wayne's father on Wayne Senior's own weakness. This suggestion prompts an Oedipal crisis in Bruce Wayne, as the implication would be that his father could no longer be perceived as the representative of Symbolic law, but as a fallible, ordinary man. Wayne therefore "refuses to go through this initiation and retains loyalty to the 'Name of the Father' while Al Ghul remains a figure of excess and Evil" (Fisher 2006: par. 14). Evey in *V for Vendetta* undergoes an identical Oedipal process, albeit again in the opposite direction: while her deceased parents have been officially branded enemies of the state, V teaches her to acknowledge that they had been political activists who died for the values she too comes to embrace. By restoring the symbolic order associated with the Law of the Father, V is accepted by Evey as a legitimate figure of power to whom she ultimately cedes authority and agency, based on the fact that he explicitly represents the values embodied by her real father.

In the film, Evey's story is therefore entirely one of patriarchal predestination. While her character is female, this in no way prevents the script from casting her development along a trajectory that is essentially Oedipal. Like Superman and Batman, she is an orphan whose Oedipal development will remain conveniently incomplete, as her martyred father will likewise go unchallenged as the bearer of complete symbolic authority. In the film, the death of maternal carer Deitrich (played by Stephen Fry) functions as a repetition of the traumatic loss of her parents, while V's sacrifice later reaffirms the absolute authority of the values these parental figures represent. While the narrative therefore superficially presents a process of education and enlightenment, this is not unlike the passive indoctrination that the infant Kal-El undergoes in *Superman* while hearing his father's voice during his journey to Earth: Evey internalizes V's authority to the point where it comes to represent the unquestionable, "natural" order. Like *Batman Begins*, the film version of *V for Vendetta* therefore organizes its narrative progression primarily in terms of characters who learn to obey the symbolic "Law of the Father."

Deitrich's capture (right) is a literal repetition
of Evey's childhood trauma (left).

Therefore, although the character of V would seem to represent "the direct literary fulfillment of the unconditionally militant subject called for by Žižek, Badiou, and Hardt and Negri," (Paik 154), his role in the film is primarily that of surrogate embodiment of patriarchal authority. Evey's Oedipal trajectory, like that of Bruce Wayne, must again remain incomplete: the obvious potential of a sexual relationship with V is never consummated, and Evey and V never become equal partners in their revolutionary project. Instead, he comes to represent the absolute authority of patriarchal power, which re-aligns Evey's ideological coordinates in such a way that the "natural" democratic order is restored at the end of the film. Evey's rejection of the evil dictator (played by John Hurt) and her embrace of the more authentic status of her biological father directly corresponds with Bruce Wayne's rejection of the evil Ra's Al-Ghul and his acceptance of his own "natural" position in the patriarchal order.

When comparing the way in which these two films' narratives represent a potential for political change, there are some obvious similarities, but also some notable differences. The most crucial similarity is both films' reliance on a highly masculine superhero figure whose intervention is required in order to affect political change in a troubled society. Without the assistance of Bruce Wayne in *Batman Begins* or the actions of V in *V for Vendetta*, individual subjects are clearly unable to act, or even to understand the true nature of their predicament. Also, both films feature a strong emphasis on the superhero's physical abilities, presenting him as an aggressive figure who relies primarily on violent action to make his points and restore his tarnished community. A third obvious similarity is the fact that in both films, the perspective of the ordinary citizen is represented by a child character, shown in both cases to be the sole believer in the hero's good nature amongst a skeptical, easily misguided population.

The choice to have the larger-than-life heroes and villains played by adults while the ordinary citizenry is represented by children fits perfectly with the form of "infantile citizenship" described by Lynn Spigel in her analysis of the way in which the media narrated the events of 9/11 to the American audience: "as if they were children, or at best, the innocent objects of historical events beyond their control" (128). This makes the superhero genre in general, and these two films in particular, clear examples of the way in which popular fantasy tends to foreclose active engagement, as all sense of political and historical agency is systematically removed from its audience. For not only are all forms of social change in these films attributed to messianic superhero figures, but the ordinary subject's point-of-view is reduced within the film's narrative to that of an awe-struck, helpless child.

In the case of *V for Vendetta*, this shifts the book's interest in the complexities and ambiguities of superhero figures in relation to both fascist and anarchist politics to a straightforward binary representation of good versus evil. Both V and Evey are heroic figures because they are clearly destined to perform these roles in the film, just as Bruce Wayne is preordained to become Batman in *Batman Begins*. The reduction of the general population's perspective to that of child characters represented in both films in terms of innocence, helplessness, and wide-eyed wonder reaffirms the notions of infantile citizenship that inform neoliberal consumer society. This is made all the more striking by the fact that in the film, no alternative to fascism is offered beyond the vaguest platitudes invoking concepts like "freedom" and "democracy." While the character of V in the comic book voices an extremely radical anarchist political agenda, his revolution in the film is ultimately—and bizarrely—apolitical in nature.

The absence of any articulated political alternative either in *V for Vendetta* or in *Batman Begins* once again confirms the basic assumption of neoliberalism that there are no longer any alternatives left to capitalism. In *Batman Begins*, the problem is not capitalism itself, but capitalism of "the wrong kind," while the film version of *V for Vendetta* clearly suggests that the horrific alternative to neoliberal capitalism is fascism and its Stalinist forms of propaganda. Both films' dystopian environments do not open up a space for utopian change, but instead point back to capitalism as the only real choice that must be restored at all costs. Their supposedly liberal politics therefore in fact imply a form of "interpassivity," where films offer an illusion of revolutionary politics, but without requiring the viewer to engage in any substantial way with the issues the text supposedly critiques. The absence of any positive form of politics or ideology in either film thus betrays their neoliberal implications: "the role of capitalist ideology is not to make an explicit case for something in the way that propaganda does, but to conceal the fact that the operations of capital do not depend on any sort of subjectively held belief" (Fisher 2009: 12-13).

The two films' endings and the seemingly opposite ways in which they represent the possibility of radical change reflect this vacuum at the core of capitalist ideology. While Batman manages to prevent a revolution from happening, V succeeds in triggering a mass movement, but both present the population in similar terms. In *Batman Begins*, the population of Gotham City is literally reduced to a psychotic, paranoid mass, while the citizens of London in the climax of *V for Vendetta* are a more benevolent, but equally homogeneous mob. The former film thus implies that ordinary subjects should not interfere with political issues, leaving them either to benevolent capitalists like Bruce Wayne and his father, or else to well-armed vigilante figures whose actions offer militarized support for the understaffed police force. The latter film allows for the perspective that hero figures ultimately must rely on the support of the population, but the "political awakening" of the public arrives in the form of hero worship and ostentatious branding.

The action that is presented as revolutionary at the end of *V for Vendetta* is therefore presented as a vapid, visually spectacular display of fireworks that reduces the revolutionary masses once again to passive spectators, gazing up at the symbol of their liberator who has already taken violent action against the villainous oppressors. In other words, the superhero "has brought about the revolution of the people and so become the apotheosis of the universalizing action" (Paik 162). The fascination with which the amassed audience gazes up at the destruction (in spectacular slow-motion) of the Houses of Parliament is uncannily reminiscent of the enthralling nature of the collapse of the World Trade Center, and seems designed to evoke this specific connection to 9/11. But again, the images are rewritten in this film to conform to a narrative of heroic triumph, the destruction refashioned into a symbolic form of spectacle from which all traces of trauma have been skillfully erased. It hardly seems a coincidence that the final shot of *V for Vendetta* is the superhero's V-shaped logo appearing in the sky above London, the film's empty politics transcended by the ubiquitous and spectacular branding that has dominated the superhero movie genre since 1989. What therefore appears on the surface to be a radical difference between these two films' endings and the different ways in which the population is represented, reveals upon closer inspection a more fundamental similarity.

The masses adopting the mask of their superhero
during their passive revolution.

For this reason, we should not interpret the film *V for Vendetta* as a superhero narrative that is revolutionary where most others are conservative. If *Batman Begins* is about a conservative hero successfully averting a threat that would change the way our world is organized, the film version of *V for Vendetta* shows a world in which society has been changed, and where the superhero's intervention is required in order to transform it back into the way it is "supposed to be": a neoliberal, multicultural consumer society in which the people are basically passive spectators, and where the frightening alternative to neoliberal capitalism takes the form of early-20th century totalitarianism. Both films are therefore based on the logic that any alternative to Western capitalist society must clearly be worse than our existing neoliberal society, and demonstrate yet again that even in politically engaged popular fantasy "there is no alternative."

3

Traversing the Neoliberal Metropolis

Superheroes are vehicles of urban representation; they embody perceptual paradigms. Through the vehicle of the superhero, as through cinema and sociology, one recovers the city as new and shifting ground. Urbanism was defined as a way of life by sociologist Louis Wirth in 1938, the year that also saw the appearance of Superman. Superheroes exist to inhabit the city, to patrol, map, dissect, and traverse it. (Bukatman 222)

The figure of the superhero is inextricably interwoven with the landscape and architecture of the modern city throughout the second half of the 20th century. As "vehicles of urban representation," they have embodied popular fantasies of navigating the daunting environment of the metropolis, glorifying the American city as a nostalgic and utopian space, while simultaneously expressing anxieties about the dangers associated with the urban jungle. The terrorist attacks of 11 September 2001 have affected the popular fantasies and fears associated with New York City as the archetypal modern metropolis, which in turn influenced its representation in popular culture. Bolstered by a heightened sense of the city's central position within global consumerism and neoliberal capitalism, the 21st-century superhero movie clearly illustrates how the contradictions of the neoliberal metropolis have come to inform the contemporary cycle of superhero films.

From *Spider-Man* (2002) onwards, superhero movies have repeatedly addressed the trauma of 9/11 in ways that seem contradictory, but which are clearly not mutually exclusive: first, by de-historicizing the present through the re-creation of a New York City in which the attacks never happened; and second, by providing narratives in which catastrophic threats against New York City are narrowly averted, thereby re-writing this history as one of triumph instead of defeat. These narratives serve as representations of a multitude of contemporary anxieties relating to globalized capitalism, the crisis of agency, the waning of historicity in postmodern culture, and the increasing virtualization of life in the contemporary global city. But due to the superhero's association with the skyscraper landscape of urban modernity, the genre's popularity during the neoliberal age has also offered a way of reconstituting a sense of individual agency and movement within the urban environment. These films can therefore also represent the city as a spectacular site that celebrates De Certeau's "unlimited diversity" by articulating an environment that provides "space to move" (103).

The Spectral Cinematic City: Fantasies and Fears

The city and the cinema have been symbiotic signifiers of modernity throughout the twentieth century, during which time film has been "constantly fascinated with the representation of the distinctive spaces, lifestyles, and human conditions of the city" (Shiel 1). Not only did the modern city provide the settings, the imagery, and the cultural conflict on which early cinema relied so heavily, but the cinema also developed a specific image of the city beyond the bustling, photogenic hive of urban activity that made it more than merely a geographical location. Instead, it became an image of a largely dystopian urban space "of an undifferentiated 'city' which is either unidentifiable with any actual place or only loosely so" (Nowell-Smith 101).

This spectral city is the environment in which the superhero figure was first introduced in the comics of the 1930s, and which remained its primary environment throughout the genre's history. The superhero genre's representation of urban spaces was simultaneously utopian and dystopian, for, as Jameson helpfully notes, "the city ... is available for anti-Utopian and dystopian functions fully as much as for more properly Utopian ones" (2005: 161). Just as the cinema developed the modern metropolis simultaneously as a utopia and as a dystopia, the popular narratives of pulp fiction and comic books also presented urban space as an exciting, dangerous, and quintessentially modern setting. In order to understand the apparent contradiction between these two co-existing perspectives, it is important to embrace the notion that rather than functioning as mutually exclusive opposites, utopian and dystopian fantasies can also be viewed as each other's dialectical counterparts. Most, if not all, dystopias are presented very specifically (and crucially) as failed utopias. Any form of dystopia therefore depends upon a concept of utopia that must both precede and define it.

This dialectical reading of utopian/dystopian phantasmal urban environments in popular narratives is particularly relevant to the superhero figure. The coexistence of utopian and dystopian representations of the modern city explains both the complementary nature and the enduring popularity of the two longest-running superheroes: DC Comics' Superman and Batman. Both Superman's Metropolis and Batman's Gotham City are thinly veiled symbolic versions of New York City that together dramatize the ambiguous nature of the modern city. Superman's "Metropolis" is traditionally presented in quasi-utopian terms as an urban space where evil is punished, where order is consistently restored, and where urban modernity is held in balance by the coexistence of provincial Smallville. Gotham City on the other hand has dominated much of Batman's long history as a film noir-inspired dystopian urban jungle, its police force eternally overwhelmed by endless crime waves, and its claustrophobia further emphasized by the absence of any pastoral spaces of refuge outside its city sphere.

This duality of urban spaces extends beyond the two characters' narrative traditions, infusing most mainstream superhero narratives with a similar dialectic. In many superhero chronologies, the Gotham/Metropolis dichotomy found expression in either a similarly utopian or radically dystopian version of New York City. For Marvel Comics, the only comics publisher to challenge DC Comics' hegemony over the industry in the early 1960s, this duality informed the introduction of main characters who lived in a more literal version of New York City. Instead of the black-and-white morality and simple binary structures of earlier superheroes, Marvel's hugely successful comic book series like The Fantastic Four, the X-Men, and Spider-Man allowed for additional nuances, as "the introduction of ambiguity into the vocabulary of the comic book superhero" became the genre's most popular form in that period (Wright 215). The ambiguity of these narratives involved the introduction of more troubled heroic characters who were often misunderstood by the public and persecuted by the government. The version of New York City they inhabited meanwhile functioned as a more pliable backdrop that could emphasize either utopian or dystopian aspects of urban life, depending upon the narrative context.

But in spite of their setting within a city that appears on the surface somewhat closer to historical reality, the Marvel characters and their "New York City" environments remain as fundamentally unhistorical as their DC Comics counterparts. What is most relevant here is the absence of political or historical change in any of these narratives throughout their long chronologies. With so much attention in superhero comic books devoted to the concept of continuity, it is precisely the decades-long accumulation of incident that has culminated in their oft-evoked status as modern myths, as described by Richard Reynolds:

> Continuity, and above all metatextual structural continuity, is the
> strategy through which superhero texts most clearly operate as
> myths ... The continuity of the individual character, and the

relationship of that character with the entire "universe" which they inhabit, provides a guarantee of the authenticity of each individual story. (45)

A strange tension thus exists between two opposing tendencies in superhero chronology: the accumulation of events and the resulting forward movement of history on the one hand, and the systematic absence of any form of political change on the other. This tension between endless narrative progression and the eradication of historical development may be considered typical of the culture industry in general, and of the superhero genre in particular.

In this sense, it is fruitful to investigate the binary division that separates superhero characters into agents of the law on the one hand, assisting the police and deliberately upholding the status quo, and their "outlaw" counterparts on the other: "heroes that fail to conform to the conservative ideology—heroes that are often seen as terrorists to the societies that they are a part of, but to the reader, existing outside of the fictional world, the truth of their heroic actions is better understood for the struggle that it is" (Wolf-Meyer 501). Interestingly, many superhero characters are divided across these categories in a way that seems largely identical to the utopian/dystopian separation discussed above in relation to their urban environments. Superman in this way constitutes the archetype for the conservative "agent of the law" superhero, while Batman embraces the position of the outsider, repeatedly misunderstood by society as a vigilante or even a criminal.

Part of the general appeal of the "Silver Age" Marvel characters like Spider-Man, X-Men and the Incredible Hulk was their lack of control over their powers and their frustrations over their sense of being marginalized and misunderstood by the world around them. Their immediate connection with rising American youth culture and adolescent identity ensured that "the young, flawed and brooding antihero became the most widely imitated archetype in the superhero genre since the appearance of Superman" (Wright 212). Although mainstream superhero comics in the 1960s and 1970s did therefore offer some reflection of changing social and political values, their narratives rarely investigated the implications such superhuman abilities would have on actual human history, theology, or politics. Remaining in essence conservative, determinedly apolitical figures, popular characters like Spider-Man "endorsed liberal solutions to social problems while rejecting the extreme and violent responses of both the left and the right" (235). In an increasingly polarized nation, superheroes on the page thereby "worked to preserve what remained of the vital center" (ibid.). Meanwhile, the strong focus on the individual subject and his actions within a political and historical vacuum unsurprisingly continued to connect to the rising culture of consumerism and the "me" generation of the 1960s and 1970s.

This sustained narrative mode is surprising given the superhero figure's obvious but rarely-realized potential to radically alter the social structures and belief systems that inform the world as we know it. The question therefore to what extent these characters and the urban landscapes they inhabit can represent some kind of utopian impulse or offer any noticeable level of political engagement becomes quite pertinent. Historically, we may briefly summarize the mainstream superhero's position as one of overwhelming conservatism: neither Metropolis nor Gotham City, nor indeed Marvel's alternate New York City, has undergone any discernible changes beyond the level of aesthetics in over seventy years of comics history, and have remained "largely removed from socio-economic context" (Pearson and Uricchio 206). Like the super-heroes themselves, adapting to changes in fashion and crossovers into other media, but never aging or altering the course of human history, mainstream superhero comics in general therefore express key aspects of the Jamesonian "perpetual present."

As a genre that is "wholly concerned with the [utopian] process and unconcerned with the results," superhero comics have dealt mostly with narratives "that reveal the inability to achieve utopia, regardless of rationale" (Wolf-Meyer 501). Apart from occasional exceptions, the superhero genre as a whole does seem to favor the repetition of narrative formulas over the exploration of their full historical implications: due to the "conservative nature of the interpretive community that is comic book fandom," the utopian goals implied by the superheroic protagonists are consistently "dissipated in the construction of the narrative" (512). The political aspect of any utopian impulse is thereby lost, with the economic concerns of the audience-based economy "contaminating utopia and imprisoning the readership in a self-imposed, conservative paradigm dependent upon hegemonic capitalism" (ibid.).

The question then becomes to what extent the modern superhero movie follows this same kind of narrative logic: does its nature as a commodified global franchise prohibit it from yielding any kind of utopian imagination within its depiction of the postmodern metropolis? Has the developing vocabulary of neoliberal discourse and globalization opened up a passage towards a more politicized form of popular narrative? Are there large differences between contemporary superhero films and the ways in which they present dystopian or (semi-)utopian urban environments? In order to answer these questions, the next two sections of this chapter will offer analyses of the two most successful 21st-century superhero film franchises, which can be organized into those two categories: first, the semi-utopian global village of a nostalgic New York in the *Spider-Man* trilogy; and second, the "world without rules" of *The Dark Knight*'s dystopian Gotham City.

The Post-9/11 Flâneur:
Spider-Man At Play in the New Global Village

All the animals come out at night - whores, skunk pussies, buggers, queens, fairies, dopers, junkies, sick, venal. Someday a real rain will come and wash all this scum off the streets.

Taxi Driver (dir. Martin Scorsese, 1976)

In Hollywood films of the 1970s and early 1980s, New York City was most often portrayed as a depraved, destitute, and dehumanizing environment. In *Taxi Driver*, Travis Bickle's wish for a "real rain" that would "wash all this scum off the streets" expressed more than a psychotic Vietnam veteran's paranoid sense of social and political alienation. It fed directly into a larger public discourse in American culture that perceived the city as the emblem of moral decline, with New York City's Times Square forming a kind of ground zero for the waves of pornography and moral decrepitude that were threatening traditional American values. Fueled by the era's economic recession and a growing culture of suburbanization that left America's inner cities in financial ruin, Hollywood's depiction of the metropolis reflected its decade's anxieties about the nation's culture and economy.

Besides *Taxi Driver*, a wide range of films sustained this perception throughout the era, with film after film demonstrating how the former "ripeness" of Times Square had "turned into rot" (Sanders 318).[5] Outside of the Hollywood mainstream, genres like Blaxploitation and grindhouse cinema seemed dedicated entirely to propagating the image of the postmodern metropolis as an overpopulated hell on earth, defined by its high levels of prostitution, pornography, and drug abuse. These films presented an image of the city that confirmed the public perception of the metropolis where "soaring crime, social crises, and countless municipal strikes were causing a precipitous decline in the quality of life" (Sanders 371).

The cinematic representation of New York in the 1970s that thus contributed to a perception of the urban jungle as a breeding ground for crime and poverty was itself the product of early neoliberalism. Under the Nixon administration, New York City had been forced into bankruptcy in the early 1970s, as the federal government drastically cut financial aid to the city. The only solution for city officials was the forced privatization of former city and state organizations and institutions, which in practice "amounted to a coup by the financial institutions against the democratically elected government of New York City" (Harvey 2005: 45). The result of this crisis was that "wealth was redistributed to the upper classes in the midst of a fiscal crisis" (ibid.) as part of what would later prove to be a crucial testing ground for neoliberal doctrine.

In the late 1980s, the image of New York as the epitome of urban decay had changed. Times Square, which for many years had represented the very worst aspects of metropolitan life, was transformed from a notoriously seedy conglomeration of porn theaters and decrepit tenement buildings dominated by prostitutes, pimps, homeless people, and drug dealers into a child-friendly tourist attraction. Republican mayor Rudolph Giuliani saw an opportunity to attract investors and clean up the city's image by collaborating with big business and private investors and transforming the area into a deregulated corporate playground. By the mid-1990s, Times Square was dominated by corporate franchises and revived Broadway theaters. And although this "Disneyfication" of Times Square was criticized by many, it met with instant financial success as a marketable commodity on the tourist market.

As the international face of New York City has been shaped throughout the twentieth century by its representation in Hollywood cinema, the city's new image was likewise popularized and distributed internationally via popular films. This resulted in a new wave of mainstream pictures that presented the city as an attractive, safe, and romantic environment. Influential films that helped re-establish the city's allure around this period included romantic comedies such as *When Harry Met Sally* (dir. Rob Reiner, 1989), *Sleepless in Seattle* (dir. Nora Ephron, 1993), *While You Were Sleeping* (dir. Jon Turteltaub, 1995), and *You've Got Mail* (dir. Nora Ephron, 1998). On television, the sitcom genre had meanwhile moved from suburban environments focused on the nuclear family, from *Leave it to Beaver* (CBS, 1957-63) to *Family Ties* (NBC, 1982-89), towards social and collegial networks in emphatically urban settings, such as *Seinfeld* (NBC, 1990-98), *Frasier* (NBC, 1993-2004) and *Friends* (NBC, 1994-2004). These many specific representations of Manhattan as an attractive marketable commodity thus solidified the city's international image as a safe and romantic destination for affluent tourists.

The irony is that as the number of popular film and television productions set in an attractive city environment increased, the vast majority of these productions were actually produced in cities that provided cheaper production facilities, like Los Angeles and Vancouver. The image of New York City presented in these films is therefore a phantasm of "New Yorkness" sustained mostly by an imaginary sense of what this urban space signifies. This fantasy version of the city fits urban theorist Edward Soja's definition of the postmetropolis, a term he has elaborated in six complementary discourses that together define postmodern urban life. Each of these six discourses is summarized by its title, which emphasizes one specific key aspect of the postmodern city:

1 FLEXCITY: on the restructuring of the political economy of urbanization and the formation of the more flexibly specialized post-Fordist industrial metropolis.
2 COSMOPOLIS: on the globalization of urban capital, labor and culture and the formation of a new hierarchy of global cities.

3 EXOPOLIS: on the restructuring of urban form and the growth of edge cities, outer cities, and postsuburbia: the metropolis turned inside-out and outside in.

4 METROPOLARITIES: on the restructured social mosaic and the emergence of new polarizations and inequalities.

5 CARCERAL ARCHIPELAGOES: on the rise of fortress cities, surveillant technologies and the substitution of the police for *polis*.

6 SIMCITIES: on the restructured urban imaginary and the increasing hyperreality of everyday life. (2002: 190)

Although all six of these discourses intersect in complex ways to make up the entirety of the conceptual postmetropolis, individual discourses are also helpful to answer specific questions raised by representations of urban life. So while Soja's discourse of carceral archipelagoes will be revisited and developed further in the next chapter, the virtual film-image of New York alluded to above is best described "as Simcity, a place where simulations of a presumably real world increasingly capture and activate our urban imaginary and infiltrate everyday urban life" (2002: 194). Drawing on Baudrillard's definition of the simulacrum, Soja argues that these imaginary versions of the postmetropolis have in fact come to precede and define reality, "more than ever before shaping every aspect of our lives, from who and what we vote for to how we feed, clothe, mate and define our bodies" (ibid.).

Soja's "Simcities" discourse of the postmetropolis therefore emphasizes the imaginary version of a city like New York that effectively supersedes and overrules any physical experience of it. According to his definition, the imaginary urban environment we encounter in forms of public discourse such as advertising and popular narratives has become strong enough to overshadow the city as a physical, social, and economic space with its endless complexity and teeming diversity. This discourse seems most compelling when applied to filmic representations of the city, which connect strongly to the way New York is articulated as a recognizable brand within the global tourist industry.

The increasing commodification of this imaginary New York as a product on the international tourist market fits into a larger trend of major Western cities (re)branding themselves as commercial products with tourist appeal. This was supported by an international wave of films that helped to resuscitate the city's image as an appealing, clean, and safe environment. The French and British film industry swiftly followed Hollywood's strategy with a range of successful films, dominated again by the romantic comedy genre, that helped restore the image of the neoliberal European metropolis as a romantic global village: *Four Weddings and a Funeral* (dir. Mike Newell, 1993), *Notting Hill* (dir. Roger Michell, 1999), and *Le Fabuleux Destin d'Amélie Poulain* (dir. Jean-Pierre Jeunet, 2001). Each of these films, and many others like them, served up a sanitized, nostalgic, and idealized articulation of its city setting, seemingly designed to serve as an advertisement for its metropolis as a tourist destination.

Again, this shift in focus of popular representations of urban space accompanied the real-world development of urban gentrification, as dilapidated city centers were restructured and fixed up by private investors, thus furthering the social and economic divisions that inform much of city life. As public space was increasingly transformed into private space and corporations came to define the organization of urban environments, the gap between the urban poor and the powerful élite increased dramatically. More than ever, living in these new urban spaces of neoliberalism meant "to accept or submit to that liberal bundle of rights necessary for capital accumulation," even as the most common popular fantasy became one of fantastical wealth, happiness, and (heterosexual) romance (Harvey 2006: 56).

The 9/11 attacks and their resulting impact on global tourism, and most particularly on tourism to New York, gave added urgency to this ongoing project of reinventing the city as an attractive consumer product. The American film industry responded to the attacks by postponing the releases of films that were now deemed inappropriate, such as *Collateral Damage* (dir. Andrew Davis, 2002) and *Sidewalks of New York* (dir. Edward Burns, 2001) (Cadorette, n. pag.). In many other films that were released in the months following the attacks, footage containing the World Trade Center was digitally altered in order to avoid the "potentially trauma-inducing" effect of being confronted with shots of the Twin Towers, the destruction of which had so visibly affected the skyline (Spigel 119). Examples of digital alteration of footage shot before the attacks includes comedies such as *Zoolander* (dir. Ben Stiller, 2001) and *Serendipity* (dir. Peter Chelsom, 2001), while several major television series, including *Sex and the City* (HBO, 1998-2004) and *The Sopranos* (HBO, 1999-2007), removed shots of the World Trade Center from the montage sequences in their opening credits.

But the 2002 popular fantasy film *Spider-Man* became a specific focal point for much of the debate surrounding New York and post-9/11 depictions of the city. This long-anticipated and aggressively advertised superhero comic adaptation was green-lit by Sony Pictures after the box office success of the more modestly budgeted superhero movies *Blade* (1998) and *X-Men* (2000). The film went into pre-production in late 2000, with a release date scheduled for summer 2002, and teaser posters and trailers started appearing in the summer of 2001 to create awareness for the next summer's major blockbuster. In both elements of this publicity campaign, the World Trade Center was featured prominently. The teaser trailer presented a mini-narrative that existed entirely separate from the film proper, with bank robbers fleeing in a helicopter only to find themselves caught in a gigantic web spun between the Twin Towers. The

Teaser poster for *Spider-Man* (2002) with the World
Trade Center reflected in the hero's eyepiece.

teaser poster meanwhile presented a close-up of Spider-Man's
masked face on the side of a towering skyscraper, the towers of
the WTC reflected in his eyepiece.[6]

One of the remarkable aspects of this poster is that it strives to
include some of the most recognizable landmarks of
Manhattan—the Empire State Building and the Chrysler Building
strangely repositioned as if they stand directly opposite each
other—while also emphatically combining the modernist architecture of "classic" New Yorkness with the sheer, reflective
surfaces of postmodernism. The glass-panel walls from which

Spider-Man contemplates the rest of the city dominate the frame, even as we realize that these impossibly tall skyscrapers do not, indeed, *could* not exist in any physical or historical reality. But even as this virtual postmodern landmark dominates the frame, its diagonal perspective bearing down threateningly on those older monuments, the modernist spire of the Chrysler Building is also reflected and thereby reconstituted upon its sheer glass surface. The postmodernism of Spider-Man's branded SimCity has thus managed to incorporate the specter of modernism, both cultural forms now co-existing uncomfortably within the new paradigm of the neoliberal postmetropolis.

The teaser poster and trailer also both illustrate the remarkable extent to which the character and the city had grown intertwined in the public imagination, with the superhero signifying a desire to successfully navigate the imposing vertical landscape of the global metropolis. And although a decision was ultimately made to not remove the World Trade Center from two shots in which it appears —all but subliminally— in the background of the actual film, some other changes were made that would identify its "post-9/11 fervor." A climactic battle scene between the hero and his nemesis the Green Goblin now saw the interference of a group of New Yorkers coming to Spider-Man's aid while yelling "You mess with one of us, you mess with all of us!" (Travers, n. pag.). This connection between the film and New York City was emphasized repeatedly by film reviewers, who consistently mentioned 9/11 in connection with the film's release. The consensus among reviewers and commentators was that the film amounted to a "towering tribute to New York," restoring some of the city's recently tarnished image (Wloszczyna, n. pag.). The debates surrounding these decisions naturally added to the film's publicity, further establishing the character's association with a particular image of New York City and making it one of the first major Hollywood productions after 2001 to revitalize the city's image as a commercial brand.

Composite image of a "Disneyfied" Times Square
during the "World Unity Festival in *Spider-Man* (2002).

Nowhere in the film is this more evident than in its first major
set piece, which takes place in an exaggerated version of the new
"Disneyfied" Times Square. This location is employed within the
narrative of the film to host the "World Unity Festival": a
corporate-sponsored outdoor concert headlined by hip-hop
superstar Macy Gray and embellished by many oversized
balloons that resemble the floats in New York's annual
Thanksgiving Day parade. Some details about this scene are
worth pointing out. First of all, there is the bricolage evident in
the construction of this location in the film. Several of the

"making of" features on the film's DVD release emphasize the tremendous complications and costs involved with creating the illusion of a coherent space out of several highly diverse elements, including studio soundstages, outdoor sets on the studio back lot, CGI elements, and location-shot background plates.[4] Rather than a consistent recreation of the actual Times Square environment, the plot required several substantial changes, including the addition of a fancy Park Avenue-style hotel overlooking the square on the eastern side of Broadway, the removal of several buildings and structures, and the widening of the space of the square itself to allow for the concert stage and required crowd scene. Because of the composite nature of this setting, the cumulative effect during the climactic action scene that takes place here is best understood via Jameson's definition of "postmodern hyperspace":

> This latest mutation in space ... has finally succeeded in transcending the capacities of the individual human body to locate itself, to organize its immediate surroundings perceptually, and cognitively to map its position in a capable external world. It may now be suggested that this alarming disjunction point between the body and its built environment ... can itself stand as the symbol and analogon of that even sharper dilemma which is the incapacity of our minds ... to map the great global multinationals and decentered communicational network in which we find ourselves caught as individual subjects. (Jameson 1991: 44)

The jumble of spatially incoherent images that makes up this World Unity Festival sequence fits not only the above description as a literal embodiment of "hyperspace." It also offers its own kind of visual mapping of "great global multinationals" in the exaggerated presence of branded billboards, even more imposing and spectacular than in real life, and in the corporate sponsoring that made this event possible as a part of the plot.

The inevitable large-scale destruction that ends this scene is brought on by Norman Osborn (played by Willem Dafoe), the former corporate CEO whose madness is the direct result of the loss of his patriarchal position of power. The members of his board of directors have used the opportunities afforded them by the principles of neoliberal finance capital to take over the company. Therefore, when Osborn kills them off, this can be read as an expression of the paradoxical desire to see this frustratingly "decentered communicational network" brought down before our eyes.

The point here is not that the footage of Times Square in this scene constitutes an artificial representation of an actual location. It is rather that Times Square in its remodeling and rebranding has been defined as fundamentally artificial, and that the garish, balloon-filled amusement park pictured in the film does not represent the location so much as it provides a specific articulation of it. In a Baudrillardian sense, this image of a "hyperreal" Times Square comes to (re)define our understanding of the "real" Times Square, thereby making the reproduction superior to the original — about which one might now legitimately ask whether it even exists at all outside of this overdetermined phantasmal image.

A second noteworthy detail is the way in which the festival in Times Square is represented by highly contradictory images that combine the spectacle of a quintessentially metropolitan setting with the reassurance of provincial camaraderie, tradition, and public safety. As the camera descends into the crowd assembled on this alternate Times Square to find Spider-Man's alter ego Peter Parker taking pictures of the festivities, the first image we pick out via his viewfinder is one of two young women dressed in some kind of folkloristic European costume. In the background, a group of Chinese women is visible, similarly outfitted in traditional wear, supposedly occasioned by this festival's ill-defined notion of world unity. The short sequence of shots meant to illustrate this bewildering interpretation of world unity is however overshadowed by the on-stage Macy Gray performance, whose real-life celebrity and status as an international mainstream hip-hop superstar gives this World Unity Festival the unmistakable flavor of American corporate-produced entertainment. Aesthetically, the pop music track being performed here creates a strong sense of cognitive dissonance with the traditionalism of the costumes worn by members of the audience, as does the incongruous absence of the security measures without which such a public appearance would be unthinkable in any urban environment. What this strange collection of confusing contradictions and exaggerations brings to mind most strongly is the popular conception of the "global village," a term first introduced by Marshall McLuhan in the early 1960s, and often used to describe the globalizing effects of the Internet and the World Wide Web.

Although the World Unity Festival of *Spider-Man* would seem to fit the utopian aspect of the "global village" perfectly, the term's origins in fact contradict the idea popularized and subsequently commodified in the 1990s. Contrary to popular perception, the author's original conception of the global village does not suggest any kind of ideal notion of benevolent and unified world capitalism. As McLuhan explained, it never occurred to him that uniformity and tranquility were properties of this Global Village. In fact, the concept instead "insures maximal disagreement on all points, because it creates more discontinuity and division and diversity under the increase of the village conditions" (McLuhan, qtd. in Stearns 314). Films like *Spider-Man* embody the contradiction wound up by these conflicting interpretations of the term in a dialectical manner: revealing first the desire to stage the postmodern metropolis as a traditional, even provincial community (in ways similar to the visual vocabulary of postclassical urban romantic comedy), only to be followed by the inevitable destruction of those very images and concepts. Within the context of the film, the film vividly illustrates Slavoj Žižek's point about this kind of popular fantasy:

> The fact that the September 11 attacks were the stuff of popular fantasies long before they actually took place provides yet another case of the twisted logic of dreams: it is easy to account for the fact that poor people around the world dream about becoming Americans—so what do the well-to-do Americans, immobilized in their well-being, dream about? About a global catastrophe that would shatter their lives—why? This is what psychoanalysis is about: to explain why, in the midst of well-being, we are haunted by nightmarish visions of catastrophes. (2002: 17)

This crucial distinction between first-world and third-world fantasies helps us understand some of the seeming contradictions that are featured so prominently in *Spider-Man* and other postclassical Hollywood films like it. On the one hand, these films, which are themselves branded commodities produced for the global marketplace, present a glorified image of a (semi-)utopian late-capitalist metropolis, offered up to its consumers as a digitally enhanced spectacle that becomes an attraction in its own right. And on the other hand, the genre conventions guarantee scenes of equally spectacular destruction, generally framed within the context of just such "global catastrophes" that embody those "nightmarish visions" that interrupt the postmodern crisis of agency.

This crisis and its resulting sense of immobilization is not merely the result of the "death of the subject" and the decentering qualities of the postmodern turn discussed in chapter one: it is also fundamentally connected to the experience of the modern city. As theorized by Georg Simmel in his 1903 essay "The Metropolis and Mental Life," "the reaction of the metropolitan person ... is moved to a sphere of mental activity which is least sensitive and which is furthest removed from the depths of the personality" (12). This desensitization of the metropolitan subject results in a fundamental attitude of "blasé-ness," which Simmel develops as follows:

> The essence of the blasé attitude is an indifference toward the distinctions between things. Not in the sense that they are not perceived, as is the case of mental dullness, but rather that the meaning and the value of the distinctions between things, and therewith of the things themselves, are experienced as meaningless. They appear to the blasé person in a homogeneous, flat and grey colour with no one of them worthy of being preferred to another. This psychic mood is the correct subjective reflection of a complete money economy to the extent that money takes the place of all the manifoldness of things and expresses all qualitative distinctions between them in the distinction of how much. (14)

The archetypal metropolitan attitude theorized by Simmel is therefore the product not only of the architecture of the modern city and its separation from the more "natural" traditions of rural life, but also, and perhaps more fundamentally, of the "complete money economy" that defines modern capitalism. In the same way that Dorothy follows a metaphorical Yellow Brick Road towards a simulacrum of New York City whose emerald glow reflects the green color of modern, paper money, the metropolis embodies the abstractions of modern capital in a way that is both visually spectacular and internally contradictory.

This is the point where Simmel's influential reflections on modernity connect most strongly with postmodern urban theorists like Sharon Zukin, who have focused their work on the transformation of public city spaces into a heavily commodified "landscape of power" (Zukin 197). She describes the "death of downtown" in terms of a far-reaching structural transformation of city spaces: "the internationalization of investment, a shift in social meaning from production to consumption, and an abstraction ... from cultural to economic values" (201). Jameson similarly describes the spectacular forms of postmodern architecture that have increasingly come to dominate our experience of the urban environment along with its own displaced simulacrum, the shopping mall, as "mesmerizing and fascinating not so much in its own right but because it seems to offer some privileged representational shorthand for grasping a network of power and control even more difficult for our minds and imaginations to grasp: the whole new decentered global network of the third stage of capital itself" (1991: 37-8). From this perspective, the postmodern city thus functions as an intensification of the metropolitan experience theorized by Simmel, as capitalism has moved into its late, post-industrial, or global stage.

The individual's inability to navigate this metropolitan maze gives rise to a fundamental sense of anxiety that partially reflects the decentering "crisis of postmodernity" and its alienating effects on the individual. The superhero figure's defining characteristic is his power to transcend this situation, either in Superman's ability to "leap tall buildings in a single bound" or Spider-Man's spectacular web-slinging trajectories through Manhattan's skyscraper canyons. Both Simmel's conception of the metropolis as a space made up of "homogeneous, flat and grey colour" and Jameson's postmodern category of hyperspace are negative categories that physically overpower the individual's body. One productive way of reading the superhero's enduring popularity as an icon of the modern cityscape is therefore as the embodiment of this public anxiety concerning the individual's position within that urban environment: "through the superhero, we gain a freedom of movement not constrained by the ground-level order imposed by the urban grid" (Bukatman 188).

Both the exaggerated plays on perspective in comic books and the effects-driven action set pieces of the superhero movie illustrate this point most strongly. *Superman* and *Spider-Man*, each in its own way a genre-defining hit, went to great lengths to foreground the sequences in which the protagonist moves through the city in superhuman ways. *Superman's* tagline "You'll believe a man can fly" spearheaded an elaborate publicity campaign that strove to communicate the notion that realistic illusions had been created for this film; *Spider-Man* adopted a similar strategy, releasing numerous Electronic Press Kits and television specials that again focused on the groundbreaking nature of the film's visual effects.

But in spite of the ostentatiously spectacular visuals of both these films, there is also a fundamental difference between the *Superman* of 1978 and the *Spider-Man* of 2002. For whereas the former relied entirely on photographic effects for its visual illusions, the 21st-century blockbuster exists within the paradigm of digital cinema. And although the commercial rhetoric surrounding computer-generated imagery focuses on the groundbreaking scope and detail of the special effects, the replacement of the human body on the screen by a digital avatar does also have far-reaching ontological consequences. Just as money "loses its material presences and turns into a purely virtual entity" in the postmodern world of late capitalism (Žižek 1997: 131), so does the human figure in these films lose its hold on the viewer, as he is increasingly replaced on the screen by uncanny digital doubles.

The rise of digital cinema has radically altered our perception of the very nature of the film medium, as it shifted irrevocably from the indexicality of the photographic trace or footprint (Bazin 18) to the concept of "a particular case of animation which uses live action footage as one of its many elements" (Manovich 1995: n. pag.). New media theorist Lev Manovich notes that in the digital age, "cinema can no longer be clearly distinguished from animation. It is no longer an indexical media technology but, rather, a sub-genre of painting" (1995, n. pag.). Previously, film had been defined in terms of its indexical relationship to observable reality, mechanically capturing indexical traces of a phenomenologically existing world. But now that computer-generated imagery has developed to the point where it is no longer discernable from live-action footage, these indexical images have become mere "raw material to be manipulated by hand: animated, combined with 3-D computer generated scenes and painted over" (ibid.). The explicit paradigm shift denoted by this change, grounded in technological and aesthetic develop-ments, has far-reaching implications for the way representations of the human body are depicted in filmic fantasies.

A crucial distinction to make here is that "computer-generated imagery is not an inferior representation of our reality, but a realistic representation of a different reality" (Manovich 2001: 202). This paradigmatic shift in our conception of film connects in many ways to the ongoing crisis of agency that is so strongly associated with theories of postmodernism. As the human body is replaced more frequently on the screen by photorealistic digital doubles, this crisis of agency becomes increasingly complex. For if the utopian promise of the Internet and the global village of new media was one of increased freedom of expression and a regained sense of agency, the filmic representations of such subjects are more and more often digital specters without any ontological connection to the human body.

Unlike the most celebrated scenes in *Superman*, in which the audience experiences the illusionistic *jouissance* of seeing actor Christopher Reeve taking to the sky, similar scenes from *Spider-Man* feature a masked protagonist who clearly has no existence outside of the digital realm. Even though the character's spectacular ability to transcend the physical limitations of the contemporary city dweller provides a pleasing fantasy of empowerment, the fundamentally non-human ontological status of the character on the screen simultaneously short-circuits the experience. The visual effects in this case become an attraction in their own right: not of the human body's ability to navigate, let alone overcome, the overwhelming urban spaces of (post)modernity, but of modern technology's ability to create such astonishing images. As Scott Bukatman has observed about just such flights of fancy: "the phenomenologic of these tactics constitutes an embodied, kinetic incursion, a means of remapping the subject (as a trajectory) onto the spaces of industrial and electronic capitalism" (3).

The transformation of the subject from a physical being into a digital "trajectory" through the abstract spaces of postmodern capitalism is the key notion in Bukatman's description of the superhero's representational implications. This perspective connects the superhero figure back to Simmel's modern city-dweller, and onward to Baudelaire's figure of the *flâneur*, both of which traverse the city with an overriding interest in safeguarding private property. Besides the "indifference toward the distinction between things" experienced by city dwellers in early modernity, later culminating in Jameson's indecipherable hyperspaces of postmodern architecture, the other central aspect of mental life in the metropolis remains that of "blasé-ness." This quintessentially metropolitan attitude was further extended by Walter Benjamin in his development of the *flâneur* as a semi-somnambulist who walks along the streets and arcades of Paris, impervious to intrusions of reality:

> Boredom is a warm gray fabric lined on the inside with the most lustrous and colorful of silks. In this fabric we wrap ourselves when we dream. We are at home then in the arabesques of its lining. But the sleeper looks bored and gray within his sheath. And when he later wakes and wants to tell of what he dreamed, he communicates, by and large, only this boredom. For who would be able at one stroke to turn the lining of time to the outside? Yet to narrate dreams signifies nothing else. And in no other way can one deal with the arcades—structures in which we relive, as in a dream, the life of our parents and grandparents, as in the embryo in the womb relives the life of animals. (Benjamin 2002: 399)

Superhero figures occupy a similarly dualistic position towards this fundamental boredom that defines our perception of life in the metropolis. On the one hand, characters such as Spider-Man and Superman seem to embody the opposite of the *flâneur*, always moving through the city with a clear sense of purpose, without any interest in the idle pursuit of commodities or social forms of exchange. The superhero persona's garish costume likewise contrasts with the drabness of the three-piece business suit that serves as the *flâneur*'s default costume, even as it effectively camouflages its wearer's true identity in similar ways. Meanwhile, the superhero's alter ego functions as a parody of one of two traditional forms of human existence: either that of the decadent playboy/aristocrat, or that of the ordinary working man.

But on the other hand, the superhero's extraordinary ability to transcend the limitations of everyday life also functions as the phantasmal escape from "capitalist realism," the compelling term introduced by Mark Fisher as an updated alternative to Jameson's definition of postmodernism (Fisher 2009: 7). The superhero's powers, which consist either of supernatural physical abilities (Superman, Spider-Man) or of a fantasy of unlimited capital (Batman, Iron Man), make him a figure of empowerment and agency in a world of consumers who are defined by their lack of these very qualities. Their crime-stopping ideological agenda is meanwhile a pure distillation of basic capitalist assumptions: the defense of private property by punishing "the transgressions of the underclass but not the conditions that give rise to these transgressions" (Pearson and Uricchio 206).

The continued popularity of these figures is to be understood by way of this structural contradiction, which is exactly what makes these superhero fantasies such potent ideological constructs. The narratives present their heroic protagonist as a role model, often citing the banal cliché that "one man *can* make a difference," while the impossibility of the superhero figure functions as "a filler holding the place of some structural impos-sibility, while simultaneously disavowing this impossibility" (Žižek 1997: 98). The structural impossibility in this case would be the existence of a utopian metropolitan environment within the system of capitalism of which it is perhaps the strongest, most recognizable signifier. The disavowal of this impossibility resides in these films' determined refusal to dwell upon the actual causes of the social problems casually represented in these pictures. In other words: the superhero movie suggests that the postmodern metropolis would be a happier, safer place if there were a force that could operate outside the bureaucracies that cripple the enforcement of the law. This offers a perfect reflection of neoliberal deregulation, alongside the mythologization of the individual in relation to private enterprise.

At the same time, the fantasy embodied by these films "teaches us how to desire" both a specific representation of this glorified urban environment and the excessive enjoyment of overcoming the limitations of the postmodern subject's crisis of agency. This enjoyment as a form of pure Lacanian *jouissance* is most evident in the web-swinging sequences in *Spider-Man*, which demand to be read in terms of excess. Not only does their obtrusive foregrounding of the use of digital visual effects draw them into Tom Gunning's category of a postclassical "cinema of attractions," but they also function as an implicit celebration of the process of film consumption itself:

This kind of cinema attracts the spectator to the spectacle of its technology, but, at the same time, aims at the fantastic element and transfers the attraction of the technology toward the diegetic. This is particularly evident in the sequences shot with the so-called "spider-cam" which is constantly showing its own virtuosity while being completely subjected to the recording of the extraordinary acrobatics of the hero. The technological device exhibits itself while highlighting, above all, the extraordinary action of the diegesis offering throughout these bewildering moments a double attraction (the attraction of the film and the attraction of the *dispositif*). (Tomasovic 315)

These sequences do indeed provide a "double attraction," sustained both by the viewer's interest in the diegetic world of the film and in the *dispositif* of movie spectatorship as an attractive and pleasurable process. But the attraction on display here is also doubly excessive: not only as a visual experience that is meant to overpower and bewilder the viewer's sensory apparatus, but also as a form of narrative excess. The most obvious example is featured at the end of all three *Spider-Man* films, where the viewer is treated to a virtuoso final "spider-cam" shot of the hero's spectacular traversal of the city. These closing sequences occur after the causal chain that makes up the plot has been concluded and full narrative closure has been achieved for that particular installment. They thus supply a spectacular coda that celebrates both the superhero's *jouissance* and the audience's excessive enjoyment of the spectacular imagery that is so prominently on display.

What the audience is being "taught to desire" here is therefore once again fundamentally contradictory: on the one hand, the fantasy of the protagonist's ability to overcome the limitations of an intensely commodified late capitalist urban landscape in which the individual consumer has little or no agency; and on the other hand, a form of enjoyment that defines the viewer as a passive consumer of the images that provide a fantasy of escape, gorging himself on spectacular scenes of mass destruction that reduce this urban hyperspace to rubble. The semi-utopian imagination of the postmodern city in films like *Spider-Man* therefore fails to provide any real sense of actual relief from the neoliberal metropolis.

The Threat of Postmodern Finance:
Dystopian Terror in Gotham City

Unlike the glossily nostalgic capitalist playground of *Spider-Man*'s New York City, *The Dark Knight* (dir. Christopher Nolan, 2008) presents a very different kind of urban environment for its superhero protagonist to inhabit and protect, as indeed may be expected given the tradition of Gothicism that has been a popular element within the Batman character's visual tradition. But unlike the preceding Batman films, *The Dark Knight* emphasizes from the very beginning that its depiction of Gotham City is not the "densely stylized urban forest of inky comic-book noir" based on a film noir version of New York City (Emerson n. pag.). Instead, it utilizes helicopter shots of existing metropolitan areas to a previously unknown degree, thereby eschewing the over-the-top aesthetics that had made the earlier Batman films so instantly identifiable as fantastical "comic book movies" that avoided any direct visible connection to an exterior reality.

A more "realist" Gotham City: downtown Chicago in *The Dark Knight* (2008).

The film's use of real locations, especially the prominence of the glass-and-steel postmodernist architecture of Chicago and Hong Kong, connects the film's familiar superhero paradigm to a different form of visual realism, while also setting itself apart from the use of location footage and background plates in the *Spider-Man* franchise. For although both films prominently feature recognizable images of Chicago's familiar city center, the selection and use of this footage reflects a radically different interpretation of what such an urban environment signifies. As I have demonstrated in the previous section of this chapter, Spider-Man inhabits a city that is branded on every conceivable level: from the literal branding of the billboards and consumer products that litter the film's squares and avenues to the extended branding of New York City itself as an attractive and spectacular commodity for the tourist market: a literal playground for the wealthy.

In Christopher Nolan's Batman films, Gotham City also functions as "a sort of exaggerated contemporary New York" (Nolan, qtd. in "Gotham Rising"), but its imagery reveals a conception of the postmodern city in which both the ubiquitous branding of late capitalism and the bustle of city life are notably absent. The Spider-Man and Superman films emphasized the dynamism of city spaces in multiple ways: by including numerous shots of crowds moving along the busy Manhattan avenues, by placing their superhero protagonists among those crowds, and by foregrounding the lively newsroom atmosphere of the newspaper workplace as a metaphorical condensation of this dynamic urban environment. Conversely, *The Dark Knight* consistently offers shots of avenues that are either entirely devoid of public life, or in which the crowds are presented specifically as

Orderly crowds and empty sidewalks in *The Dark Knight* (2008).

organized and controlled, thereby emphasizing order and discipline over the implied freedom of movement in public urban space. Whenever this sense of public order is threatened or temporarily suspended, this is always due to disruptive actions undertaken by the movie's main villain.

These different conceptions of urban space relate back to the difference between utopian and dystopian imaginations of the city, as described earlier in this chapter: Spider-Man's Manhattan represents the metropolis as a lively, attractive space in which the superhero counteracts the occasional calamity, while Batman's Gotham City on the other hand presents the urban landscape as a far more threatening environment, constantly plagued by terror, civil unrest, and the systematic failure of its democratic institutions. Ways of thinking about how these different types of urban environment and the narratives that take place within them relate to the films' ideological implications are best approached from the perspective of the following quotation:

> As always, the way to understand ideology is not to ask "what does the film think," nor "what can I think through the lens of this film," but "what does thinking 'with' the film prevent me from thinking." [Popular films] are not interested in making "arguments" ... their job is to reinforce premises. Not because their creators have malicious intentions, but because it is important for their financial backers and consequently for them to ensure that those premises remain profitable. For example, the baseline pessimism and dependency that supports big-screen violent fantasies along with the notion that it is "easier to imagine the end of the world than the end of capitalism" is comforting, enabling to all kinds of fantasies, and serves as ground zero for a set of trained assumptions about the world, along with the opinions, laudatory, apologetic, or critical, derived from them. This is one definition of "popular." (Vu n. pag.)

The strength of this perspective on how to decode popular texts from an ideological point of view is that it demonstrates that these texts should not be interpreted as cohesive statements of ideology (as they are too easily read). Instead, they should be understood as mechanisms that reflect ideological assumptions by providing narratives that systematically limit the viewer's choices.

This approach may be viewed as a sensible strategic choice for texts that are produced first and foremost as commodities that require a large audience to yield the required profits. As many others have observed, the postclassical Hollywood film represents politics in a way that is strategically ambiguous, thereby opening itself up to a larger number of contradictory readings and interpretations. If a popular movie then triggers discussion or even some mild controversy, then all the better: a limited degree of controversy translates into free publicity, and the larger the audience, the higher the profits. But in spite of this room for strategic ambiguity, which applies most strongly when attempting to read these texts as literal political allegories, their narratives do tend to limit our options in systematic, highly controlled ways. Productive interpretation must therefore include not only what is on the screen, but also (and perhaps especially) what has been omitted, as "we can locate the trace of pernicious ideology not in the choices themselves but rather in what the authors choose to leave off the menu" (Pistelli n. pag.).

The Dark Knight serves as a particularly potent example of this type of ideological manipulation through limitation, best encapsulated by neoliberalism's familiar "There Is No Alternative" mantra. In the film's plot, the citizens of Gotham City are faced with a series of choices between two available options that literally leave no room for alternatives. In the film's self-professed "world without rules," the preferred option can consistently be described as opting for the lesser of two evils. This binary narrative logic is embodied most explicitly by the central conflict between the film's protagonist and its primary antagonist: Batman stands for order, and the Joker stands for chaos, while all the characters that seem to fill in the middle ground are swiftly eliminated from the playing field.

The central division between the two main characters goes beyond the Manichean binary of good vs. evil that is so familiar from the standard formula of the popular fantasy film. Instead, it introduces the Joker as the embodiment of a paradigm shift that forces the other characters to redefine their definitions of such terms, effectively constituting not so much an opposing force to Batman, but even an attempt to hijack the entire film: "the Joker is whom we have come to see, the Joker what we have been waiting for, the Joker who generates nearly all of the pleasure of the film" (Canavan 2010: 4). While attempts are made within the narrative to make sense of the Joker's actions, all such efforts are repeatedly contradicted at key points in lines of dialogue, both by the Joker himself and by several other characters:

The Joker: Do I really look like a guy with a plan? You know what I am? I'm a dog chasing cars. I wouldn't know what to do with one if I caught it. You know, I just... do things.

Alfred: Some men aren't looking for anything logical, like money. They can't be bought, bullied, reasoned or negotiated with. Some men just want to watch the world burn.

Harvey Dent: The Joker's just a mad dog.

These none-too-subtle characterizations are confirmed at the visual level as well as by the mechanics of the plot, which endow the Joker with an all but supernatural ability to predict and disrupt even the most ingenious plans that are laid out against him. These narrative choices have encouraged critics and audiences alike to interpret *The Dark Knight* as an allegorical representation of America's Bush-era War on Terror, in which the Joker "can very easily stand in propagandistically for 'America's enemies'" (Pistelli n. pag.), and which conservative critics have described as "a paean of praise to the fortitude and moral courage that has been shown by George W. Bush" (Klavan n. pag.).

As superficial as these readings of the film as a literal political allegory may be, they do illustrate the strong general tendency to interpret the film as a topical text that reflects contemporary political and ideological choices and dilemmas, rather than a fantastical alternate universe without any bearing on a perceived form of "reality." This is very different from the response to superhero movies in the 1980s and 1990s, which were rarely discussed as political allegories or topical debates. Instead of simply adopting the binary narrative mechanisms of the film and projecting them onto an external geopolitical reality, we must therefore strive to reveal the more complicated ways in which *The Dark Knight* encourages such readings while systematically sealing off others.

With the Joker defined so explicitly as a new form of an irrational, essentialist evil, the "good" for which Batman stands can remain much more loosely defined (as can the definition of "order" as opposed to the Joker's "chaos"). As the embodiment of patriarchal capitalism, he can even be presented within the narrative as a reluctant avenger who uses his repressive forces of violence only after all other options have consistently failed. What is therefore most interesting to note here is that these "other options" in fact hardly figure in *The Dark Knight*'s narrative universe at all:

> The moral is as old, and as conservative, as Hobbes: we can live in a wild, murderous wasteland or a lawless, authoritarian police state. It doesn't matter which of these options the film presents as more

appealing or fun; all that matters is that no other options—e.g., left-wing anarchism, participatory democracy, decentralized communism, democratic socialism etc.—present themselves. (Pistelli n. pag.)

One way of describing this type of narrative logic is through the term "crisis management": for most superhero movies, as for many other popular film genres, the plot is so strongly focused on averting a particular crisis that no time is taken to investigate or even touch upon the hero's methods, let alone the ideological values he embodies and perpetuates. In geopolitical terms, this mode of thinking is extremely similar to the previous chapter's description of disaster capitalism, reflecting our seemingly constant state of crisis. As ever, the hero does not distinguish himself so much by his methods, which are usually similarly violent, but by the fact that "superheroes, by dint of their emplotment and alignment with the status quo, can be understood as distinguishable from their opponents not through the nature of their violence ... but through their political objectives" (Dittmer ch. 1). In other words: we do not mind that the superhero is fighting, as long as we implicitly share the values he is fighting for.

These values in most popular genres of entertainment are firmly embedded in capitalism, from James Bond with his vintage sports cars and playboy lifestyle to Bruce Wayne with his reliable butler and corporate empire. In the case of Batman, this myopic devotion to capitalism is even endemic to the character's basic conception: "other popular heroes such as Sherlock Holmes and Superman may support the status quo, but doing so does not constitute their *sine qua non*" (Pearson and Uricchio 203). For since Bruce Wayne must depend wholly on his billionaire status to maintain his alternate crime-fighting persona and pay for his arsenal of technological gadgets, vehicles and costumes, Batman's superpower may indeed be defined as Capital in the most literal sense. As the heir to his father's fortune and as CEO of a multi-billion dollar corporation Wayne Enterprises, Bruce Wayne therefore obviously has a clearly defined interest in sustaining the status quo of patriarchal capitalism, which is illustrated so vividly by the main plot of *Batman Begins*.

As Mark Fisher has pointed out as well, the name of the hero's father is literally synonymous with that of capitalist enterprise, thereby establishing both aspects as fundamental to the symbolic order that defines the hero's worldview. In the film's narrative, the Fordist corporate empire of Wayne Enterprises is threatened by a hostile take-over in the form of post-Fordist finance capital, represented in the film by the character Earl (played by Rutger Hauer). This economic threat directly mirrors the physical threat of terrorism that Wayne/Batman must simultaneously avert. The rise of speculative, virtual capital that has taken place in the years since Wayne Senior's demise is meanwhile reflected by the social and economic downfall of Gotham City, thus neatly forcing Bruce Wayne to take up the predetermined role he had previously abandoned:

> There is no doubt that the film poses finance capital as a problem that will be solved by the return of a re-personalised capital, with "the enlightened despot" Bruce taking on the role of the dead [father] Thomas. It is equally clear … that *Batman Begins* is unable to envisage an alternative to capitalism itself, favouring instead a nostalgic rewind to prior forms of capitalism. (One of the structuring fantasies of the film is the notion that crime and social disintegration are exclusively the results of capitalist failure, rather than the inevitable accompaniments to capitalist "success.") (Fisher 2006: par. 19)

Batman Begins nostalgically re-establishes the dominance of this more conservative form of patriarchal capitalism by successfully challenging the threatening emergence of neoliberal finance capital. But even as it superficially rejects the rise of finance capital, the film's systematic glorification of a corporate CEO as a new kind of capitalist superhero plays upon the most successful rhetoric of the neoliberal and neoconservative movements.

This deeply contradictory mobilization of contemporary political discourse is further heightened in the sequel *The Dark Knight*. As this second film in the new Batman cycle begins, the protagonist's efforts to rebuild Gotham City appear to be successful on two different levels: petty criminals have grown reluctant to take to the streets for fear of being attacked by the new vigilante, while the visual splendor of the modern highrises and office buildings that represent Gotham in this film suggest that the economy has similarly improved, and that Wayne's corporate empire of benevolent patriarchal capitalism has flourished. But once again, the hegemony of this neoliberal empire is challenged, in this case by what the film's dialogue ironically refers to as "a better class of criminal." Whether this line is an intentional play on the topic of social class or not, *The Dark Knight* certainly turns out to be singularly obsessed with class warfare, and with radical changes to the socio-economic order.

This focus is introduced straightaway in the film's spectacular opening scene, where the Joker orchestrates a complex bank robbery with his gang of clown-faced henchmen, whose masks cannot disguise their working-class accents. What sets this sequence apart from similar heist scenes in crime films like *Heat* (dir. Michael Mann, 1995) is the fact that the Joker's crew eliminates each gang member as soon as his task has been carried out: "The boss told me when the guy was done, I should take him out. One less share, right?" This strategy reflects the kind of logic based on short-term individual gains over long-term benefits that typifies the dangers of neoliberalism and speculative finance capitalism: gang members are dispatched as soon as the application of their particular skill-set has been carried out, thereby literalizing the logic of neoliberalism's infamous "disposable workforce" (Petras and Vieux 2594).

Although this dog-eat-dog "world without rules" of *The Dark Knight* sets itself apart from the honorable crooks in the afore-mentioned *Heat*, one may point out that the Joker's modus operandi in reality simply sees the paradigmatic changes implied by Mann's film through to their logical conclusion:

> One of the easiest ways to grasp the differences between Fordism and post-Fordism is to compare Mann's film with the gangster movies made by Francis Ford Coppola and Martin Scorsese between 1971 and 1990. In *Heat*, the scores are undertaken not by Families with links to the Old Country, but by rootless crews, in an LA of polished chrome and interchangeable designer kitchens, of featureless freeways and late-night diners. All the local color, the cuisine aromas, the cultural idiolects which the likes of *The Godfather* and *Goodfellas* depended upon have been painted over and re-fitted. (Fisher 2009: 31)

It is remarkable that the other crime bosses in Gotham City, who are similarly threatened by the appearance of the Joker and his methods, are presented entirely along the lines of the old-school "crime families," their identities defined by ethnicity, dialect, and "Old Country" traditions. On the basis of the scene in which Gotham's three major gangs meet to discuss their plans, they consist of easily recognizable groups: the old-fashioned Italian gangsters led by Salvatore Moroni (played by Eric Roberts); an African-American gang headed by "Gambol" (played by Michael Jai White); and an Eastern-European faction of drug dealers led by an unnamed, heavily accented gangster identified in the credits merely as "The Chechen" (played by Ritchie Coster). These are typical petty criminals of the Batman series, where each bad guy "conforms to the stereotype of a different marginalized subculture" (Pearson and Uricchio 205).

Unlike the Joker's seemingly inexhaustible resources, both human and otherwise, these more traditional crime families are easily out-maneuvered, both by Batman and by the new kind of competition represented by the Joker. The crime families' main problem throughout the film is their floundering ability to keep track of their money. It is relevant to note here that the gangsters' financial resources, unlike those of Batman or the Joker, are distinctly visualized as cash money, and "money is, to be sure, not the same as capital, as Marx tirelessly and vigorously reminds us" (Jameson 2005: 230). Bruce Wayne can of course rest assured that money remains irrelevant for someone with his kind of capital:

> Big business, the so-called ruling class, has projects and ideologies: political plans for future change, in the spirit of privatization and the free market. But the mass of people who either desperately need money or are in a position to make some and to invest, do not themselves have to believe in any hegemonic ideology of the system, but only to be convinced of its permanence. (ibid. 229)

The criminals of Gotham City on the other hand clearly depend upon physical access to actual money, and are now forced to rely on unsavory Asian finance capitalists like the duplicitous and cowardly Lau (played by Chin Han) in order to keep track of it in today's world of global, virtual finance. After having demonstrated his tactical superiority in the scene where he interrupts their meeting, the Joker ultimately demonstrates the conceptual chasm that separates them by literally burning a large mountain of the gangsters' money. Unsurprisingly, the Joker's grasp of the virtualization of money brings him conceptually closer to his nemesis Batman, who consistently adopts the persona of the wasteful billionaire playboy whose financially irresponsible behavior reflects a similarly decadent disdain for cash. Like Batman, the Joker is more akin to the famous caricature of the

The Joker: a Scrooge McDuck-like capitalist
burning a mountain of money in *The Dark Knight.*

Scrooge McDuck-like capitalist, lighting his cigar with a hundred-dollar bill, than to the criminal class he associates with.

The Joker may therefore be interpreted more productively as a new signifier for the systemic threat of the permanent disposable workforce of post-Fordist capitalism than as an allegorical representation of globalized terrorism: "we must be careful to resist readings of *The Dark Knight* as an uncomplicated, one-to-one mapping of the major players in the War on Terror into comic-book terms" (Canavan 2010: 4). Both the anxiety and the obvious attraction that surround the figure of the Joker in this film point to a wider public ambivalence in the face of post-Fordist, globalized capitalism:

> The slogan which sums up the new conditions is "no long term." Where formerly workers would acquire a single set of skills and expect to progress upward through a rigid organizational hierarchy, now they are periodically required to re-skill as they move from institution to institution, from role to role. (Fisher 2009: 32)

With the traditional crime families of Gotham City thus representing "the hierarchical Fordist structure" of the age of entrepreneurial capitalism, the Joker's gang signifies the network-based form of organization that has come to define postmodern finance capital. It makes sense therefore that neither the old-school crime gangs nor the liberal-minded representatives of democratic government are able to thwart the rise of the Joker and the new kind of criminality he represents within the post-historical age of neoliberalism.

The other characters' inability to grasp the Joker's true motivations also makes sense in the context of a historical period in which the individual lacks the conceptual vocabulary to describe with any accuracy the larger cultural and economic shifts of postmodernity. The political rhetoric in 21st-century public discourse has relied heavily on the stability of the nation state in terms derived from twentieth-century historical events. In his incisive analysis of the key speeches given by George W. Bush in the first twelve months after 9/11, J. Maggio explains how the former president drew on such historically specific notions of citizenship and statehood to define those events:

> Bush's term "Axis of Evil" itself employs unique rhetoric. First, it creates ... a "condensation symbol" for the complex web of anti-American governments and networks. Hence, one does not need to analyze the complex structures or causalities of separate nations and/or groups ... Second, it associates these regimes and groups with one of the United States' greatest enemies, the Axis Powers of World War II ... And third, by equating these countries with the "Axis" —as well as the biblical notion of "evil"—Bush defines the regimes as inherently our enemies. (830)

However, as many cultural, political and economic theorists have repeatedly pointed out in recent years, the notion of the nation state as the basic constitutional order of Western societies is now in many ways outdated. Indeed, "there has been increasing recognition for the fact that ... we are entering the transition from one constitutional order to another—from the nation state to the market state" (Bobbitt 86). This has resulted in a widespread if understandable sense of confusion as to the motivation of new enemies in this age's political and military conflicts.

The lack of any generally convincing geopolitical narrative in the wake of the 9/11 attacks has therefore led to the kinds of questions that are dramatized in *The Dark Knight*. In this changing paradigm, it becomes difficult to adopt appropriate narrative metaphors for wider anxieties related to this transition from nation-state to market state:

> The emergence of the twenty-first century market state is the principal driver of the Wars against Terror. The same forces that are empowering the individual and compelling the creation of a state devoted to maximizing the individual's opportunity are also empowering the forces of terror, rendering societies more vulnerable and threatening to destroy the consent of the individual as the essential source of state legitimacy. (Bobbitt 85-86)

Historian and political theorist Philip Bobbitt here connects the rise of terrorist groups like Al Qaeda to the economic development of the market state, the postmodern, decentralized form of statehood that also fits the familiar post-Marxist definition of global capitalism. While cultural and political discourse on 9/11 and the continuing Wars against Terror have emphasized the religious and ideological conflicts that seem to typify this conflict on the surface (as in Samuel Huntington's "clash of civilizations" thesis), Bobbitt argues that Al Qaeda is in fact the product of the very postmodern capitalism that presents itself as its binary opposite: "it is becoming increasingly clear that Al Qaeda is not only a reaction to globalization but that it is a manifestation and exploitation of globalization" (83). Like the division between Batman and the Joker, the seemingly absolute difference between postmodern multicultural liberalism on the one hand and global terrorism on the other is therefore similarly illusory.

The fact that "the unifying element among the groups to which Al Qaeda outsources its elements is not a mystical, retrograde form of Islam" (ibid.) but the methods of an outsourced, networked corporation helps us understand why the Joker was interpreted by so many as "a perfect reflection of their view of Al Qaeda" (Ackerman n. pag.). Indeed, it is hardly a coincidence that connections have been made between the phenomenal appeal of the Joker and the rise to power of 21st-century neoliberal politicians like Berlusconi:

> Beneath [Berlusconi's] clownish mask there is a mastery of state power functioning with ruthless efficiency. Even if Berlusconi is a clown without dignity, we should therefore not laugh at him too much — perhaps, by doing so, we are already playing his game. His laughter is more like the obscene-crazy laughter of the superhero's enemy from a Batman or Spiderman movie. To get an idea of the nature of his rule, one should imagine something like the Joker from *Batman* in power. (Žižek 2009: 50)

But if the Joker represents the most unsettling aspects of post-Fordist capitalism and the development of the market state, to what extent then does Bruce Wayne/Batman and his relentless quest to end the Joker's reign of terror constitute a possible alternative?

As in *Batman Begins*, the protagonist's struggle in *The Dark Knight* is fuelled by his desire to restore the Fordist patriarchal order that symbolizes an older age of entrepreneurial capitalism. The worldview represented by the superhero in this film can therefore be defined as fundamentally reactionary, the dramatic conflict between protagonist and antagonist revolving around the question whether this older worldview has become obsolete or not. As the Joker explains: "I'll show you: when the chips are down, these 'civilized' people, they'll eat each other. You see, I'm not a monster—I'm just ahead of the curve." In the most literal sense, Wayne/Batman as the standard-bearer of entrepreneurial Fordist values represents a nostalgic fantasy of the past that revolves around notions of patriarchal hegemony. The Joker meanwhile proudly proclaims a future of absolute neoliberal dogma and radical deregulation: "The only sensible way to live in this world is without rules."

But without the neoconservative values that fill up the empty core of neoliberal practices, the true nature of "fundamentalist capitalism" stands revealed. The compromise offered by Batman/Bruce Wayne is therefore that of capitalism "with a human face," or at least: with a face *more* human than the hideous but strangely compelling visage of this particular arch-villain. In this sense, the attraction we feel for the Joker in *The Dark Knight* reflects our ambivalence in the face of a new form of capitalism that is as monstrous, chaotic, and unpredictable as it is insecapable. As the Joker tells Batman in their final dialogue in *The Dark Knight*: "I think you and I are destined to do this forever." The dramatic deadlock between the two characters therefore points yet again towards our inability to imagine a world without capitalism, and these films' failure to articulate a society that offers an alternative to our own is therefore indicative of the larger cultural failure to imagine viable alternatives to capitalism.

4

Surveillance, Control and Visibility in the Neoliberal City

Superman: Listen; what do you hear?
Lois Lane: Nothing.
Superman: *I hear everything.* You wrote that the world doesn't need a savior, but every day I hear people crying out for one.

Superman Returns (emphasis added)

Whether the superhero is presented within his diegetic world and narrative tradition as the enforcer of government policies (like Superman) or as a lone vigilante whose costumed crime-fighting is only fully understood by the reader (like Spider-Man and Batman), the superhero figure consistently embodies ideological values of discipline and control. Moreover, the superhero represents a form of power that is centered on his abilities that make him able to observe the general public: Superman uses his super-hearing and X-ray vision, his gaze penetrating the privacy of city homes; Batman perches gargoyle-like atop skyscrapers, using his technologically sophisticated gadgets to monitor the inhabitants of the urban jungle; and Spider-Man relies on his supernatural "Spidey-sense" to alert him to impending crime or danger.

This "panoramic and panoptic gaze" (Bukatman 188) functions as a deterrent for criminal behavior in ways that resemble Michel Foucault's description of the Panopticon as a metaphor for the invisible forms of control exerted on the individual. As legislation, political rhetoric, and public debate have increasingly focused on issues surrounding surveillance in recent years, the Panopticon and Foucault's conception of the "carceral society" have re-emerged as dominant theoretical paradigms in contemporary critical discourse. The sustained popularity of the superhero in post-9/11 popular culture therefore raises several important questions: are today's superhero figures the literal embodiments of hegemonic state control? If they do indeed represent forms of normative discipline, then what ideological values do they represent? Can they also be convincingly interpreted as sites of resistance that provide models of social difference, heterogeneity, and individual agency? And perhaps most importantly: what can these seemingly contradictory aspects of superhero discourse teach us about the politics and ideology of 21st-century popular culture?

Foucault and Surveillance Culture: Panopticon and Synopticon

In *Discipline and Punish: The Birth of the Prison*, Michel Foucault argues that the central institutions that have come to define Western modernity have all been based on the model of the prison: factories, schools, hospitals, mental institutions, and government bureaucracies form an immense virtual network that rigorously documents and regulates the individual subject (Foucault 1995: 228). As he develops his frightening central image of a society "in which the carceral circles widen and the form of the prison slowly diminishes and finally disappears altogether," the most important effect on the individual is that of a fully internalized sense of discipline (298).

The best-known visual model for this form of institutionalized disciplinary power is Jeremy Bentham's Panopticon: the architectural penal experiment that placed prisoners in cells distributed across the exterior of a massive spherical structure, with a central tower from which an invisible observer can view each prisoner in every cell at any time. Fundamental to the operation of this system of control is firstly the fact that the individual prisoner never knows whether he is being observed or not, and secondly that the observing guard has no actual power, as he is merely an anonymous and replaceable part of a larger system. As a conceptual, easy-to-visualize synecdoche for the decentered power structures that make up (post)modern Western society, the Panopticon visualizes how such power networks produce and subsequently legitimize forms of individual subjectivity along lines of discipline and control.

Remains of the abandoned Presidio Modelo prison, a once-operative Panopticon in Cuba. (Source: commons.wikimedia.org)

The swift transformation of modern Europe into forms of carceral society was a crucial element in the ongoing development of capitalism, which became both the force behind these changes and the product created by them. For on the one hand, the capitalist model with its central concepts of profit and industrialization led to new forms of power, as it became "more efficient and profitable in terms of the economy of power to place people under surveillance than to subject them to some exemplary penalty" (Foucault 1980: 38). On the other hand, the adoption of these models of profitability, automation and efficiency for penal law, surveillance and incarceration further enforced the institutionalization and naturalization of capitalism as a grounding concept at all levels of society.

As Foucault emphasizes, the forces that defined these specifically modern forms of power, discipline, and subjectivity were not so much the imposition of a malign force from above as they were the introduction of systematic processes that were internalized by the public and legitimized by scientific discourse. The adoption of these panoptic forms of modern power as a mechanism that operated from within the social body rather than from above it is relevant for an appropriate definition of contemporary discourses of surveillance. The popular perception of surveillance may still revolve around the top-down exercise of state control in the Orwellian sense, with a dictatorial government strictly monitoring individual actions for possible transgressions. The film version of *V for Vendetta* perfectly reflects this early-modern model of control, with its evil government directly manipulating the population by surveillance combined with ubiquitous propaganda.

But Foucault's use of the term is actually closer to the "reality TV" paradigm of *Big Brother* (CBS, 2000-present) than it is to that of the ubiquitous telescreens of *Nineteen Eighty-Four* (1949). The power mechanisms he describes have moved beyond the exclusive domain of the state apparatus into other areas that are not directly controlled by government operations, but that ultimately still function as a disseminated network of control that operates with great efficiency:

> I do not mean in any way to minimise the importance and effectiveness of State power. I simply feel that excessive insistence on its playing an exclusive role leads to the risk of overlooking all the mechanisms and effects of power which don't pass directly via the State apparatus, yet often sustain the State more effectively than its

own institutions, enlarging and maximising its effectiveness. (Foucault 1980: 72-73)

With the development of computer systems that have made the circulation and ubiquitous institutionalization of data a central part of economic and social practices, Foucault's theoretical construct of panopticism had already gained a heightened sense of relevance and urgency. The concurrent development of surveillance technology, increasingly the domain of corporate interests rather than government institutions, meanwhile gave new form to Bentham's controversial views on the disciplinary power of invisible observation. Indeed, the American shopping mall with its omnipresent CCTV cameras was soon recognized as the most literal kind of postmodern Panopticon; and as the infra-structure and architecture of urban centers was subsequently reverse-engineered to mirror and absorb the contained, priva-tized public spaces of the shopping mall, "the panoptic technology of power has been electronically extended: our cities have become like enormous Panopticons" (Koskella 292).

Whether such broad claims about the carceral nature of contemporary urban life are more substantial than paranoid hyperbole is a legitimate question. As the previous chapter has indicated, the neoliberal postmetropolis must be recognized as a complex entity rife with internal contradictions. While surveil-lance has developed to the point of near-ubiquity in a metropolis like London, the city can also be considered a space the individual subject is still free to traverse and explore, certainly to a greater extent than was the case in pre-modern communities. In *The Practice of Everyday Life*, Michel de Certeau adopted a point of view that transforms Foucault's notion of panoptic control by focusing on how the city allows the individual subject an unprecedented degree of freedom of expression and of movement:

The act of walking is to the urban system what the speech act is to language ... Walking affirms, suspects, tries out, transgresses, respects, etc., the trajectories it "speaks." All the modalities sing a part in this chorus, changing from step to step, stepping in through proportions, sequences and intensities which vary according to the time, the path taken, and the walker. These enunciatory operations are of an unlimited diversity. (97)

Although this perspective counterbalances the carceral logic of Foucault's panopticism, it has failed to provide a convincing response to the radical proliferation of 21st-century surveillance culture. A problem here is that the postmodern subject seems to lack the ability to create a "cognitive mapping" of the opaque, convoluted nature of contemporary urban spaces (MacCabe, qtd. in Jameson 1992: xiv). One major topic in contemporary urban theory and surveillance studies does indeed concern the extent to which the postmetropolis is experienced as a panoptic, disciplinary space. As public spaces are increasingly privatized and corporate interests remain the driving force in the commodification of both actual cities and their spectacular representation in popular entertainment, the public anxiety related to panoptic forms of surveillance and control is easy to understand. But the term "panoptic" requires some further development in order to explain how it relates to city life and its many different forms of mediation.

Firstly, Foucault's original use of the term suggests a basic powerlessness in the face of the rigorous discipline imposed by the panoptic mechanism. This normative power strips the individual subject of any ability to resist it, firstly by making him complicit in the process. Not only does this concept therefore require to be reinterpreted in light of Foucault's later writing on bio-power and its notion that power inherently produces forms of resistance; it also demands more nuance in order to seem appropriate in the context of postmodernism and its more fluid, mobile forms of subjectivity. In order to introduce a dialectical element into the power dynamic of panopticism, Thomas Mathiesen and David Lyon have therefore argued for the necessity to incorporate the complementary concept of "synopticism":

> The few may well watch the many, as they do in surveillance situations of constantly increasing magnitude, but this does not mean that the many no longer watch the few, as Foucault suggested in his analysis of the demise of public executions and other punitive spectacles. Indeed the same communication and information technologies today permit an unprecedented watching of the few by the many—mainly through television—as well as an unprecedented watching of many by the few through visual surveillance and dataveillance of various kinds. (Lyon 42)

The addition of the "Synopticon" as a theoretical concept that expands our understanding of panopticism in the context of the neoliberal city is all the more essential when examining the crucial role played by popular representations of urban spaces and panoptic mechanisms. As I argued in the previous chapter, audiovisual representations of city spaces are better understood as articulations of said spaces than as representations of physical realities. These images function along the logic of Baudrillard's precession of simulacra, as the phantasmal images of city life shape our conception of these cities at least as much as the actual cities shape such representations (2001: 1733). Therefore, just as these images of contemporary urban space shape our understanding of them, so do the characters that inhabit these narratives contribute to our shared discourses on the forms of subjectivity they produce. When we seek to apply the theoretical concepts of panopticism and synopticism to contemporary popular narratives, we do so in order to chart the complex ways in which these concepts inform such narratives, thereby contributing to the ideological choices they represent.

David Lyon has demonstrated how the popular 21st-century television genre dubbed "reality TV" embodies the double logic of the surveillance society. In programs like *Big Brother*, the synoptic effect is that of the many (i.e. the television audience) watching the few (i.e. the contestants). This process seemingly represents the opposite of Foucault's definition of panopticism, with the few (i.e. the guards) watching the many (i.e. the prisoners). But rather than canceling each other out, the two instead serve to legitimize and strengthen each other in contemporary mass culture. As Lyon argues, the 24-hour surveillance embodied by forms of entertainment such as *Big Brother* is not presented as an invasion of privacy that has even the remotest negative effects on the subjects under observation. For not only do the participants engage in the complex *dispositif* of surveillance, exhibitionism, and scopophilia willingly, but they even appear to benefit from it through the accumulation of financial gain, celebrity, and social status. The implicit ideology of this type of television is therefore that panoptic surveillance is beneficial rather than dangerous.

24: Heroic Narratives of Neoliberal Surveillance

But reality TV is not the only popular form of entertainment that embodies this double logic of the panoptic and the synoptic. With the emergence of surveillance as a central concern within discourses of neoliberalism, it has increasingly come to structure fictional television narratives as well. The first season of real-time spy thriller *24* was conceived, written, and produced before the 9/11 attacks occurred, but was not broadcast until November 2001, making it the first TV phenomenon to capitalize explicitly — if accidentally — on post-9/11 anxieties. This shows that the issues that would come to be defined as central elements of 9/11 discourse after the attacks were already present before, but had not necessarily been identified as central points of public concern and political debate.

Once the first season of 24 became phenomenally popular in the wake of the terrorist, with its super-heroic government agents racing against the clock to avoid ever-impending catastrophes, subsequent seasons confirmed the series' explicit connection with ongoing issues in the War on Terror by foregrounding topics such as government-sanctioned torture, Islamic fundamentalism, ethnic profiling, and surveillance technology. The show's subject matter thus connected it consistently to the discursive formation that was swiftly transforming recent historical events into a way of speaking and thinking about the world. In this way, protagonist Jack Bauer (played by Kiefer Sutherland) came to represent the indestructible superhero who embodied American fantasies of mastery and revenge in the developing War on Terror.

As with *Big Brother*, the choice for a particular narrative form represents specific ideological choices and limitations. In reality TV, the 24-hour surveillance of participants is subsequently edited into a half-hour selection of moments that follow familiar dramatic patterns. Reversing this pattern, 24 presents its action in a way that simulates the passage of real time. This formal device has the benefit of adding an intense sense of immediacy and dramatic urgency to a spy narrative that runs the obvious risk of seeming overly contrived and implausible. As the on-screen clock ticks away the minutes of every hour-long episode directly before and after each commercial break, the narrative rushes headlong towards the next cliffhanger moment, deliberately leaving the viewer little opportunity to reflect on the reasons behind the ongoing events.[7]

Beyond the obvious ideological issues raised by the series' basic themes, this formal device can also be viewed as the prototypical embodiment of neoliberal practices. In his article "Fox and Its Friends: Global Commodification and the New Cold War," Dennis Broe argues that the show's formal elements reflect a perception of the world that perfectly replicates the basic principles of global capitalism:

> The corporatization of time and space can be seen in the basic formal organization of 24. The program takes place in real time; each segment shows a clock that marks the passing not only of the hour of the episode but of the series as well. Each twenty-four-episode season tells one ongoing story that plays out over a single day. Advertising time is figured into the space the space of the hour ... Locales shift continually, usually among four spaces, and each segment begins and ends with a four-way split screen, tracking the different elements of the story. Narrative time is submitted to the rigors of the clock, similar to that of the global markets, with their tightly run periods of trading ... Narrative flow thus expresses the flow of capital. (100)

In addition to the genre requirements of surprise and suspense being met by the show's distinctive formal features, the logic that underlies its organization of time and space thus reflects that of global capitalism, of which the Fox Network is one of the better-known corporate embodiments.

Throughout the consecutive seasons of 24, the single location around which the action revolves is the headquarters of fictional counterterrorist unit CTU, where the heroes struggle to avoid impending terrorist attacks. The show's entire plot defined by the "ticking time bomb scenario," the narrative logic of the series is predicated on the fact that there is never any opportunity for thought or reflection. Indeed, superheroic protagonist Jack Bauer is constantly reminding other characters of the urgent time constraints with repeated lines like "There's no time to explain!" His narrative thereby comes to embody the purely intuitive action of the morally superior superhero figure. Empowered by his position within a well-funded government espionage organization and equipped with advanced surveillance technology, Jack

Bauer functions as an ideological legitimization of panopticism that conveniently strips the concept of its more unsettling implications.

First among these is the decentered, invisible form of power that is produced by the panoptic machinery of ubiquitous surveillance technology. Foucault emphasizes the fact that the invisible observer at the center of this device can be literally anyone, and that his reasons for adopting this role are equally immaterial:

> It does not matter who exercises power. Any individual, taken almost at random, can operate the machine ... Similarly, it does not matter what motivates him: the curiosity of the indiscreet, the malice of a child, the thirst for knowledge of a philosopher who wishes to visit this museum of human nature, or the perversity of those who take pleasure in spying and punishing. (1995: 202)

In 24, a team of experts operates the surveillance technology that provides easy and immediate access to virtually any kind of personal information, from telephone conversations to GPS data revealing individual subjects' geographical location. This team is made up of sympathetic characters defined on the one hand by specific, highly professionalized skill sets, and on the other by interpersonal relationships familiar from other television narratives centered on the workplace (rivalries, flirtations, comic relief, etc.). By the series' presentation of CTU's main office as a familiar, recognizable central location populated by a stable group of sympathetic characters, 24 gives surveillance technology a comforting human face, reassuring its audience that those in control of the apparatus are skilled professionals with consistent personalities and the best intentions.

The second troubling implication of surveillance culture concerns the possibility of those in power abusing it, and this anxiety is indeed frequently addressed in 24. As in most popular narratives in the spy thriller genre, much of the series' narrative suspense revolves around the conceit that someone within the hero's team is in fact a mole who is abusing his or her power to assist the enemy. While some characters therefore become suspects at various points in the narrative, others—most notably protagonist Jack Bauer—remain beyond reproach, and the mole is systematically rooted out before the season ends. The representation of the authority in charge of the panoptic machinery is therefore one that functions in terms of familiar narrative patterns and devices, and in which order is systematically restored. This demonstrates on a weekly basis that there is nothing wrong with the system itself: like capitalism, it merely needs to rid itself of the occasional bad apple, for which it relies on the heroic intervention of those already occupying positions of power.

With the threat of abuse of power by those with bad intentions thus dispelled by the self-regulating nature of the CTU team, another concern that is repeatedly raised by Jack Bauer's exploits is that of illegal actions carried out by those in a position of power with good intentions. But in this regard, the narrative game is rigged, and the audience is consistently reassured that CTU's investigative efforts are directed only towards those who deserve such attention. When the innocent are unrightfully monitored, detained, or even tortured, this is shown to be the result of enemy manipulation, not the systemic abuse of power: "[tortured] CTU employees are portrayed as victims and they survive, while the tortured terrorists are always guilty and often die" (Scott 11). The fundamental efficacy of "enhanced interrogation techniques," GPS tracking, and ubiquitous surveillance is demonstrated in every season by the basic fact that Jack Bauer and his team do indeed manage to avoid catastrophe and save the world on a weekly basis.

A form that favors actions over consequences therefore largely assuages both main concerns raised within the narrative context of 24 in its commonly embraced role as "the Official Cultural Product of the War on Terror". The potentially disturbing illegality of Bauer's renegade methods is meanwhile systematically curtailed by a series of narrative choices that reassure the viewer about the character's sympathetic and trustworthy persona, which is primarily achieved by identifying him as a devoted father and loyal patriot. The ideology represented by 24 thus offers a compelling embodiment of the double logic of the Panopticon and the Synopticon, in which each process is strengthened and sustained by the other. The panoptic power represented by CTU, with its elaborate surveillance technology working alongside its legal mandate to apprehend and punish individual subjects, is legitimized by the synoptic role it plays as a popular text in mass culture: "the synoptic helps justify the panoptic, which in turn provides some of its most telling images" (Lyon 50).

This is not to say that popular narratives such as 24 leave no room for ideological negotiation, or even for what Stuart Hall would describe as oppositional readings. In such readings, the audience is aware of and able to understand "both the literal and the connotative inflection given by a discourse but [decodes] the message in a *globally* contrary way" (Hall 1999: 517). Indeed, there are clearly "complex ways in which people negotiate and reconcile their political identity and media preferences when they are in tension with one another," as is often the case with 24 and its diverse global audience (Tenenbaum-Weinblatt 383). This is partly due to the long-running serialized form of a text like 24, which inherently accrues a certain level of ideological polysemy as it continuously introduces new issues, surprise reversals, and moral quandaries. But given the highly consistent range of ideological choices reflected by this series' narrative and form, and its universally recognized conservative viewpoint, it would make more sense to speak of this text in terms of its Gramscian "common-sense" reception:

> It is precisely its "spontaneous" quality, its transparency, its "naturalness," its refusal to be made to examine the premises on which it is founded, its resistance to change or correction, its effect on instant recognition [that] makes common-sense, at one and the same time, "spontaneous," ideological and *unconscious*. (Purvis and Hunt 479)

Just as Stuart Hall explained how a "common-sense" reading of the 9/11 attacks came into being "through the repeated performance, staging or telling" of one particular kind of narrative (Procter 67), a general, common-sense reading of 24 quickly emerged that saw it as a series that focused exclusively on the fundamental necessity of an aggressive government policy to combat seemingly non-stop terrorist threats, and to legitimize every conceivable form of action taken against them.

American conservatives have therefore tended to defend the show in terms of its politics, with politicians such as former Secretary of Homeland Security Michael Chertoff praising Jack Bauer "for his gut-wrenching efforts to make the best choices from a bad set of options" (qtd. in Scott 1). Liberal American politicians on the other hand have emphasized the lack of correspondence between the show's premise and the realities of contemporary counterterrorism: "[Bill] Clinton, a self-professed fan of 24, ... argued that the 'ticking bomb' scenario, which occurred regularly in 24, rarely happened 'in the real world'" (Tenenbaum-Weinblatt 368). With political hawks thus describing the series as an honest depiction of contemporary realities and the doves emphasizing its lack of realism, both sides clearly recognize its central position within this debate and its constant interplay with forms of political and ideological discourse.

Therefore, whether it was perceived as a politically charged fantasy that addresses anxieties about terrorism in a post-9/11 environment or as a formally inventive spy thriller that is enjoyable in spite of its political implications, 24 quickly became the clearest example of popular culture taking up a central position within 9/11 discourse:

> In the case of the torture debate, for example, proponents of torture used *24* as evidence that supported torture, whereas opponents of torture presented the show as either a fantasy that had no bearing on the actual effectiveness and morality of torture or, alternatively, as being a cause of positive attitudes toward torture or even of actual interrogation techniques. (ibid. 382)

Both sides of the debate thus serve to demonstrate the extent to which the complementary functions of the Panopticon and the Synopticon operate successfully within contemporary popular culture. Whether they are being criticized or defended, the panoptic privileges and technologies that empower Jack Bauer within the series are ultimately legitimized for both sides by the show's synoptic quality, with the many of the audience watching the few.

The implicit legitimization of the benefits of panoptic surveillance is grounded in the double logic that makes Jack Bauer and his CTU staff members a subject within this very process. For not only are they on display at the metatextual level as a character in a weekly TV drama, but they are also under constant video surveillance within the narrative itself. Like most technological elements that feature prominently in *24*, this form of panoptic surveillance can be both beneficial and obstructive to the protagonist and his main goals. Access to security tapes can reveal the identity of a mole within CTU (as occurs in season 1), but it can also pose a hindrance when Bauer finds himself forced to operate as a free agent, freely setting aside the rules of the organization in order to get the job done. Although it is clear from this narrative that surveillance technology can be a benefit as well as a hazard, its ubiquitous nature is never questioned, and the benefits clearly outweigh the disadvantages.

Discipline and Control in the Post-9/11 Superhero Film: The Cyborg Superhero

Batman's controlling gaze watches over the city
in a promotional image for *The Dark Knight.*

The role played by popular culture in the legitimization of panoptic surveillance as a natural and necessary part of contemporary public life relies as much on the Synopticon as it does on the Panopticon: the notion of the few watching the many is given dramatic form within mass media narratives in which the many watch the few. In the case of *24,* the character of Jack Bauer provides a fantasy figure whose clearly defined persona can serve to alleviate anxieties about the potential abuse of such power. Not only does his character dispel concerns about the decentered nature of power by providing "a masculinity compatible with globalization" (Scott 20), but the narrative also consistently demonstrates that his actions and intuitive responses are always justified.

The more literal superheroes in post-9/11 Hollywood cinema frequently perform a similar role. Many of them are easy to read as attempts to address public anxieties related to agency and masculinity in a decentered postmodern world in which the new enemies have incorporated the logic of late capitalism and the market state. In the previous chapter, I argued that the figure of the Joker in *The Dark Knight* should be interpreted as a metaphorical embodiment of this specifically postmodern economy that requires the chaos of destructive capitalism and the flexibility of a permanent disposable workforce. In this section, I will examine more closely how superheroes utilize their panoptic powers to counterbalance these threats, and how they are thereby transformed into a form of this panoptic machinery, their bodies literally inscribed by the surveillance technology they utilize.

The superhero arose from American popular culture in the 1930s, alongside the development of the metropolis in its modernist form of geometric glass-and-concrete buildings and architectural designs that attempted to remove all traces of bourgeois nineteenth-century cityscapes. The modernist ambitions of transforming the proliferating chaos of nineteenth-century urbanization into a transparent, multifunctional environment gave architectural form to the utopian desire to control urban space: "by changing structural conventions one could alter consciousness and produce social change, even if the inhabitants of these glass towers were unable to comprehend the political significance of these radical innovations" (Collins 1992: 329). The imposing skyscrapers of Manhattan and Chicago that arose in the 1920s and 1930s thereby embodied the heroic modernist quest for power through order, transparency, and visibility.

The superhero figure became the pop-cultural figure most easily associated with the forms of power and control implied by the architecture of the International School and its utopian aspirations. The two archetypal superheroes of comic books' Golden Age, Batman and Superman, each patrol the city in their continuous efforts to provide a sense of safety and order for its citizens, while neither figure can truly be considered an inhabitant of the city he safeguards. Both Batman's residence at Wayne Manor and Superman's arctic Fortress of Solitude suggest a strong connection to the older, European traditions of the aristocracy and its pre-modern forms of power. These superhero archetypes and their many descendants thus represent not only a fantasy of overcoming the obvious limitations of the human body within the physically and mentally overpowering vertical landscapes of the modern metropolis; they can also be read as the literal embodiments of modernist aspirations, reframed from within the context of popular culture.

If the original ascendance of superheroes in the 1930s and 1940s constituted a popularized and more accessible incarnation of modernist visions of urban order and control, the superhero's popular resurgence in post-9/11 mass culture indicates a paradoxical nostalgia for older imaginations of the urban environment. As I argued in the previous chapter, the superhero movie genre strives to present the postmetropolis as a coherent space in which modernist and postmodernist architecture coexist comfortably under ubiquitous capitalism, while social and architectural contradictions are subsumed by the superhero's panoptic, controlling gaze. A large part of the attraction of these narratives therefore resides in the fantasy they offer of a postmodern urban environment that is made safe by the traditional forms of power associated with an older form of capitalism.

While *Batman Begins* offers the most obvious example of this desire to re-establish entrepreneurial capitalism when faced with the threat of global terrorism, *The Dark Knight* elaborates in more detail how this hegemonic position can be enforced and maintained, and how strongly the exercise of this kind of power has come to rely on panoptic forms of surveillance. Christopher Nolan's second Batman film foregrounds issues of visibility and the implied empowerment of the gaze at several levels, the first

of which is encapsulated by the film's visual aesthetics. Its predecessor *Batman Begins* offered a more traditional Gothic presentation of a Gotham City that seemed all but impossible to master:
"a city askew, defined by angular perspectives, impenetrable
shadows, and the grotesque inhabitants of its night" (Bukatman
203). *The Dark Knight* however presents a vastly different
conception of the postmetropolis, which is here depicted as a
public space defined entirely in terms of visibility.

This shift is obvious from the opening helicopter shot that
provides a spectacular, panoramic view of downtown Gotham
City. It displays the city in broad daylight, the blue morning sky
reflected in the vast surfaces of one of the many postmodern
high-rise office buildings of central Chicago. The use of high-
definition IMAX film stock for all such panoramic shots of
cityscapes in the film further emphasizes the importance of
visual detail on prominent display. The larger film stock
employed by IMAX cameras yields an image in which one can
distinguish far more detail than is possible in standard 35mm
film projection. Unlike *Batman Begins*, which was also shown on
IMAX screens, but in prints that had been blown up from 35mm
negatives, the imagery of *The Dark Knight* provides an
overwhelming amount of visual detail that becomes an
important part of the value of the film as a commodity.[8] Indeed,
much of the film's promotional material focused on both the
visual rewards and the technical challenges of its extensive use
of IMAX technology:

> The reality is that you see every little detail — that piece of camera
> tape down the street in the frame, the one you don't normally worry
> about, had to be removed. We had to condition everyone on the crew
> to a higher level of discipline, especially [production designer]
> Nathan Crowley and his team. Everyone had to be meticulous.
> (cinematographer Wally Pfister, qtd. in Heuring, n. pag.)

The foregrounding of the city as a visible and therefore manageable and controllable space is evident not only in the numerous panoramic shots of Chicago and Hong Kong, but also in the many scenes that display the city through the windows of locations occupied by characters associated with state power. In scenes that take place in the offices of the District Attorney, the police commissioner, and the city judge, enormous windows frame spectacular and panoramic views of the city's downtown area. Bruce Wayne, while awaiting the reconstruction of Wayne Manor, now resides in the penthouse of Chicago's Trump Tower, where one notices that his easy chair offers a controlling view of the city that lies both physically and metaphorically at his feet.

Bruce Wayne's controlling gaze from Chicago's
Trump Tower penthouse in *The Dark Knight*.

By contrast, characters who are ethnically or economically marginalized are shown in locations that are confined, without a view of the panoptic city that seeks to exclude them. They are consistently presented in sheltered interior environments where they are momentarily safe from the controlling gaze of state power. The black, Italian and Chechen criminal gangs meet in isolated, low-ceilinged environments such as parking garages and basements. And on the rare occasions where they make themselves visible to the outside world, they frequently pay for this with their lives. Benevolent state power is thus systematically associated with transparency and visibility, while illegal and subversive activity is linked to confined, enclosed spaces and the desire to elude the penetrating gaze of state authority.

The thematic importance of the film's high-definition aesthetics is further compounded by the narrative's increased focus on the importance of visibility, data visualization, and surveillance technology towards its climax. In one of the film's most-discussed scenes, Bruce Wayne reveals to Lucius Fox (played by Morgan Freeman) that he has modified his "sonar cell phone technology" to create a device that will allow him to listen in on all of Gotham City's cellular telephone network:

Batman: Beautiful, isn't it?

Lucius Fox: Beautiful. Unethical. Dangerous. You've turned every cell phone in Gotham into a microphone.

Batman: And a high-frequency generator-receiver.

Lucius Fox: You took my sonar concept and applied it to every phone in the city. With half the city feeding you sonar, you can image all of Gotham. This is wrong.

Batman: I've got to find this man, Lucius.

Lucius Fox: At what cost?

Batman: The database is null-key encrypted. It can only be accessed by one person.

Lucius Fox: This is too much power for one person.

Batman: That's why I gave it to you. Only you can use it.

Lucius Fox: Spying on 30 million people isn't part of my job description.

As this quotation illustrates, the surveillance technology on display here goes beyond the mere eavesdropping on telephone conversations: the monitors of his surveillance device make it possible to "image all of Gotham." The wall-filling array of screens closely resembles the familiar collections of CCTV surveillance camera screens that are monitored by security guards in shopping malls, office buildings, and any number of other public and private spaces that make up the postmetropolis.

The panoptic surveillance device in *The Dark Knight.*

The notion of ubiquitous surveillance as a means of enforcing social control is addressed by Edward W. Soja in the fifth of his six discourses that together make up his definition of the postmetropolis (as discussed in the previous chapter). Drawing on the work of Mike Davis, he describes the discourse of the city as Carceral Archipelago as follows:

> The globalized post-Fordist industrial metropolis, with its extraor-dinary cultural heterogeneity, growing social polarities and explosive potential, is being held together largely by "carceral" technologies of violence and social control, fostered by capital and the state. (2002: 194)

It is important to emphasize that this perspective on the postmetropolis as a carceral archipelago where individual subjects have been reduced to the status of prisoners must be understood as only a partial discourse on the contemporary city. Without Soja's other five discourses to add nuance, perspective, and the necessary diversity, our understanding of the carceral postmetropolis becomes too much like the kind of top-down exercise of state power associated with the classic Orwellian dystopia.

But the fictional postmetropolis of Gotham City in *The Dark Knight* represents a way of imagining the city without any need for such complexities. Like most other popular narratives, it is free to draw on just one or two concepts associated with the postmetropolis and allow this to largely define the way the urban environment is presented. As in *24*, surveillance technology in this narrative context becomes a potent tool of empowerment and virtual omniscience that makes literally the entire city and its inhabitants visible on surveillance screens. And although the dialogue indicates a token sense of disapproval, Batman's use of this technology is justified by the fact that he employs it successfully, and only after all other methods have failed. Meanwhile, Batman's moral responsibility is reassuringly confirmed by the fact that he destroys the device after having used it.[9]

This form of empowerment by way of panoptic surveillance technology subsequently moves beyond its traditional twentieth-century form when it is extended outside the traditional surveillance monitors and is physically embedded in Batman's costume. After using the imaging device to pinpoint the Joker's location, Batman is able to gain the upper hand by feeding the input from the sonar device directly into his mask. He thereby replaces his actual field of vision with the visualized data that renders the building he enters literally transparent, like a three-dimensional blueprint or a videogame environment. This technological ability provides him with a form of mastery over the chaotic situation that supersedes the attacking police force's misreading of direct visual information. Because the gang members have exchanged costumes with their group of hostages, only Batman's panoptic use of data visualization technology makes him able to interpret the situation correctly and take the appropriate kind of action.

At the same time, the incorporation of Batman's surveillance technology into the costume that defines his identity transforms him into a cyborg: "a hybrid of machine and organism, a creature of social reality as well as a creature of fiction" (Haraway 150). Donna Haraway's classic essay "The Cyborg Manifesto" envisioned the cyborg as a semi-utopian "creature in a post-gender world," liberating the subject from the traditional binary divisions that have served as the conceptual paradigms of oppressive militarism and patriarchal capitalism (151). However, most cyborg-like figures that have been featured so prominently in postclassical Hollywood, from *The Terminator* (dir. James Cameron, 1984) and *RoboCop* (dir. Paul Verhoeven, 1987) to *Iron Man* and *The Dark Knight*, fulfill little of this revolutionary potential. Instead, they seem to function as technologically enhanced versions of the hard-bodied icons of masculinity from the Reagan era:

> Where the Rambo films were structured to leave audiences desiring the externalized strength of Rambo's national hard body, *RoboCop* invites audiences to desire a protective figure who not only can enforce the law … but who can wield it fairly and faithfully, without corruption or compromise. The system, such desires whisper, is already in place. All we need are a few good (white) men to make it work. (Jeffords 117-8)

In many ways, Batman in *The Dark Knight* represents the cyborg as an image of empowered masculinity similar to that of *RoboCop*, but one that is politically much more problematic. It goes so far as to suggest that the technologically enhanced superhero is in fact free to disregard the laws he is expected to uphold whenever he decides that circumstances demand it. Just as Jeffords relates the popular narratives of the 1980s to the political and ideological discourses of that era, it is easy to read this current wave of popular heroes as similarly supportive of neoliberal American government policy. The fantasy they provide constitutes a militarized form of masculine power that functions as the explicit extension of patriarchal capitalism. Nowhere in the films under discussion is this more evident than in the superhero's appropriation of surveillance technology.

But while Batman's costume integrates high-tech imaging software as an effective tool of panoptic empowerment, its use in the film meanwhile severs an important link between character and audience. For as soon as Batman activates the imaging technology, it covers up the actor's eyes, leaving only his mouth and chin as a recognizable part of the human face, and precluding the film's use of effective eyeline matches. *Iron Man*, another superhero film in which the protagonist wears a costume that denies us access to the actor's face, found a way to visualize the incorporation of similar technology without sacrificing the expressiveness that makes the character a recognizable and sympathetic human figure. For as soon as billionaire playboy Tony Stark (played by Robert Downey Jr.) dons the suit that transforms him into the super-powered cyborg Iron Man, the film inserts close-ups that show Stark's face inside the suit, operating a complex but visually elegant Graphical User Interface before his eyes.

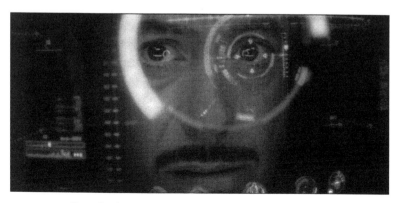

Tony Stark controlling the GUI of his suit in *Iron Man*.

Tony Stark's skillful operation of the suit's GUI with what appears to be a combination of voice control and eye movements shows the extent to which this kind of intuitive, "natural" operation of advanced technology represents a popular fantasy. The film continuously cuts back and forth between these close-ups of Stark's face surrounded by dynamic GUI elements, external shots of the Iron Man suit in action, and the character's point-of-view shots. These POV shots vary from views of the data visualization offered to Stark by his suit's computer system, which are similar to the videogame-like visuals in *The Dark Knight*, to photographic images enhanced by crucial computer information.

This use of data-enhanced images is more prominent in *Iron Man*, as it reveals the full extent of this popular cyborg fantasy, in which organic perception and technological data have become not merely inextricably intertwined, but also — and crucially — mutually beneficial and empowering. In one spectacular action sequence, Iron Man intervenes in an Afghan village where a massacre is about to occur. When faced with multiple terrorists who have taken the innocent villagers hostage, the computer system that is embedded in his costume automatically differentiates between the guilty and the innocent, making Iron Man able to target only those who supposedly deserve to be killed.

The impressive functionality of this system and its obvious effectiveness illustrates the logic that typifies postmodern

Distinguishing terrorists from civilians via data visualization in *Iron Man*.

American warfare. Slavoj Žižek has described our fantasies of this kind of "clean war" as that of "the Colin Powell doctrine of war with no casualties (on our side, of course)," or therefore even as "war without war" (2004b n. pag.). Like the uncanny images of smart bombs flying down the chimneys of targeted buildings in the first Gulf War, or the "Shock and Awe" tactics of the Rumsfeld doctrine in the more recent military conflict, Iron Man's use of high-tech weaponry is depicted as something that is possible without civilian casualties. In spite of the film's surface rejection of the military-industrial complex, *Iron Man*'s ideal soldier is presented as a cyborg figure who has incorporated this military technology into his outfit and made it into an essential, even natural part of his physique. As in Batman's use of "immoral" surveillance technology, the film's superficial rejection of the military-industrial complex is contradicted by its ongoing celebration of militarized (and privatized) cutting-edge technology.

Such fantasies of masculine empowerment through the subject's transformation into a technologically enhanced cyborg are not limited to the fantastical narratives of comic books and Hollywood action films. The U.S. Army's infamous 2001 advertising campaign that adopted the slogan "An Army of One" tried to draw in new recruits on the basis of exactly this kind of image. The text that accompanies the advertisement's photograph of a lone futuristic soldier, all but anonymous in the heavily armored and helmeted costume he is wearing, runs as follows:

The U.S. Army's "Army of One" recruitment advertisement (2001).

What you see is a Soldier system that gives me 360° vision in pitch black. Makes me invisible to the naked eye. Lets me walk up a mountainside. And run in a desert. You've never seen anything like me. But don't worry. They haven't either. I AM AN ARMY OF ONE. And you can see my strength.

As this advertisement illustrates so vividly, the ideal 21st-century soldier is here imagined as an invincible figure whose complete control of advanced technology grants him the opportunity to "become a high-tech superhero in the army" (Lawrence and Jewett 2002: 200). This kind of superheroic figure therefore vividly illustrates Žižek's description, in which military conflict is presented not merely as a war without innocent victims, but as a virtual experience that resembles a videogame, undertaken by soldiers who operate as invincible, completely self-sufficient cyborgs.

These particular incarnations of Iron Man and Batman make so much sense to contemporary audiences because they are both embodiments of such real-world fantasy figure associated with postmodern warfare. They each appropriate high-tech military equipment and surveillance technology as ways of enhancing their bodies, and then employ these abilities to stave off the threatening advances of post-Fordist capitalism. Tonal differences aside, *Batman Begins* and *Iron Man* feature identical plots, with their billionaire protagonists transforming themselves into superheroes by first building their own militarized body armor, then using their abilities to keep the villain from selling off their fathers' companies. This makes their position as fantasy representations of the postmodern subject once again contradictory. On the one hand, they embrace the possibilities offered by the virtual, technologically enhanced body that is the product of postmodernism, while on the other hand rejecting the perceived threats of a virtual, post-Fordist economy that itself generates these new, more fluid forms of identity.

This extreme ambivalence concerning the individual subject's position in a technologically advanced postmodern environment is typical of many contemporary popular narratives. *The Matrix* is perhaps the most frequently cited text in that regard: "on the one hand, reduction of reality to a virtual domain regulated by arbitrary rules that can be suspended; on the other hand, the concealed truth of this freedom, the reduction of the subject to an utter instrumentalized passivity" (Žižek 1999, n. pag.). Žižek's words here help us understand how these narratives dramatize anxieties about the contradictions inherent in postmodernism without ever truly resolving them: simultaneously nostalgic and future-minded, liberating and oppressive, reactionary and subversive, they offer a momentary illusion of escape from the passivity associated with postmodern consumerism.

As fantasy archetypes and even role models, these characters' use of surveillance technology and its incorporation into the superhero's very body is therefore entirely emblematic of the panoptic/synoptic double logic that informs the neoliberal surveillance society. In the above examples, the superhero figure legitimizes the use of panoptic and controlling forms of surveillance due to the fact that his actions are always justified by the narrative's outcome. This justification meanwhile becomes all the more effective by the superhero's visibility, both as a cultural icon (Batman as metatextual icon and brand) and as a public figure within the diegesis (Bruce Wayne and Tony Stark's status as billionaire celebrities in their own fictional cities).

This contradictory way of imagining the postmodern subject via popular superhero characters is most typical for the genre, just as *24* is most typical for the conservative politics of the post-9/11 spy thriller. But just as a television series like *The Wire* (HBO, 2002-2008) demonstrates that there is also room within the wider context of television culture for alternative frameworks that question the dominant perspective, there is also some space within the superhero movie genre for texts that challenge the politics of surveillance culture. The final sections of this chapter will therefore investigate popular texts that provide an alternative point of view. Alan Moore's comic book *Watchmen* focuses on the ways in which panoptic technologies are used for abusive forms of power, while Guillermo del Toro's *Hellboy* films offer ways of reading the superhero as a figure who can also represent forms of radical alterity. The focus in this concluding section will remain that of visibility and surveillance as a form of social control, seeking to investigate to what extent popular culture can successfully adopt an ideological position that resists the unrelenting conservatism of the neoliberal age.

Panoptic Power and Neoliberalism: Visibility and Control in *Watchmen*

As the previous section has demonstrated, the most typical superhero films fully incorporate the cultural logic of contemporary popular narratives, using the protagonist's unquestioned heroic status as a legitimization for the panopticism of the post-9/11 surveillance society. Whether the superhero's panoptic abilities are (super)natural, as with Superman's X-ray vision, Spider-Man's "Spidey-sense," and Daredevil's acute hearing, or technological, as in the cyborg-like technological enhancements of Batman and Iron Man, the fact that the narratives consistently demonstrate that masculine power figures use such abilities for good justifies their existence and contributes to their public acceptance. But even though most popular culture, from *24* and *CSI* to *The Dark Knight* and *Iron Man*, does function along predictable lines of Barthesian mythology, there is also room for alternative perspectives in postmodern popular culture. And although it certainly seems to be the case that films in the superhero genre are usually more alike than different, there is also some space within the superhero movie genre for characters and narratives that challenge this dominant paradigm.

The importance of establishing such counter-narratives arises from the social consequences of contemporary panoptic and synoptic surveillance culture. One such element is the increased marginalization of groups and individuals that are presented and perceived as "other," and therefore find themselves singled out for surveillance by controversial post-9/11 measures like the Patriot Act. Racial profiling is one such policy that has been the subject of much debate in the decade since the 9/11 attacks, and one in which the combination of panoptic and synoptic mechanisms has played a key role. On the one hand, panoptic surveillance software has been developed to single out subjects whose appearance fits a particular cultural and ethnic model associated with modern-day terrorism (i.e. young males of Arab or North African descent). On the other hand, there have been sustained government efforts in North America and Western Europe to mobilize the general public as a synoptic form of surveillance, the many being asked to report any form of unfamiliar or suspicious behavior.

With surveillance and panopticism therefore occupying such a pivotal position both in neoliberal politics and in popular culture, the need for narratives that question or challenge the cultural myths that inform these assumptions increases. And although such sites of ideological resistance are quite common in the "high culture" of fine art and literature, these texts not only have a more limited audience, but they also generally offer a form of commentary that is explicitly ideologically charged, drawing attention to aspects of social and political discourse from the institutional safety of the art gallery or the museum. Popular culture on the other hand draws attention away from its ideological implications, presenting itself as entertainment based on familiar cultural myths that are masquerading as "natural."

This systematic form of signification offers yet another example of the workings of the Barthesian myth and its second-order semiological system: by showing a diegetic world that appears internally coherent, "a world wide open and wallowing in the evident," these texts suggest that the same logic applies to real-world ideology (Barthes 1972: 143). If a large part of post-9/11 neoliberal discourse is centered on the legitimization of panoptic surveillance as a necessary means of enforcing security, one way to view the resulting operations of popular culture in response to this is via the Barthesian myths it develops and propagates. And like the required visibility of the superhero character both within these texts and on the metatextual level, these myths are similarly explicit about their own visibility:

> Myth does not deny things, on the contrary, its function is to talk about them; simply, it purifies them, it makes them innocent, it gives them a natural and eternal justification, it gives them a clarity which is not that of an explanation but that of a statement of fact. (ibid.)

The moral, ethical and ideological implications of the superhero figure's panoptic powers were explicitly foregrounded in mainstream comics for the first time in Alan Moore's influential work of the 1980s. While previous superhero comics had sided automatically with the protagonist, even if characters like Batman and Spider-Man were wrongly perceived by the public as dangerous vigilantes, *Watchmen* (1986) develops Juvenal's phrase "Who Watches the Watchmen?" into a deconstruction of the values inscribed in the superhero tradition.

In *Watchmen*, the arch-conservatism of popular superhero figures is no longer merely subtext, and the question what kind of politics these characters represent is brought to the foreground for the first time. The superheroes of *Watchmen, Batman: The Dark Knight Returns* (1986) and *V for Vendetta* (1989) were no longer separated from the forces of history in these comic books: "these superheroes, unlike those of fantastic worlds and abilities, are caught up completely in ideology" (Hughes 548). *Watchmen's* dystopian version of New York City is radically different from that of Marvel's superhero continuity, or even that of Gotham City. The text develops an elaborate alternate history of post-World War II America in which costumed vigilantes are a daily reality, and where the first appearance of a man with super-human powers (the Superman-inspired Dr. Manhattan) has had far-reaching consequences for politics, theology, and popular culture. In his first outline for the *Watchmen* project, author Alan Moore described the world he envisioned as follows:

> For one thing, I'd like the world that the ... characters exist in to be at once far more realistic in conception than any super-heroes the world has been before, and at the same time far different to our own world than the worlds as Earth One, Earth Two or Marvel Earth. To see what I'm trying to get at, you have to try and imagine what the presence of superheroes would actually *do* [to] the world, both politically and psychologically.
>
> Imagine, for the sake of argument, that Captain Atom was one of the first heroes with actual super powers to appear on the world we're dealing with. ... What would his appearance do to the world psychologically... the actual manifestation of a real being with powers similar to a god? Would there be widespread feelings of inadequacy in people who had suddenly realized that even if they did their best and became the best long distance runner in the world, Captain Atom was always going to be faster and stronger and cleverer? Or would there be a sudden blossoming of crank religious groups who worshipped superheroes? How would the media respond to such an attractive and presentable image? Would they try to buy the rights from super heroes to the manufacture of dolls and lunch-boxes in their image? Would religion be altered by the sudden inarguable presence of demonstrably real superbeings? (Moore, qtd. in Gibbons 3)

Alan Moore's faux-naïve questions are remarkable, if merely for the fact that they seem to have been posed so rarely in nearly five decades of comic book history. *Watchmen*'s appeal therefore lies primarily in the way it stages a deliberate confrontation between the preconceptions that underlie all of superhero mythology and a genuine sense of historicity. So even if the conclusion of *Watchmen* does not offer a way out of this dystopian alternate present, the text's emphasis on the ways in which the existence of actual superheroes would alter human history makes it the rare exception to the generally unhistorical nature of popular narratives.

Because the traditional superhero represented an unchallenged form of ideological order, its politics left no room for explicit ideological debate. With the protagonists safely enshrined "on pedestals as champions of justice and perfection, their creators also positioned them outside of the realm of ideology" (Hughes 546). For as the narrative reveals the characters' various motivations for donning a costume and fighting crime, the book's superhero characters become far more emphatically immersed in ideology:

> Superman, Batman, Green Lantern, and the rest of the traditional good guys become superheroes for some intrinsic responsibility, but the brood in *Watchmen* choose to do it for much more mundane reasons—money, power, fame, or to promote their own ideology. (548)

Unlike the countless superhero teams that have populated mainstream comics for decades, the group of costumed characters in *Watchmen* do not pursue a single ideology that thereby naturalizes and mythologizes the worldview presented by the narrative. Instead, these characters are clearly marked as distinct embodiments of concrete ideological positions:

> Rorschach is a radical conservative, Dr. Manhattan is a conservative, Silk Specter indifferent or neutral, Dan Drieberg [sic] a liberal, and

> Veidt a radical liberal; The Comedian's politics, while rather conser-
> vative in nature, are representative of the American public ... The
> narrative can then be read as a conflict between ideologies rather
> than conflicts between characters. (Wolf-Meyer 508)

While each of the main characters in *Watchmen* clearly illustrates
one individual aspect of the superhero myth, the issue of social
control by way of surveillance is most explicitly represented by
that of "radical liberal" Adrian Veidt, the ambiguous
mastermind whose actions drive the plot forward, and who
brings about the apocalyptic destruction of New York City in the
book's final chapter.

Like all but one of the superhero characters in *Watchmen*,
Veidt has no supernatural abilities. His athletic prowess is the
result of physical self-improvement courses, his millionaire
status is the product of the successful commercial exploitation of
his own superhero celebrity, and even his legend as "the world's
smartest man" is suggested to be his own doing (Moore 1986: ch.
11). Not only does Veidt's character present the most explicit
embodiment of the Nietzschean "Übermensch" as someone who
"simply overcame humanity, [who] transcended the bounds
yoked upon him by culture and achieved his genetic potential"
(Wolf-Meyer 498); he is also the text's most obvious representative of neoliberalism, with his position as powerful CEO of a
multinational corporation strongly associated with the visual
motif of his panoptic surveillance device.

Veidt uses his wall of television screens in two distinct ways:
as a tool to scan the full range of television's multiple broadcast
images simultaneously, and as a device to monitor and control
his own surroundings by way of CCTV surveillance cameras.
Both applications of audiovisual technology revolve around
power and control, with the panoptic screens giving him the
ability to decode messages that remain indecipherable to others
who lack this all-seeing perspective. The first moment that intro-

duces Veidt's wall of TV screens illustrates how his interpretation of subtext and subliminal imagery on television gives him an advantage as the head of a diversified and deregulated global corporation:

> *Adrian Veidt*: Hm. Let me see… First impressions: oiled muscleman with machine gun… cut to pastel bears, valentine hearts. Juxtaposition of wish fulfilment [sic] violence and infantile imagery, desire to regress, be free of responsibility… This all says "war." We should buy accordingly.
>
> *Servant*: But… Sir, we have never bought into munitions…
>
> *Adrian Veidt*: Of course not. You're ignoring the subtext: increased sexual imagery, even in the candy ads. It implies an erotic undercurrent not uncommon in times of war. (Moore 1986: 10; 24)

Even as a device that merely monitors the images of broadcast television, the fact that his panoptic machinery displays the images side-by-side rather than consecutively grants him a form of mastery over the situation. The kind of neoliberal capitalism Veidt represents is therefore directly associated with panoptic forms of control that can effectively monitor and decode complex forms of simultaneity. As a figure who so obviously represents a form of disaster capitalism that uses its power to profit finan-

Adrian Veidt observing the approach of his attackers
in *Watchmen* (Moore and Gibbons: 11; 2).

cially from any given situation, Veidt's utopian ideals, along with his incorporation of the Nietzschean Übermensch, are revealed as a destructive force against which even the super-powered Dr. Manhattan can offer no defense.

Later in the narrative, when the other superhero characters converge on his headquarters in an attempt to foil Veidt's plan, he employs these same screens as a surveillance device that gives him control over the situation as it develops. As Rorschach and Nite Owl move toward his headquarters in what is meant to be a surprise attack, the screens reveal their approach from every conceivable angle, demonstrating in advance that the plan is doomed to failure. Whether Veidt is using his wall of screens to monitor and interpret the cultural signals of broadcast television or to track the movements of other characters via surveillance cameras, his use of panoptic technology is therefore consistently associated with the exercise of power. More specifically, the fact that Veidt "acts more like a businessman than a hero-type" establishes the text's most explicit criticism of the neoliberal politics that had come to define the decade in which *Watchmen* was published (Dubose 926).

What has occurred in that era's neoliberal shift from nation state to market state is not so much that the neoliberal agenda of late capitalism has subverted the established order, but that it has come to supersede it, taking the place of the establishment while forcefully eradicating its former institutions. Placing one's faith in icons like the clean-cut, attractive, and wildly popular Veidt, as the book suggests, is "to give up responsibility for our lives and future to the Reagans, Thatchers, and other 'Watchmen' of the world who [were] supposed to 'rescue' us and perhaps lay waste to the planet in the process" (Wright 273). *Watchmen* therefore may be read as a popular text that criticizes the assumptions that underlie the superhero myth and its ideological implications. It establishes a connection between the politics of the superhero figure and the neoliberal political agenda that defined the economic policies of the 1980s, employing the structural motif of panoptic forms of control in its representation of corporate power.

If *Watchmen* stands as a clear example of a pop-cultural text critiquing the ideological framework that informs and largely defines its own narrative tradition, its use of panoptic devices is presented in terms of explicit power relationships. An example of a popular film franchise that offers an alternative way of employing the superhero to conceptualize these issues is director Guillermo del Toro's *Hellboy* (2004) and its sequel *Hellboy II: The Golden Army* (2008). Rather than presenting the superhero as a figure who uses panoptic devices to enforce his own brand of normative power, the Hellboy films develop a very different perspective on the topic of surveillance and control. Both films present narratives and imagery that instead revolve around issues of difference, marginalization, and minority groups' right to forms of visual representation.

The "Freaks" of *Hellboy*: Representing the Marginalized

Maybe it's the cold wind that chills you to the bone.
Or the strange rumblings beneath the city streets.
It's the unnerving sense that *there's a world around us we cannot see.*
It's not your imagination.
This world is very real. And it's very, very angry.

(Narration from the *Hellboy II: The Golden Army* trailer, emphasis added)

Based on Mike Mignola's comic book superhero, a property of independent comics publisher Dark Horse, Del Toro's two Hellboy films offer an unusual blend of diverse elements. Both pictures were financed and distributed by major American film studios, and offer the kind of action-oriented spectacle that is typical of postclassical Hollywood franchises, with regular action set pieces, iconic characters, and simple narratives. Very much an amalgam of diverse yet familiar elements, writer-director Del Toro describes *Hellboy* as "something that combined the superhero/action genre with a much more human approach, and at the same time had the trappings of a great Gothic fantasy" (qtd. in *'Hellboy': Seeds of Destruction*).

But unlike the superhero movies featuring characters with long track records as mainstream popular icons, the Hellboy films are not preoccupied with a nostalgic desire to re-establish the hegemony of white, patriarchal, entrepreneurial capitalism. As the voice-over from the trailer indicates, the Hellboy films are about the "world around us we cannot see": a hidden world that eludes the panoptic power associated with normative visibility, and one that is presented primarily in terms of its visual richness and cultural diversity. If the transparency and panoptic visibility of the worlds of *The Dark Knight*, *Spider-Man*, *Iron Man* and *Superman Returns* ultimately result in a reactionary emphasis on cultural and ethnic homogeneity, the Hellboy films instead foreground characters that are excluded from such a world, and who voice their desire to reclaim visibility in the public sphere they too inhabit.

The issue of visibility is central to most superhero narratives. By dressing up in an elaborate costume, the superhero clearly sets himself apart from normality, causing the ordinary citizens of the metropolis to stop, stare, and point (cf. the familiar phrase from Superman: "Look, up in the sky..."). In that sense, the superhero trope dramatizes the modern subject's desire to stand out from the crowd and take on a more performative identity within a culture of postmodernity. However, most mainstream superheroes alternate between the garish performativity of their costumed personas and the relative anonymity of normative contemporary identity. Whether their transformation is a voluntary choice involving a change of costume (e.g. Batman,

Superman, Spider-Man) or the involuntary transformation of the protagonist's body (e.g. the Incredible Hulk, the Human Torch), the character's identity remains grounded in forms of white heterosexual masculinity.

For Hellboy, his appearance as a superhero is inextricably connected to his natural physical appearance. As the literal spawn of Satan, brought into our world as the result of paranormal experimentation by the Nazis during World War II, Hellboy (played by Ron Perlman) is a red-skinned demon who files down his horns in an attempt gain control of his own identity, and whose granite forearm and supernatural origins grant him unusual physical powers. With features so radically different from those of normative society, Hellboy's overwhelming desire in both films is to gain public acceptance and receive recognition as a heroic crime-fighter in spite of his unusual skin color and exotic appearance. The government, as represented in the film by the secret Bureau for Paranormal Research and Defense, insists on keeping his existence a secret, continuously denying rumors of the government employment of such a radically "other" being. The main challenge that defines Hellboy's character arc in the films is thus defined by issues of visibility, representation, and the social acceptance of non-normative subjects.

This perspective extends as well to the other two protagonists in the films, both of whom are similarly challenged and excluded by the normative workings of their society. The other characters that make up the central superhero team are Liz (played by Selma Blair) and Abe Sapien (played by Doug Jones): Liz has the super-natural power of pyrokinesis, able to start fires by force of will, and Abe Sapien is a sophisticated, highly literate amphibian with telepathic abilities and effete diction and mannerisms. Flashback scenes in the first film establish how Liz has been ostracized by her peers for being a "freak" since early childhood, and is shown to have retreated into institutionalized care as the result of her experience of social exclusion. Abe Sapien is similarly cast as a marginalized figure in two ways: his amphibian physique requires him to wear a special breathing apparatus to survive outside of water, which brings his character into the paradigm of the physically disabled. His effeminate demeanor meanwhile offers an alternate form of heterosexual masculinity that counter-balances Hellboy's more macho persona.

Although none of these characters is literally presented as the member of an established real-world minority group, the fact that they are all perceived by "normal" characters as "other" opens them up to numerous metaphorical readings in exactly that way. Their reluctant supervisor Tom Manning (played by Jeffrey Tambor) points out Hellboy's marginalized, socially unacceptable status as "freak" to him on several occasions, unsubtly underlining the film's intention to offer social commentary:

> This whole thing is a farce, because in the end, after you've killed and captured every freak out there - there's still one left: you.

Del Toro's only previous superhero film, *Blade II* (2002), is one of the rare examples of a black protagonist within a genre where minority superheroes have been few and far between. Instead, superheroes have very consistently embodied a hegemonic and ostensibly neutral whiteness as a normative ethnic constitution: "always highly visible but with their race generally deemed tacit and unworthy of attention, nationalist superhero bodies are constitutive of the larger (racialized) bodies politic with which they are aligned" (Dittmer ch. 3). And while the Hellboy films focus strongly on their characters' strengths and abilities, they are emphatically shown as socially marginalized subject who are ostracized by their peers and rejected by society. As the represen-tatives of power and authority within the films make use of their unique abilities while insisting that they also remain hidden from the public eye, the films open up a space for identification with forms of identity that are either marginalized or completely excluded from most other superhero movies.

The importance of popular franchises that embrace models of social and ethnic diversity in the contemporary landscape of globalized cross-media narratives is emphasized by Henry Jenkins in his book *Convergence Culture*. In his analysis of the fan cultures surrounding the Harry Potter universe, Jenkins has shown how these fan groups flourished as "people of many different ethnic, racial and national backgrounds (some real, some imagined) formed a community where individual differences were accepted" (180). Although the Hellboy films may primarily address a different audience demographic than the Harry Potter stories, their strong focus on "otherness" gives the film franchise similar strengths in how it is able to address minorities in a more inclusive manner.

A direct comparison with Batman and Iron Man provides a telling illustration. As I have shown in chapter two, Christopher Nolan's cinematic reboot of the Batman film franchise introduced an "othering" of its superhero in *Batman Begins*, as Bruce Wayne is trained and indoctrinated by an Orientalist eastern sect. But as the narrative progresses, Wayne quickly comes to reject this environment and the kind of cultural and ethnic identity it implies, instead incorporating his experience into a self-made form of assembled subjectivity that is based on high-tech American military equipment and the re-establishment of patriarchal order. In an almost identical manner, Tony Stark in *Iron Man* builds his first crude suit of body armor while imprisoned by Afghan terrorists, which he later modifies into a more sophisticated version equipped with the newest military technology.

The Hellboy films, on the other hand, reverse the traditions of Orientalism, in which the East is explicitly associated with the primitive, the mystical, and the irrational, while the West is associated with sophistication, technological innovation, and reason. Instead, the technological capabilities of the BPRD consistently prove to be largely useless against the threats that occur in the films, with Hellboy, Liz and Abe Sapien relying on their physical abilities to defeat their monstrous enemies. The kinds of technology that they are able to use effectively are either objects with magical powers or archaic objects rejected by modern science. This different perspective on surveillance technology is evident not only in the protagonists' lack of techno-logical enhancements, but also in how the most common forms of visual representation of the Panopticon are presented within the narrative.

As in *The Dark Knight*, *Iron Man* and *Watchmen*, the Hellboy films include many shots of the superhero in his secret basement or cave, surrounded by a large collection of screens. But whereas these screens function in other superhero films as a tool for surveillance, mastery, and panoptic control, the screens in *Hellboy* perform a very different function. First of all, Hellboy's screens are not organized into an orderly bank of monitors associated with the disciplinary control of surveillance screens, but are strewn around his living room in a seemingly arbitrary

Radical eclecticism and *bricolage*:
Hellboy's diverse collection of television monitors.

fashion. And rather than presenting any kind of unified perspective, the images displayed on the screens offer a diverse selection of audiovisual content, ranging from Saturday morning cartoons and news broadcasts to home movies of Hellboy's colleague and love interest Liz. Rather than using his collection of screens to suggest the mastery of an all-seeing panoptic vision, the television sets strewn around his den instead imply the fragmentary, constructed identity of postmodern *bricolage* (Collins 1992: 342).

In the second Hellboy film, the use of these screens extends to a more complex form of intertextuality, as the incorporation of scenes from classic horror films begins to comment directly on the action. For instance, in the scene where he is rejected by Liz, the screen beside Hellboy displays the moment from *Bride of Frankenstein* (dir. James Whale, 1935) in which the creature played by Boris Karloff is rejected by his newly created mate. The use of similar images from *The Wolf Man* (dir. George Waggner, 1941) and other classic horror movies in the background of several shots confirms Hellboy's implied status as a sympathetic but publicly misunderstood "monstrous" Gothic protagonist. This desire to establish an intertextual connection with old horror movies reflects another way in which the superhero film can indeed be identified as "post-genre," freely mixing and matching from established generic frameworks as diverse as horror, romantic comedy, action, epic, fantasy, and science fiction, often within a single film. More than most other superhero films, the Hellboy cycle places particular emphasis on its fantasy trappings while rejecting most of the more common science-fictional elements.

Both Darko Suvin and Fredric Jameson have elaborated on the theoretical distinction between science fiction and fantasy, framing the two genres as each other's "generic and marketing opposite number" (Jameson 2005: 56) due to science fiction's reliance on speculative narratives:

Science fiction is ... a literary genre or verbal construct whose
necessary and sufficient conditions are the presence and interaction
of estrangement and cognition, and whose main formal device is an
imaginative framework alternative to the author's empirical
environment. (Suvin 7-8)

The science fiction genre is thus theorized as structurally
removed from, or even opposed to the fantasy genre and "the
fundamental role it assigns to magic" (Jameson 2005: 58). While
most superhero films are indeed organized around "the ethical
binary of good and evil" that is one of the characteristics of the
fantasy genre (ibid.), the occurrence of anything like magic is
generally limited to the superhuman powers of heroes and
villains (which are in turn paradoxically explained in science-
fictional terms: as the result of radiation, genetic mutation, etc.).
The Hellboy films however draw much more explicitly on the
tropes of the fantasy genre, their diegetic world populated by all
kinds of fantastical creatures such as fairies, goblins, elves, trolls,
and demons. Like the Harry Potter universe, the Hellboy films
thereby reveal a secret world of magical powers and fantastical
beings hidden behind the everyday facade of postmodern urban
life.

But unlike the Harry Potter series, the Hellboy films steer
clear of the "Christian (or even Anglican) nostalgia particularly
pronounced in Tolkien and his fellow-travelers" (ibid.). For the
secret magical world in these films is not presented as a fantasy
of pre-modern Britain, but instead as a diverse mix of exotic
cultures and oriental imagery. The best example is the Troll
Market scene in *Hellboy II: The Golden Army*, in which Hellboy
and his team discover the existence of a thriving bazaar hidden
beneath the Brooklyn Bridge. The market's production design
incorporates visual elements from Eastern Europe and Moorish
architecture, all of which are set within the larger context of a
market that is remarkably similar to the iconic bazaars of the

Middle East. While some of the visual elements of this "hidden public space" answer to conventional Orientalist stereotypes, the overwhelming diversity grounds the scene first and foremost as the establishment of a thriving space of uncontrolled "otherness" in an unusually positive sense.

The kind of space represented in this part of the film therefore corresponds very strongly with Foucault's concept of the "heterotopia" as a place that exists in society in which marginalized and forbidden elements can reside:

> There are also, probably in every culture, in every civilization, real places – places that do exist and that are formed in the very founding of society – which are something like counter-sites, a kind of effectively enacted utopia in which the real sites, all the other real sites that can be found within the culture, are simultaneously represented, contested, and inverted. Places of this kind are outside of all places, even though it may be possible to indicate their location in reality. Because these places are absolutely different from all the sites that they reflect and speak about, I shall call them, by way of contrast to utopias, heterotopias. (Foucault 1967: n. pag.)

Foucault's term "heterotopia" has become central to the development of postmodern urban spaces that reject the totalizing frameworks of modernist architecture, moving instead towards a form of urban planning that emphasizes issues of difference and identity in multicultural cities. Given the superhero movie genre's ongoing fascination with the modernist structures that impose a rigid formal sameness onto the cityscape, which is monitored and controlled by white male power figures, the need for the representation of such heterotopias within this pop-cultural realm should be evident.

For unlike the utopian context that defines the futuristic urban environments of other superhero narratives, the Troll Market heterotopia in *Hellboy II* represents what Foucault calls a "heterotopia of deviation," where "individuals whose behavior is deviant in relation to the required mean or norm are placed" (ibid.). Although Foucault's original use of this term referred mostly to institutions like psychiatric hospitals, contemporary urban theory has re-appropriated it to signify physical spaces where cultural difference can manifest itself freely. By presenting this fantastical environment as a hidden part of New York City, the film therefore suggests that this kind of cultural richness and diversity is able to thrive within the postmetropolis in spaces that are not surveilled by the technologies associated with corporate and state power. Moreover, within this reversal of the more traditional ways of representing Orientalist imagery, issues of ethnicity are further destabilized by having the most obvious kinds of Orientalist characters (like the veiled Princess Nuala) portrayed by blonde-haired Caucasian cast members.

The reversal of Orientalist stereotypes
in the heterotopias of *Hellboy II: The Golden Army.*

It is quite common for contemporary popular texts to reverse the relationship between "us" and "them," between "West" and "East," and between "European" and "Oriental." This all too often results in the romantic glorification of colonial subjects and those who are ethnically or culturally "other," while simultaneously maintaining the inherent superiority of a white male protagonist. Some of the most egregious examples of this simpleminded cultural liberalism are films such as *Dances with Wolves* (dir. Kevin Costner, 1990), *Pocahontas* (dir. Mike Gabriel and Eric Goldberg, 1995), *The Last Samurai* (dir. Edward Zwick, 2003), and *Avatar* (dir. James Cameron, 2010). The superficial cultural reversal of stereotypes in these films leaves intact the fundamental difference between the two, thereby falling into the trap of what Žižek describes as "liberal tolerant racism at its purest: this kind of 'respect' for the Other is the very form of the appearance of its opposite, of patronizing disrespect" (2010: 46).

Hellboy II: The Golden Army manages to avoid this pitfall by destabilizing the clear separation between a Western "us" and an Orientalist "them." Rather than dealing in direct representations of other cultures and ethnicities, minorities are represented in ways that open the film up to multiple readings. Like the fantasy novels of China Miéville, Del Toro's film uses alien beings and fantasy tropes to present a complex and ambiguous perspective on the modern cityscape. Instead of acting as direct metaphors for specific social or ethnic groups, the diverse alien beings are frequently hybrids that upset traditional representational clichés. The character of Hellboy himself for instance unites the traditional performance of working-class white American masculinity with a radically non-Caucasian skin color and traditional Japanese hairstyle. Such hybrid cultural and ethnic representations contrast sharply with the casual racism of *Batman Begins*, *Iron Man*, and many other popular texts that leave the fundamental binary division of the Orientalist cultural dynamic largely intact.

The third and final element that makes the Hellboy films different from most other superhero movies is their treatment of patriarchal lineage and its association with narratives of predestination. As the previous chapters have demonstrated, the most enduring superhero archetypes systematically foreground notions of patriarchal heritage: Superman carries out the instructions of his deceased father Jor-El; Bruce Wayne uses his martyred father's inheritance to avenge his parents' death; Tony Stark must restore his dead father's original corporate vision to ensure the company's future, and so on. Although these classic superheroes initially reject the paternal call to destiny, their narratives repeatedly dramatize the necessity that leads them to follow in their father's footsteps, thereby reaffirming the natural superiority of patriarchal mythology. The films therefore systematically reinforce essentialist notions of power and agency, as each superhero is ultimately preordained to carry on his father's work and continue the cycle of white patriarchal hegemony.

Such questions of patriarchal tradition and biological predestination are also prominent elements in the Hellboy films, both of which revolve around the question to what extent the protagonist's satanic lineage defines his identity. Characters attempting to bring about the end of mankind continuously remind Hellboy of this, emphasizing the fact that his biological identity contradicts his involvement with humanity and his attachment to his adopted human father. But although both films present scenes in which Hellboy is tempted to embrace this idea, he always rejects the concept of predestination in the end, in spite of the fact that the "otherness" of his skin color and appearance effectively isolates him from normative society.

Therefore, unlike most traditional characters in contemporary superhero films, *Hellboy* and *Hellboy II: The Golden Army* disavow the nostalgic values of patriarchal capitalism, presenting instead a superhero figure who embodies values of otherness, self-determination, and postmodern *bricolage* as most vital to identity. As a character and popular icon, Hellboy is presented as "living proof of the nurture-over-all theory in that despite his demonic origins, his all-American upbringing has led him to feel like a real boy and act like a regular, grouchy, cigar-chomping action man"

(Newman 2004: 50). His hybrid ethnicity and cultural identity gives him and other characters the ability to stand in symbolically for a variety of real-world social and ethnic groups that suffer similar forms of marginalization: from the discarded working class and the disabled to homosexuals and any number of ethnic minorities. Most other superhero characters leave no such room, instead endlessly re-establishing the absolute hegemony of the white heterosexual male.

Moreover, these films employ the visual motifs and technologies associated with panoptic control in a form that challenges the questionable ways in which most popular narratives incorporate and legitimize neoliberal discourses of surveillance. Like *Watchmen*, these films challenge the legitimacy of panoptic forms of social and political power, while opening up a space for otherness and diversity as essential categories with a right to public visibility and acceptance. But Del Toro's films move beyond Moore's critique of neoliberal panopticism in their attempt to carve out a domain for characters that are presented in terms of their status as marginalized minorities.

In this regard, the Hellboy films are not entirely unique within the superhero film genre. Bryan Singer's two X-Men films for instance are often cited as narrative allegories for queer theory and civil rights issues, both films' mutant characters "explicitly analogized to Jewish bodies, gay bodies, adolescent bodies, Japanese or Native or African American bodies—they are first and foremost, subjected and subjugated and colonized figures" (Bukatman 73). And the TV series *Heroes* has similarly foregrounded categories of ethnic and sexual diversity in its various groupings of super-powered characters. But within the larger landscape of mass culture and contemporary popular entertainment, these potential sites of ideological resistance remain themselves a small but essential minority.

5

Neoliberal Capitalism and the End of the World

> Watching *Children of Men*, we are inevitably reminded of the phrase attributed to Fredric Jameson and Slavoj Žižek, that it is easier to imagine the end of the world than it is to imagine the end of capitalism. That slogan captures precisely what I mean by "capitalist realism": the widespread sense that not only is capitalism the only viable political and economic system, but also that it is now impossible even to *imagine* a coherent alternative to it. (Fisher 2009: 2)

The popular entertainments of the postmodern era have seen an ongoing proliferation of apocalyptic narratives and imagery. From the science fiction B-movies of the 1950s to the millennial disaster revival of the late 1990s, end-of-the-world scenarios have maintained a constant grip on the popular imagination in the post-World War II era. The spectacular visual effects that make up the main attraction for films about global catastrophe have continued to ensure the marketability of the apocalypse: in Cold War genre films like *Earth vs. The Flying Saucers* (dir. Fred F. Sears, 1956), in digital cinema blockbusters like *2012* (dir. Roland Emmerich, 2009), and even in arthouse favorites like *Melancholia* (dir. Lars von Trier, 2011).

This succession of apocalyptic film cycles in American popular culture has flourished alongside the historical development of a particular form of capitalism. From the development of consumer society in the 1950s onward, American capitalism has undergone a series of intensifications that have culminated in the past three decades in the establishment of neoliberalism as a global paradigm. Each series of disaster movies has reflected historically determined anxieties that were specific to its own phase in the development of capitalism: the cycle of Cold War science fiction films in the 1950s can be read as an expression of anxieties triggered by ubiquitous consumerism, while the successful series of disaster films in the 1970s reflected the concerns about a decade of inflation and economic crisis. In the contemporary age of neoliberal capitalism and its "There Is No Alternative" mantra, the apocalyptic motif in popular culture has extended beyond its traditional genre boundaries, now appearing in many kinds of narrative entertainment. Besides the zombie film, the disaster film, and the post-apocalyptic action movie, the superhero film has become another expression of this post-historical worldview.

In this chapter, I examine the relationship between the post-WWII disaster film and its complex relationship with capitalism as it developed from late-Fordism to post-industrial neoliberalism. I develop my analysis of this relationship between popular genre fiction and ideology by first discussing the dialectical structure of the classic monster movie, concluding my initial argument with a close look at the contemporary disaster film *Cloverfield* (dir. Matt Reeves, 2008). These monster movies have a great deal in common with the contemporary superhero movie genre, and will help articulate more clearly the contradictory nature of many such popular narratives. The second part of the chapter then extends this argument by examining the first season of the television series *Heroes*, which offers one of the most compelling examples of the relationship between post-9/11 neoliberalism and the superhero genre, and which also brings together many of the conceptual strands from earlier chapters. By examining the apocalyptic elements that can be identified in these popular narratives, this chapter will argue that these end-of-the-world scenarios reveal how one of the pervasive elements of neoliberalism is the false notion that we have indeed reached the end of history.

The Antinomies of Apocalyptism

The audiovisual depiction of large-scale destruction in Hollywood entertainment has often been placed in the context of Tom Gunning's "cinema of attractions" paradigm, which elevates the attraction of spectacular imagery above the traditional emphasis on narrative. This perspective certainly has relevance for the formulaic and narratively shallow disaster film, which emphasizes kinetic thrills and spectacular visual effects over elements such as character development, complex plotting, and verisimilitude. But although these films do give precedence to visual effects over characterization and plot, there is also a narrative motif in these end-of-the-world scenarios that connects strongly with postmodern anxieties.

As Frank Kermode pointed out in his discussion of apocalyptic narratives in literary history, apocalyptic fantasies offer an illusion of order and progression by providing history with a sense of closure. Just as origin stories supply a comforting sense of narrative beginnings and mythological predestination, the apocalypse promises a revelation that all too often serves to reboot a system that has gone into crisis. Furthermore, it is an extremely flexible motif that is adaptable to a seemingly infinite range of historical periods, genres, and narrative forms:

> Apocalypse can be disconfirmed without being discredited. This is part of its extraordinary resilience. It can also absorb changing interests, rival apocalypses, such as the Sybilline writings. It is patient of change and of historiographical sophistications. It allows itself to be diffused, blended with other varieties of fiction—tragedy, for example, myths of Empire and of Decadence—and yet it can survive in very naïve forms. (Kermode 8-9)

Among such naïve forms of apocalyptic narrative are clearly the pop-cultural texts that range across numerous genres in multiple media, including post-World War II Hollywood cinema. But perhaps most remarkable about the systemic occurrence of these apocalyptic narratives is that such popular films—with very few exceptions—ultimately show the world being saved from disaster on the eve of its destruction, frequently due to the direct intervention of a martyr figure. Such martyr figures have become increasingly commonplace in apocalyptic blockbuster films of the late 20th century, where "the Hollywood appropriation of martyrdom situates it in the larger context of the redemption of mankind" (Copier 174).

While most Hollywood films of this kind avoid explicit religious references that would limit the films' popular appeal in a predominantly secularized Western culture, Biblical notions of martyrdom and sacrifice do continue to dominate these pictures. In *The Poseidon Adventure* (dir. Ronald Neame, 1972) as much as in *Armageddon* (dir. Michael Bay, 1998), Hollywood disaster films have indulged in the fantasy of a heroic martyr sacrificing his own life to redeem a corrupt, stagnant world from the brink of destruction. The contemporary superhero movie is certainly no exception to this pattern: *Superman Returns* for instance represents only one of the many ways in which the genre has appropriated messianic imagery and themes in connection with apocalyptic scenarios. As I have developed in more detail in chapter 1, Kal-El's acceptance of the messianic role determined by his father connects his origin story to a larger mythical discourse of predestination and patriarchal power.

While apocalyptism makes up a continuous cross-genre motif in classical and postclassical Hollywood cinema, its individual movie cycles have reflected the specific anxieties of their own historical circumstances. The 1950s wave of apocalyptic monster and science fiction films can, for instance, be read as symptomatic of wider socio-cultural fears and anxieties relating directly to the paranoia of its era's cultural and political discourses:

While the science fiction of the long 1950s responds in a particularly direct and obvious way to the threat of nuclear holocaust, it is also the case that this fiction is influenced by a number of other concerns and anxieties that were crucial to the texture of American life in the decade. Indeed, these other concerns and anxieties are ultimately inseparable from the nuclear fears of the decade, the synergies among these various fears accounting for the otherwise seemingly inexplicable level of Cold War hysteria that informed American attitudes during this period. (Booker 4)

Similarly, the 21st-century cycle of superhero movies has incorporated apocalyptic imagery and motifs in ways that reflect contemporary anxieties related to post-9/11 neoliberalism and the War on Terror.

These films stand as a telling example of how the absence of historicity in late capitalism triggers a desire for Kermode's "rectilinear views of the world," the resulting re-establishment of order, and perhaps even a promise of redemption. The disaster film acts out the wider fantasy that the postmodern world has reached the point of collapse, while promising a nostalgic form of rebirth and renewal. This is why the disaster film connects so strongly to discourses of 9/11 and the neoliberal agenda: the spectacular imagery of the attacks automatically led the public to interpret the events as part of a postmodern culture of spectacle. This contributed to the ease with which the events and their media representation were effectively severed from any socio-historical context, and came to circulate as lurid spectacles in their own right. These images subsequently came to serve a cultural and political agenda that embraced neoliberalism's "There Is No Alternative" logic in the articulation of the Bush Doctrine and the War on Terror.

Most films in the disaster movie genre embody a strong sense of nostalgia for a pre-modern world, using the films' cataclysmic events as a kind of societal and historical reboot, returning the world to an earlier form of capitalism. The apocalyptic mode of superhero movies however reflects a more ambivalent attitude towards postmodernity. For while the superhero films typically do include spectacular scenes of mass destruction that define much of these films' drawing power, the narrative tradition of the superhero also requires that the world be saved from this calamity. The preservation of a status quo that will inevitably lead to a similar crisis in the next installment is thereby ensured. The superhero film thus serves as an excellent example of the specific kind of postmodern culture that has developed in the neoliberal era. For instead of the repeated fantasy/anxiety of a devastating attack on New York City, these 21st-century films circulate in a culture where this has already happened, and where the conflicting desires to revisit those events while also fantasizing that they never took place creates an uncanny narrative/historical short circuit. The endlessly repeated superhero cycles fulfill this antinomy: the world is both saved and destroyed, the hero both sacrifices himself and survives, the events in the films both did and did not happen.

Disaster Movies and America's Addiction to Catastrophe

> Only a catastrophe gets our attention. We want them, we need them, we depend on them, as long as they happen somewhere else. (DeLillo 1985: 66)

The above passage from Don DeLillo's postmodernist novel *White Noise* (1985) is frequently quoted in reference to the central role occupied by catastrophic imagery in the American public imagination. In response to the question why the postmodern subject finds himself so enthralled by images of large-scale devastation, the character Alfonse Stompanato memorably replies: "Because we're suffering from brain fade. We need an occasional catastrophe to break up the incessant bombardment of information" (65).

This perspective on the postmodern desire for moments of spectacular disaster that briefly interrupt the deadening monotony of late capitalist consumerism indicates the contradictory nature of postmodern popular culture. According to this logic, the disaster film is symptomatic of both the desire to upset the status quo, and the opposite wish to see that same balance endlessly and immediately restored. This negative dialectic is typical of the schizophrenic nature of the capitalist system, as well as its tendency to move towards crisis: "with its ceaseless boom-and-bust cycles, capitalism is fundamentally and irreducibly bipolar" (Fisher 2009: 35). A similar idea was suggested by Susan Sontag as early as 1965, in her influential essay "The Imagination of Disaster":

> Ours is indeed an age of extremity. For we live under continual threat of two equally fearful, but seemingly opposed, destinies: unremitting banality and inconceivable terror. (42)

As Sontag pointed out so accurately, the spectacular and repetitive nature of cataclysmic imagery in Hollywood films from the 1950s onward became a crucial element in the historical development of postmodernism. As science fiction and horror movies from the Cold War era offered more depictions of large-scale destruction, the public perception of catastrophe was increasingly defined by fantasy representations, with movies setting the standards by which real-life disasters came to be judged.

Unlike the more speculative, science-oriented narratives of early-20th century science fiction novels, the Cold War disaster films offered the audience a more haptic form of involvement. These spectacular films with their emphasis on visual effects allowed the viewer to engage in a fantasy of seeing recognizable landmarks of the modern Western world destroyed and capitalist civilization brought to a sudden, violent end. The ubiquitous nature of disaster footage in the Hollywood movies of the 1950s therefore "owed a good deal of their fascination to the therapeutic opportunity they presented for working through anxieties about the frightening prospect of global annihilation, particularly because they so consistently supplied happy endings and comforting resolutions" (Rozario 168).

It has become commonplace to interpret these films' alien invasions, atomic mutation, and identity theft as metaphorical representations of anxieties related to the threats of nuclear warfare, communism and McCarthyism. More recent studies of these film genres however have focused on the way in which they articulated and acted out wider resentments against modernity itself, and the complex relationship with capitalism they seem to represent. If the period of late or globalized capitalism has indeed ushered in an era in which the Baudrillardian simulacrum has usurped our perceptions of reality, then "the postmodern culture of calamity may well be defined by a collision or collusion between the apocalyptic and the hyperreal" (Rozario 188).

In the history of the disaster film, this simultaneous collision and collusion started with the cycle of science fiction films of the 1950s, beginning with *When Worlds Collide* (dir. Rudolph Maté, 1951), including the "paranoia subgenre" of *The Thing from Another World* (dir. Christian Nyby, 1951), *Invaders from Mars* (dir. William Cameron Menzies, 1953), and *Invasion of the Body Snatchers* (dir. Don Siegel, 1956), and culminating in the cycle of monster movies featuring visual effects produced by Ray Harryhausen: *The Beast from 20,000 Fathoms* (dir. Eugène Lorié, 1953), *It Came from Beneath the Sea* (dir. Robert Gordon, 1955), *Earth vs. The Flying Saucers* (dir. Fred F. Sears, 1956), and *20 Million Miles to Earth* (dir. Nathan Juran, 1957).

The Dialectics of the 1950s Monster Movie

Harryhausen's monsters offered audiences a productive way of engaging with the dialectical view of (post)modernity that is embodied by the disaster film as the product of a mass culture in which "everything becomes a *spectacle*, that is, essentially *non-participatory*" (Lefebvre 1995: 337). One of the primary postmodern anxieties concerned the breakdown of the distinction between the natural and the cultural, the modernist opposition that was being challenged by the swift development of technology and commodification in the 1950s. Resentments against this cultural shift were articulated in these films by monsters wreaking havoc on the major American cities that represented modern discourses of progress. Whether the monster in the film took the form of a giant lizard, a gargantuan octopus, or the monstrous yet endearing alien "Ymir" from *20 Million Miles to Earth*, the creatures represented a primitive, peculiarly innocent force of nature that responded violently and spectacularly to the arrogance of modern humanity. These films thereby came to perform "valuable, if problematic, therapeutic work for a modern people living in a world of constant turmoil and turbulence, in a world haunted by violence" (Rozario 188).

The therapeutic work these popular texts perform is itself deeply contradictory, as we desire to see resentments against modernity acted out from within the context of these formulaic narratives in which the upset balance is also systematically restored. This desire is indicative of some of the doubleness that typifies the historical period of the 1950s. The schizophrenia that Deleuze and Guattari have described as an essential characteristic of postmodernism may be witnessed here: "the overt doubleness of American culture in the 1950s can ... be taken as a reflection of the increasing hegemony of capitalism in the decade, as the last remnants of agrarian alternatives to capitalism were swept from the American scene once and for all" (Booker 4). Just as Marx adopted a dialectical form of analysis in order to chart the complexities and contradictions of capitalism, an analysis of American Cold War popular culture should be similarly dialectical in order to recognize the embedded contradictions that fueled this cultural period.

The Hollywood disaster films of this era present us with such overwhelming contradictions that their narrative logic becomes a form of shorthand for dialectical thought. Firstly, the films' entire existence is predicated on the depiction of apocalyptic imagery, yet they consistently present narratives of historical redemption. Secondly, the films' articulation of the communist threat is allegorically represented in the form of mind-controlling aliens that transform American citizens into a homogeneous mass, while American commodity culture of the period represents exactly this kind of cultural homogeneity. Thirdly, the destructive monsters provide a form of therapy for postmodern audiences that lack a sense of agency, even as this "therapeutic activity" takes the form of a passive consumer spectacle. Both Lefebvre and Debord have criticized such visual spectacles for being essentially non-participatory, emerging precisely at "the historical moment at which the commodity completes its colonization of social life" (Debord 29). If the popular culture of the 1950s can thus be interpreted as a symptom of this historical moment in which we see the beginnings of late capitalism and an emergent postmodernism, it could be rewarding to compare the features of this period's allegorical disaster films with more recent texts that share this apocalyptic motif.

Such a comparison between similar texts from different eras can clarify shifts and possible ruptures in ideological values over time, as popular culture adapts to changing cultural concerns. This allows us to focus on the ways in which they represent the dialectical values of continuity, in the form of stable intertextual genre conventions, and change, in the form of modifications to the formula that connect to historically specific reading positions. One of the traditional ingredients of the disaster movie genre is the hero's vocation as a scientist. The disaster movie typically "opens with the scientist-hero in his laboratory, which is located in the basement or on the grounds of his tasteful, prosperous house" (Sontag 43). The protagonist thereby represents not only the Enlightenment ideals of scientific knowledge and rational thought, but also the conservative ideological values associated with white heterosexual patriarchy, his female assistant an important but subservient accessory in his ongoing investigation.[10]

Not only is the scientist-hero in these disaster films instrumental in saving the world from the aggressors; his cooperation with the American military also represents the efficacy of the military-industrial complex that provided the economical engine for post-WWII America. In this sense, the narratives of 1950s disaster movies dramatize the successful cooperation between the government and the enlightened individual, often overcoming initial conflicts and misunderstandings to rise together and overcome seemingly insurmountable odds. At the most superficial symbolic level, these narratives therefore seem to offer thinly veiled metaphorical representations of American superiority, always in the form of explicitly masculine and patriarchal fantasies of social and technological control.

Although this kind of "common-sense" interpretation does indeed hold true at the most basic narrative level, the monster movies of the 1950s simultaneously provide an altogether different level of engagement that runs counter to what one may call the "preferred reading" of this surface meaning. For although the scientist-hero is nominally the protagonist and therefore theoretically the primary locus of audience empathy and identification, he simultaneously offers a more ambiguous representation of the "one who releases forces which, if not controlled for good, could destroy man himself" (Sontag 46). The protagonist thereby stands not only for the positive aspects of scientific progress and Enlightenment values, but also for the destructive powers associated with nuclear power, ultimately making him responsible for the disasters that take place in the film. In other words: the protagonist occupies a position that could with equal legitimacy be described as that of dramatic antagonist.

By the same token, the monster that functions as the picture's nominal villain may also be said to be the film's actual protagonist-hero, and the primary focus of audience engagement. Like the eponymous main character in archetypal monster movie *King Kong* (dir. Merian C. Cooper, 1933), the stop-motion animated creatures in the 1950s cycle of monster movies constitute "a narratively centralised special effect … whose singular nature not only forms the basis for the diegetic story, but also supports a meta-narrative *about* spectacular display" (North 66-67). In marked contrast to the bland, interchangeable leading men who portray these films' scientist-heroes, the spectacular monsters in the 1950s disaster movies are colorful, larger-than-life characters, given forceful and distinctive personalities. Indeed, these films' longevity within fan culture and genre film history derives from the creature effects more than anything else. Even the film posters' design usually emphasized the dominance of the creature over the human characters in the film, who dwell in the margins as the monster overshadows every other aspect of the image.

The original poster for *20 Million Miles to Earth* (1957)
and the centrality of its monster protagonist.

With hero and villain thus occupying opposite yet inter-changeable roles in the genre, the monster movie provides an opportunity for viewers to navigate between these two positions. Rather than limiting the viewer's options to a binary choice between good and evil, these films provide a deceptively complex interface through which the dialectical nature of capitalism is clearly reflected: the scientist-hero/villain embodies Jameson's notion that "capitalism is at one and the same time the best thing that has ever happened to the human race, and the worst" (1991: 47). This helps us understand why the disaster film became such a ubiquitous genre within global cultures of postmodernism, as it reflects most accurately how we must view "the cultural evolution of late capitalism dialectically, as catastrophe and progress all together" (ibid.). Even if the films themselves are commonly perceived as hollow, superficial forms of postmodern spectacle, the contradictions that exist at every level of their structure make them quintessentially symptomatic of postmodern culture.

Cloverfield and the Post-9/11 Disaster Film

From a psychological point of view, the imagination of disaster does not greatly differ from one period in history to another. But from a political and moral point of view, it does. (Sontag 48)

As Susan Sontag implies in the above quotation, the imagination of disaster within this popular genre reflects wider social concerns that allow contemporary audiences to engage with these texts at a level beyond that of mere plot. In their ambivalent treatment of apocalyptic imagery and narratives, distinct cycles in the disaster movie genre's history can be related to political and ideological values of their periods. For instance, just as the 1950s cycle of monster movies reflects concerns about the Atomic Age, the post-WWII rise of Western consumerism, and the loss of individual identity this cultural shift entails, the late 1990s "millennial" cycle, spearheaded by the success of *Independence Day* (dir. Roland Emmerich, 1996), represents the contradictions of the fully globalized capitalism of Clinton's post-Cold War "Pax Americana." Throughout this cycle, which also includes films like *Deep Impact* (dir. Mimi Leder, 1998) and *Armageddon*, the focus is placed squarely on America's leading role in world politics, willing to sacrifice a martyr figure to redeem the world while a benevolent, patriarchal American president succeeds in uniting the world and leading a global response to the cataclysmic event at hand.

When the 9/11 attacks occurred, the popular genre of the disaster movie took up a pivotal role within the forms of public discourse that would come to define the event. Many commentators, including *New Yorker* film critic Anthony Lane, immediately emphasized the film-like qualities of the attacks: "People saw—literally saw, and are continuing to see, as it airs in unforgiving repeats—that day as a movie" (qtd. in Rozario 177). And while the spectacular images of the destruction of the World Trade Center buildings were endlessly repeated, the public response to the uncanny way in which these images seemed so familiar from countless disaster movies created a strangely contradictory response. On the one hand, there was a public outcry against Hollywood images that sensationalized mass destruction, as "numerous critics summarily declared that the attacks ... had brought about the 'end of irony'" (Spigel 120). But this was simultaneously contradicted not only by the public's addiction to the ceaseless repetition of these images, but also by a widely shared private interest in the disaster movies that were publicly deemed unacceptable: "even while industry leaders were eager to censor out trauma-inducing images of any kind, video outlets reported that when left to their own discretion consumers were eagerly purchasing terrifying [disaster films] like *The Siege* and *The Towering Inferno*" (ibid.).

This contradictory relationship with 9/11 and its connection with the spectacles of the disaster movie genre confirms Slavoj Žižek's explanation of the unreal qualities of the attacks and their imagery:

> What happens at the end of this process of virtualization ... is that we begin to experience "real reality" itself as a virtual entity. For the great majority of the public, the WTC explosions were events on the TV screen, and when we watched the oft-repeated shot of frightened people running towards the camera ahead of the giant cloud of dust from the collapsing tower, was not the framing of the shot itself reminiscent of the spectacular shots in catastrophe movies, a special effect which outdid all others, since—as Jeremy Bentham knew—reality is the best appearance of itself? (2002: 11)

This Baudrillardian reversal of real and representation, of authenticity superseded by simulation, clarifies this apparent desire to revisit the disaster films that had defined the spectacle of catastrophe for us, as this allows us to measure the "reality" of the 9/11 footage by the yardstick of the "fantasy" of the disaster film. Using Lacanian theory to illuminate the importance of fiction in our understanding of reality, Žižek employs the notion of "traversing the fantasy" as a way of negotiating our fears and desires without having to confront them directly: "we should be able to discern, in what we experience as fiction, the hard kernel of the Real which we are able to sustain only if we fictionalize it" (ibid. 19). In other words: the fantastical representations of spectacular apocalypse do not truly represent an escapist flight from reality into the realm of fantasy and entertainment. Rather, at a more fundamental level, they act out a perverse desire to see this drive fulfilled, while the troubling implications of this desire are inoculated by the emphatically non-realist trappings of the genre film.

This is again a point where we should clearly differentiate between the two conflicting notions of popular fantasy and what it represents. Fantasy is not merely a cultural expression of how one wishes things were: "it is a 'story' that both naturalizes a state of affairs – *that's just the way that things are* – and makes it a personal configuration – *that's just the way that I am*" (Williams 212). Apocalypticism in popular narratives therefore articulates both a desire for historical linearity to re-impose itself forcefully, and the post-historical anxiety of neoliberal capitalism. Such forms of fantasy thus allow one to engage with the tension between structured desire and unmediated *jouissance*, allowing us to "approach what [we] desire without ever getting any closer to it" (ibid.).

Therefore, whether they deal with the anxieties caused by the Cold War and its threat of nuclear annihilation or by 9/11 and the threat of global terrorism, monster movies function as sites where audiences can negotiate these issues therapeutically within the safety of a genre that confronts these fears indirectly. Matt Reeves, the director of the post-9/11 monster movie *Cloverfield* (2008), acknowledges this perspective on the genre in his audio commentary from the film's DVD release:

> From the beginning a lot of people were saying: "... Does it have this 9/11 angle to it?" And in a certain sense I was always aware that it did, in that it felt like it was a way of dealing with the anxieties of our time ... Genre movies ... deal with very real anxieties that people have. That's why they're effective. *Godzilla* came out of that whole A-bomb nightmare for Japan, and the idea of this terrible, unfathomable destructive force ... and all the anxiety that came out of the atomic and nuclear age ... So that was always the entry point for our movie. But then we felt that once you call up those feelings, I think genre films enable you to approach those feelings in a safe environment, and to experience them, but in the safety of ultimately knowing it's a giant monster movie.

In many ways, the "9/11 angle" to which Reeves refers in *Cloverfield* is all too obvious. For while the film establishes itself

in the generic tradition of the disaster movie by forging intertextual connections with the classic Ray Harryhausen monsters,
it repurposes the genre's familiar narrative and visual tropes as
an extension of post-9/11 culture.

The teaser trailer for the film immediately established not
only the subjectivity and immediacy of the digital-video
aesthetic associated with 9/11 and its various media representations, but also the tradition of the monster movie, alongside the
resulting nature of the film as defined primarily by its entertainment value. Besides the associative connections between the
handheld digicam conceit and the endlessly recycled 9/11
footage, the film re-stages iconic images from within the safety of
its own monster movie context. These obvious symmetries
largely shaped the critical response to the film, with reviewers
and audiences alike voicing the film's uncanny appropriations of
9/11 imagery. Dubbing the film's nameless monster "Al-
Qaedzilla," *Village Voice* film critic Nathan Lee was one of many
writers to observe that "street-level 9/11 footage would fit
seamlessly into *Cloverfield*'s hand-held, ersatz-amateur POV; the
initial onslaught of mayhem, panic, plummeting concrete, and
toxic avalanches could have been storyboarded directly from the
CNN archive" (n. pag.).

Given the fact that *Cloverfield*'s multiple and deliberate articulations of 9/11 discourse were equal to (if not larger than) its
disaster movie genre trappings, the film's enormous critical and
commercial success may indeed testify to the audience's
readiness to engage with these issues from within the relative
"safety" of its explicit monster movie context. Hollywood films
that have presented aspects of the 9/11 attacks in a more literal
way (such as *United 93* and *World Trade Center*) were surrounded
by controversy and public debate, and attracted only a fraction
of *Cloverfield*'s blockbuster-sized audience. An often-heard
complaint was that audiences were still too traumatized by the
attacks to confront a cinematic recreation of the events directly,

thereby once again foregrounding the traumatic aspects of 9/11, as discussed previously in chapter 2. These films' narratives however provided little more than generic tales of heroic American martyrdom aimed at transforming a passive and victimized America into an image of heroic masculinity.

This general lack of a coherent geopolitical narrative to contextualize the attacks has been frequently discussed and criticized in studies of 9/11: "the events of September 11 were converted into a human-interest story, into a commodity that could generate substantial profits for commercial news organizations" (Rozario 194). With the bombardment of spectacular images and sentimental human-interest narratives about individual victims, the attacks were presented within a historical and political vacuum that reduced complex issues to familiar patterns of heroes and villains:

> The entertainment media and apocalyptic theology both tend to present politics and morality in black-and-white terms, treating the world as a place where "innocence" is always imperiled and where retribution is demanded against violators of virtue. Both discourses privilege the sentimental and favor personal morality over political knowledge to such an extent that complexity can begin to feel like the last refuge of fools and the corrupt. (ibid. 200)

This simplistic reduction of historical events into ready-made generic binary patterns conforms once again to Lynn Spigel's description of "infantile citizenship," as I have developed previously in chapter 2. With the mass media coverage presented in ways that are both sensational and sentimental, while entirely lacking in historical or geopolitical context, both the news footage of 9/11 and its various depictions in Hollywood movies patronize their viewers as if they were children. This position helped the American public adopt a role of victimized exceptionalism "that allows adult viewers comfortably to confront the horrors and guilt of war by donning the cloak of childhood innocence" (Spigel 128).

Cloverfield incorporates several elements of this a-historical media response to 9/11 as well, firstly by re-staging familiar representations of those catastrophic moments as an unforeseeable attack by a nameless, unidentifiable monster. In an inspired break with genre traditions, *Cloverfield* offers no explanation for the monster's actions, or even any indication of its origins. And unlike the traditional scientist-hero of the disaster movie, the protagonists of *Cloverfield* are young "neo-yuppies" with no idea of the nature of the events they encounter. But the fact that there is no central voice of authority represented within the narrative maintains the protagonists' ambiguous position in the film. For just as the unforeseen consequences of technological progress made the scientist-hero at least partially responsible for the impending apocalypse, it is here implied that the ignorance and incompetence of these new global capitalists is to blame for our current predicament. As Nathan Lee suggests, a subversive reading of *Cloverfield* may indeed be the most compelling one:

> With its emphasis on corporate infrastructure and the unimaginative consumer class that enables it, *Cloverfield* makes for a most satisfying death-to-New-York saga. Which is to say, the fatal flaw of Drew Goddard's script—shallow, unlikable heroes—can be flipped to an asset: death to the shallow, unlikable heroes! (n. pag.)

Furthermore, while this oppositional reading of the heroes' traditional dual role of protagonist/antagonist certainly applies within this post-9/11 cultural context, the monster's similarly dialectical nature is equally convincing. As in the Ray Harryhausen films of the 1950s, the monster acts out wider resentments against (post)modernity in ways that allow viewers to indulge in such fantasies indirectly.

SOME THING HAS FOUND US

C L O V E R F I E L D
01·18·08

"Some Thing Has Found Us":
smoke-covered Manhattan on
the *Cloverfield* film poster.

As the film's poster illustrates, the monstrous attacks on New York constitute *Cloverfield*'s quintessential attraction: the notion of a post-9/11 New York under attack by a mysterious creature is the sole focus of the poster's design. While the image on the poster recreates familiar images of the attack that showed downtown Manhattan from the water, enormous smoke clouds rising from the Financial District, it adds the tag line "Some Thing Has Found Us" as its sole indication of the force behind this destruction.

With the film's monster literally described by the term "Some Thing," one is tempted to perceive it as a metaphorical embodiment of the Lacanian concept "Das Ding": the lost object of desire and *jouissance* that must be continually re-found, representing the unknowable "abyss/void of the Other beyond every empathy and identification" (Žižek 2010: 312). *Cloverfield*'s monster posits the threat to the city precisely in the form of this "unknowable void" that acts out our own repressed fantasies:

> Not only were the media bombarding us all the time with talk about the terrorist threat; this threat was also obviously libidinally invested — just remember the series of movies from *Escape from New York* to *Independence Day*. That is the rationale of the often-mentioned association of the attacks with Hollywood disaster movies: the unthinkable which happened was the object of fantasy, so that, in a way, America got what it fantasized about, and that was the biggest surprise. (Žižek 2002: 15-16)

The monster thus comes to represent a far more accurate embodiment of how 9/11 was given shape by the media, and therefore of the way it was experienced by much of the public. Unlike the more literal recreations of the attacks, post-9/11 disaster movies like *Cloverfield*, *War of the Worlds* (dir. Steven Spielberg, 2005), and *Children of Men* (dir. Alfonso Cuarón, 2006) offer more productive ways of "traversing the fantasy" of 9/11. The fundamental ambiguity of genre cinema perfectly accommodates the "Janus-like structure" that is required of such a fantasy: "simultaneously pacifying, disarming (providing an imaginary scenario which enables us to endure the abyss of the Other's desire) *and* shattering, disturbing, inassimilable into our reality" (Žižek 2008: 329).

In direct contrast with the human-interest media depictions of 9/11 and the sentimental Hollywood features that frame the attacks in terms of heroism and victimization, the post-9/11 disaster film fully embraces the antinomies of contemporary culture. Unlike the monster movies of the 1950s, there is no happy ending that restores the former status quo, nor is there a return to pre-modern fantasies of an Edenic agrarian society. Moreover, the traditional representatives of political authority and scientific progress, which were still such a strong presence in the late-1990s disaster movie cycle, are strikingly absent, leaving the individual subjects to fend for themselves in a catastrophic situation they fail to understand, and in which both the traditional authority figures and themselves may very well be implicated.

9/11 and the "End of History"

Each apparent movement of history brings us imperceptibly closer to its antipodal point, if not indeed to its starting point. This is the end of linearity. In this perspective, the future no longer exists. But if there is no longer a future, there is no longer an end either. *So this is not even the end of history.* We are faced with a paradoxical process of reversal, a reversive effect of modernity which, having reached its speculative limit and extrapolated all its virtual developments, is disintegrating into its simple elements in a catastrophic process of recurrence and turbulence. (Baudrillard 1994: 10-11)

What we may be witnessing is not just the end of the Cold War, or the passing of a particular period of postwar history, but the end of history as such: that is, the end point of mankind's ideological evolution and the universalization of Western liberal democracy as the final form of human government. (Fukuyama 4)

Of the many genres incorporated and appropriated by the "post-genre genre" of the superhero movie, the disaster film is certainly one of the most obvious. Most superhero movies directly invoke the threat of an impending apocalypse; most superhero narratives are structured around set pieces that foreground spectacular visual effects of mass destruction; and most superhero franchises feature a superhero-versus-supervillain dynamic that functions in a similarly dialectical way as the ambivalent scientist-hero-versus-monster binary of the classic disaster film.

The previous section of this chapter demonstrated that the historical development of the disaster film reflects both continuity and change in relation to its cultural context. The superhero movie functions similarly, as a popular film genre that began to take shape in the late 1970s, when the cultural logic of postmodernism had taken hold, but which did not become a sustained cycle until the first decade of the 21st century. Previous chapters have argued that neoliberalism and the superhero movie genre both revolve around central themes of origin stories, trauma, the postmodern city, and panoptic surveillance. Another element that binds these two discourses together is that of apocalyptism and end-of-the-world scenarios.

The systematic presence of such apocalyptic motifs in the most popular forms of contemporary entertainment suggests a connection with the postmodern subject's diminished sense of historicity. According to theorists such as Jameson and Žižek, contemporary events in late capitalism are presented and experienced in a historical vacuum, leading to a new set of public anxieties of which these films are clearly symptomatic. The superhero movie offers a way of mobilizing the contradictory desire to see spectacular images of mass destruction repeated over and over from the safety of a genre that is constructed around such endless repetition in serialized form. This helps sustain the kind of widely shared cultural amnesia through which the public "too easily forgets and forgives the transgressions of the capitalist class and the periodic disasters its actions precipitate" (Harvey 2010: 219). Or, as one of the superheroes in *The Incredibles* (dir. Brad Bird, 2004) comments with obvious irony: "No matter how many times you save the world, it always manages to get back in jeopardy again!"

The perpetual threat of the world coming to an end takes many forms in the superhero movie, ranging from the "moral apocalypse" represented by the post-historical, post-ethical world of *The Dark Knight* to the more traditional last-minute postponements and reversals of the world's destruction. The motif of both organizing and reversing moments of crisis was established in the 1978 *Superman* when the protagonist turned back time to undo the effects of a catastrophic attack, and has continued in many contemporary superhero narratives. As with the disaster film, the structural logic of these films embodies the contradictory desire to witness the physical destruction of the world while also seeing it saved by way of the traditional Hollywood "happy ending." Not only does this present a worldview that dramatizes the capitalist logic of perpetual crisis and "creative destruction," but it once again organizes this as a spectacle that itself takes on the form of a capitalist commodity.

This desire to see a spectacularly physical apocalypse may be read as an expression of the logic of the postmodern condition, which has been repeatedly described in terms that suggest that we have entered an era that exists outside of the traditional continuity of history. From the utopian claims of Francis Fukuyama to the hyperbolic pessimism of Jean Baudrillard, the tendency to identify our age as the "end of history" has been a pervasive, unifying element among otherwise highly diverse and often contradictory postmodern theorists. But whatever their political or theoretical views, they do also have in common their emphasis on establishing a connection between the current state of global capitalism and the wider sense of cultural apocalypticism they describe:

> The global capitalist system is approaching an apocalyptic zero-point. Its "four riders of the apocalypse" are comprised by the ecological crisis, the consequences of the biogenetic revolution, imbalances within the system itself (problems with intellectual property; forthcoming struggles over raw materials, food and water), and the explosive growth of social divisions and exclusions. (Žižek 2010: x)

Whether we follow Žižek's claim in stating that our system is indeed approaching a truly apocalyptic endpoint, or Baudrillard's thesis that "history, meaning and progress are no longer able to reach their escape velocity" (1994: 4), the apocalyptic imagination of superhero movies offers a way of dramatizing such irresolvable contradictions. It is therefore less important to define what kind of "post-historical" thinking they represent than it is to emphasize how such texts act them out in a way that leaves intact their fundamental incommensurability.

One popular superhero text that focuses strongly on an impending apocalypse from the context of neoliberal culture is the first season of the television series *Heroes*. Not only did this phenomenally successful television narrative bring together numerous strands of the increasingly popular superhero genre, but it did so in a way that was typically postmodern in its use of intertextuality, hyperconsciousness, and convergence culture. This makes it an ideal case study for the complex ways in which popular culture mobilizes and enacts the circular motion of late capitalism. This cycle creates a self-sustaining feedback loop that bizarrely seems to reinvigorate itself by endlessly repeating its own catastrophes. Its closed circle is simultaneously repeated on another level in the narrative of *Heroes*' first season, in which the repeated use of apocalyptic threats ultimately takes the form of a temporal short circuit that offers an uncanny example of the "post-historical" aspects of contemporary culture.

Heroes: Reversing the Flow of Time

In recent days, a seemingly random group of individuals has emerged with what can only be described as "special" abilities.

Although unaware of it now, these individuals will not only save the world, but change it forever. This transformation from ordinary to extraordinary will not occur overnight. Every story has a beginning.

Volume One of their epic tale begins here…

Opening text crawl from *Heroes* (episode 1: "Genesis")

The weekly television series *Heroes* premiered on September 25, 2006, its pilot episode drawing 14.3 million viewers, making it

NBC's most successful post-9/11 drama series debut. Throughout its first season, the series maintained this level of popularity, its success further compounded by spin-offs in the form of comic books, novelizations, and other licensed merchandising and fan fiction. Although the show's popularity decreased over the subsequent three seasons, ultimately leading to its cancellation in 2010, *Heroes* was for a time a popular phenomenon that brought together several strands of the ongoing superhero movie cycle. It incorporated the superhero genre's cultural association with discourses of fandom and subcultures, while broadening its appeal to multiple socio-demographic groups. Moreover, by incorporating elements from the superhero's narrative genealogy (most notably from the X-Men series and from *Watchmen*), it offered a re-reading of the genre through the specific prism of post-9/11 mainstream popular culture.

The superhero movies discussed in previous chapters demonstrated a complex form of interaction with genre traditions on the one hand and the historical specificities of their contemporary cultural context on the other. My analysis of *Heroes* will similarly focus on the ways in which the series follows certain familiar genre tropes while explicitly breaking with others. This combination of continuity and change can provide insight into the ways in which discursive formations do not emerge out of a vacuum fully formed, but draw on an established archive of historically determined material that functions as "the general system of the formation and transformation of statements" (Foucault 2002: 146). By viewing a concept like capitalist realism as a discursive formation that draws on an established archive that "forms and transforms" groups of statements and thereby potentially alters the episteme of our discursive reality, one must also emphasize this aspect of simultaneous change and continuity. As Foucault explains in his archaeological approach to the differentiation of discursive formations:

To say that one discursive formation is substituted for another is not to say that a whole world of absolutely new objects, enunciations, concepts, and theoretical choices emerge fully armed and fully organized in a text that will place that world once and for all; it is to say that a general transformation of relations has occurred, but that it does not necessarily alter all the elements; it is to say that statements are governed by new rules of formation, it is not to say that all objects or concepts, all enunciations or all theoretical choices disappear. (191)

This Foucauldian perspective illustrates that historical change must be viewed as a process in which continuity and genealogy play as great a role as rupture and revolution. His approach is particularly helpful when using popular genres to chart shifts in cultural discourse. This view offers a productive way of countering the "shock doctrine" associated with the seemingly abrupt and world-changing events of postmodern disasters. For the "shock doctrine" of disaster capitalism becomes all the more effective in a culture "where everything now submits to the perpetual change of fashion and media image," and which therefore becomes post-historical because "nothing can change any longer" (Jameson 1996: 16). So although the popular texts themselves may be said to reproduce the logic of late capitalism and the "perpetual present" that isolates audiences from any actual engagement with history, a closer analysis of the inter-action between such texts, their place in relation to genre history, and their relationship to their own historical context can help us dissect the ideological positions they articulate.

Like the superhero movie genre and many other popular 21st-century narratives, *Heroes* may also be said to inhabit a space that is "post-genre." It follows the postmodern logic of a television series like *Twin Peaks*, firstly because it no longer approaches its audience "as a homogeneous mass, but rather as an amalga-mation of microcultural groups stratified by age, gender, race, and geographic location" (Collins 1992: 342). In *Heroes*, this is expressed not only through the show's large group of protagonists, which is made up of a diverse selection of characters that allow for interpellation along lines of gender, ethnicity, age, nationality, and subculture, but also through the interweaving of various popular genres. Just as other 21st-century television series such as *Lost* (ABC, 2004-2010) and *Battlestar Galactica* (SyFy Channel, 2003-2008) each offer similarly diverse genre hybrids, *Heroes* combines elements from fantasy, science fiction, high school drama, situation comedy, and superhero tropes within the episodic framework of the weekly drama series. This polysemy of genres and characters makes the series accessible to a wide variety of audience groups, each of which may be interpellated by one or more aspects of the series.

Another aspect of *Heroes* that makes it fit this definition of typically postmodern television so neatly is the series' repeated use of "generic and tonal variations" in its treatment of the diverse genres it incorporates:

> At one moment, the conventions of a genre are taken "seriously"; in another scene, they might be subjected to the sort of ambivalent parody that Linda Hutcheon associates with postmodern textuality. These generic and tonal variations occur within scenes as well as across scenes, sometimes oscillating on a line-by-line basis, or across episodes when scenes set in paradigmatic relationship to one another (through the use of the same character, setting, or soundtrack music) are given virtually antithetical treatments. The movement in and out of parodic discourse is common in all of the episodes. (ibid. 345-6)

Collins' description of *Twin Peaks* applies equally to the postmodern *bricolage* of *Heroes*, which opens up a similar space to navigate between different viewer positions: from melodramatic sincerity to ironic detachment, and from parodic hyperconsciousness to immersive forms of intertextuality, often even within a single scene. The characters on the show whose positions most strongly express this radical kind of tonal fluidity are the series' central duo of Japanese characters Hiro Nakamura (played by Masi Oka) and Ando Masahashi (played by James Kyson-Lee).

These two characters embody the subculture of comic book fandom, responding to the events around them with a full awareness of the rules and conventions of exactly the kind of genre fiction they inhabit metatextually. As their highly coded form of discourse illustrates, both characters belong to a specific subculture of comic book fandom that Matthew Wolf-Meyer has described as a Foucauldian "discourse of comics":

> Comic book fandom is a subculture predicated upon its language of difference, which relies, in part, upon continuity similar to Foucault's critique of the theoretical construction of history with a vocabulary of names, places, and events particular to the community, employed within the culture to communicate, and outside of the culture to promote itself as culturally important while retaining difference. This continuity, and the knowledge of this continuity ... is an essential component of the discourse of comics. (499)

As representatives of this specific subculture, the characters present an obvious entry point into the series for audiences who recognize and appreciate this "discourse of comics." When Hiro first discovers that he has supernatural abilities, the two characters repeatedly engage in detailed discussions of familiar superhero figures such as Superman and Spider-Man in order to determine their next course of action. This explicit acknowledgment of the series' relationship to ongoing genre traditions performs several functions at once: it establishes character in a way that makes these figures easily relatable to viewers who share their perspective on cultures of comic book fandom; it signals the text's awareness of its own position within a specific form of popular culture; and it establishes a relationship towards older superhero traditions that is both playful and respectful.

But unlike most other explicitly self-reflexive characters in these types of hyperconscious texts, Hiro and Ando do not merely comment on the ongoing action around them. They also participate actively and sincerely in it, thereby transforming their passive consumption of fan cultures into an active engagement with the genre's narrative. In many ways, Hiro can in fact be viewed as the series' primary protagonist, as he simultaneously discovers and explains the narrative's basic rules for the audience while also giving new form to the traditional superhero figure (with Ando as his conventional sidekick). The character's continuous oscillation between the roles of genre expert and increasingly competent superhero figure makes Hiro a particularly successful audience substitute for viewers who recognize and share his discourse of comics fandom. For this group, he therefore offers both a "realistic" character and the traditional adolescent fantasy of developing actual superpowers of one's own.

On the other hand, an exclusive focus on Hiro as protagonist might have limited the series' audience to viewers who felt both comfortable and familiar with the kind of fan-community discourse these two characters represent. For as likely as it is that viewers of the show might single out Hiro (who was indeed the most popular character among internet fan communities) as the cheekily tautological "hero" of *Heroes*, he shares both screen time and narrative prominence with several others, who could just as easily be identified as central characters within the ensemble cast. Each of these other characters provides a different audience segment with a point of identification and ideological interpellation in the text: Claire Bennet (played by Hayden Panettiere) as the independent-minded teenage cheerleader from rural Texas; Peter Petrelli (played by Milo Ventimiglia) as a feminized, postmodern embodiment of masculinity; Matt Parkman (played by Greg Grunberg) as the more traditional archetype of the blue-collar working man; Niki Sanders (played by Ali Larter) as both sides of the clichéd female sex object (alternately submissive and aggressive); and so on.

While each of these numerous lead characters in *Heroes* can therefore be viewed as possible points of identification for a diversified and explicitly heterogeneous postmodern audience, they can also function as multiple points of entrance simultaneously. In the kind of diversification embodied so forcefully by the semiotic multiplicity of the 1989 *Batman*, the show attempts to make itself accessible to numerous possible readings at the same time. Claire for instance can be embraced by teenage girls as a sympathetic way of dramatizing issues they recognize and identify with, such as parental conflicts, social issues, and the character's drive towards self-mutilation. But at the same time, her scenes can be enjoyed by male audiences as a pleasurable, heavily eroticized depiction of the culturally fetishized cheerleader sex fantasy. The series' employment of such a diverse cast of characters in prominent roles thereby constitutes another viable postmodern strategy of appealing directly to a large variety of individual subcultures, lifestyles and audience groups.

Meanwhile, the main narrative of the first season of *Heroes* frames these multiple and fluid forms of postmodern subjectivity within a cultural context that foregrounds specific ideological choices. As with so many superhero narratives, the larger story arc deals with the threat of an apocalyptic crisis that must be averted, and which a group of individuals with supernatural abilities ultimately overcomes. In this sense, *Heroes* establishes a sense of genre continuity that connects it explicitly with other similar superhero movies and narrative franchises across numerous media. Like any other capitalist commodity in the age of neoliberalism, the series thus seeks out as many possible audience groups as possible across any number of available channels, including intertextual references to established successful franchises.

The most obvious parallels are firstly with the X-Men series, which became a lasting favorite among comic book fans from the 1960s "Silver Age" onward. The high-profile film adaptation *X-Men* (2000) was also one of the first in the 21st-century cycle of superhero movie blockbusters that established the genre's viability. As in *X-Men*, the protagonists of *Heroes* discover that some form of genetic mutation/evolution has endowed them with superhuman powers that generally conform to those of the most familiar superhero characters (e.g. invulnerability, physical strength, invisibility, pyrokinesis, the ability to fly, etc.). As in *X-Men*, this discovery leads the characters towards concerns about how they will be perceived by others, while government organizations seek to regulate and contain them. And as in *X-Men*, the sympathetic characters move towards working together in a collaborative team in order to save the world from a looming apocalyptic threat. Secondly, *Heroes* resonates as well with Alan Moore's *Watchmen*, numerous structural elements of which are copied or mirrored in its first season. This is particularly noticeable in the part of the plot in which the destruction of New York is planned in order to avoid a larger-scale apocalypse.

But *Heroes* also sets itself apart from its genre roots by eschewing some of the more iconic motifs associated with the superhero tradition. First among these is the series' total abandonment of the superhero costume. In recent films like *X-Men* and *Hancock* (dir. Peter Berg, 2008), superhero characters have expressed a parodic form of self-reflexivity by commenting sarcastically on their costumes, offering the viewer a form of ironic engagement with these traditional genre elements. Nevertheless, most films in the post-9/11 movie cycle maintained the semantic genre motif of the costumed vigilante, even if it was presented as a knowing reflection on genre traditions. In *Heroes*, this tradition is jettisoned completely, as the eponymous heroes work together without the apparent need to organize themselves into a costumed band of crime-fighters.

In one sense, this can be understood as another way of making the series more accessible to audiences that do not feel included by the discourses of fandom that have historically limited the superhero's primary appeal to particular socio-demographic groups. By abandoning the most visually garish iconography associated with the genre and its ghettoized culture of adolescent males, the series' treatment of similar narrative material is rendered more formally "realistic," and is thereby opened up to new audiences. Meanwhile, the traditional cultures of fandom were offered the opportunity to embrace the series' "innovative" way of presenting superheroes more realistically, while seeing their own form of discourse validated by the show's many references to other superhero authors and characters, and by its sympathetic treatment of fan culture.

The tradition of the costumed superhero, like so many other genre elements, is contradictory in a way that demands further analysis. On the one hand, the eccentric costumes seem to offer "ordinary" modern subjects like Clark Kent, Bruce Wayne and Peter Parker a performative mode of standing out from the crowd: their iconic tights, capes and logos brand them with an identity that establishes them as unique individuals with transcendent identities. Much of the performative essence of the superhero traditionally resides in these outfits, since "the use of costumes and masks only emphasizes that the body is a vision meant to be beheld (if not fully comprehended)" (Dittmer ch. 3). As I have noted in previous chapters, the superhero's costume thus comes to function as a mask that makes it possible to overcome the limitations of free-floating postmodern subjectivity and to enact a form of masculine authority. This points however towards the other side of the costume's inherent paradox, which is that the costume simultaneously functions as a uniform that by its very definition robs the individual subject of his unique identity, transforming him into a part of a Symbolic order that points toward Lacan's concept of the "big Other."

The "Big Other" in Post-9/11 Superhero Narratives

In Lacanian terms, the Symbolic order represents the structuring aspect of language that is associated with the "Law of the Father" and which allows individual subjects to experience the world as coherent and organized. Although this Symbolic order is—like language itself—riddled with gaps and inconsistencies, it allows the individual to imagine the existence of this "big Other" that functions along lines of "fetishistic disavowal." As Žižek explains this concept, it involves the classic Lacanian disavowal strategy of "*je sais bien, mais quand même...*" ("I know very well, but still..."). The strongest example Žižek provides of this is the figure of the judge, who is treated with respect not because of the way this individual person is perceived (i.e. as a normal man with the usual abundance of human flaws and inconsistencies), but because "it is the Law itself which speaks through him" (389).

This disavowal is one of the fundamental elements that drive the system of capitalism. For whereas other ideological systems require a form of belief in order to sustain themselves, capitalism in fact demands a systematic form of ironic distance and disavowal: only by embracing the notion that money is worthless are we able to act in exactly opposite terms. Therefore, "so long as we believe (in our hearts) that capitalism is bad, we are free to continue to participate in capitalist exchange" (Fisher 2009: 13). This observation demonstrates the extent to which Capital has truly become the Real that underlies all aspects of contemporary life: the supposedly "post-ideological" framework of postmodernity "is not that of an illusion masking the real state of things but that of an (unconscious) fantasy structuring our social reality itself" (Žižek 1989: 30).

This imagined "big Other" as the fantasmatic embodiment of an operational and effective symbolic order therefore comes to represent the existence of a coherent socio-symbolic force that structures our daily reality. The paradoxical nature of postmodernity is now that the individual's faith in this "big Other" has effectively collapsed:

> The problem today is not that subjects are more dispersed than they were before, in the alleged good old days of the self-identical Ego; the fact that "the big Other" no longer exists implies, rather, that the symbolic fiction which confers a performative status on one level of my identity, determining which of my acts will display "symbolic efficiency," is no longer operative. (Žižek 1999: 399)

The dissolution of this public belief in "the big Other" has been expressed in various ways from the perspective of postmodern theory. It is evident in one form in Jean-François Lyotard's postmodern condition and his description of the collapse of the Grand Narratives. It is recognizable in Jean Baudrillard's development of the simulacrum as the contemporary short-circuit of semiotic signification that prevents us from engaging with reality. It informs Foucault's description of the Panopticon as a modern emblem of power, occupied by an "empty center." And it informs Fredric Jameson's definition of postmodernism as a cultural dominant that blocks the individual's experience of historicity.

While all these postmodern theorists share this concern for how individual subjectivity takes shape within contemporary culture, Žižek's use of Lacanian theory brings them together in a way that helps explain not only how this relates to politics and ideology, but also to apocalyptic narratives:

> Fredric Jameson's old quip holds today more than ever: it is easier to imagine a total catastrophe which ends all life on earth than it is to imagine a real change in capitalist relations—as if, even after a global cataclysm, capitalism will somehow continue... We may worry as

much as we want about global realities, but it is Capital which is the [Lacanian] Real of our lives. (Žižek 2010: 334)

As the constitutional order of the nation state developed into that of the market state, and entrepreneurial capitalism was transformed into virtual, post-Fordist finance capitalism, the symbolic fiction of the "big Other" came to dissolve and the symbolic function of the father was increasingly undermined. Popular apocalyptic texts are clearly symptomatic of this form of anxiety, staging on the one hand a return of the symbolic mandate of patriarchal figures, and on the other an apocalyptic threat that provides the final *telos* so crucial in allowing our acts to be properly located and accounted for.

To return now once more to *Heroes* in order to illustrate this theoretical perspective, our first observation must be how strongly patriarchal power is presented as a structuring force throughout the series. The mysteriously omniscient organization that tracks individuals with special powers and seeks to control them is led by Noah Bennet (played by Jack Coleman). Bennet is one of several prominent father figures in *Heroes*, his character defined most strongly by his conflicting responsibilities as a father and as a secret agent. Like the three other most prominent patriarchal figures in this season, Linderman (played by Malcolm McDowell), Chandra Suresh (played by Erick Avari), and Kaito Nakamura (played by George Takei), Bennet's character is associated emphatically with secret organizations that secretly control and organize the major characters and events throughout the narrative.

As the series' protagonists struggle throughout the season's narrative arc to solve the mysteries they encounter, their key moments of revelation repeatedly involve the discovery that their own father had been secretly orchestrating and monitoring their actions from the start. Their struggle (like that of Batman, Superman, and Iron Man) therefore comes to revolve around the question how to deal with these father figures, and to what extent their individual destinies have been predestined by a hidden symbolic order and a "big Other" traditionally organized around patriarchal power. The series' diverse range of characters demonstrates a variety of strategies for dealing with this anxiety: from Hiro's complete acceptance of his destiny in the patriarchal chain to Claire's ambiguous, perpetually shifting relationship with her foster father, and the question to what extent he can be embraced as an authentic surrogate.

But while most of the series' father figures are shown to be benevolent, the key character representing this conjunction of patriarchy and capitalism is that of Daniel Linderman, the sole malevolent father figure in the series. His leading role within "the Company" along with his prominence as CEO of a powerful multinational corporation establishes an explicit link between patriarchal authority and capitalist enterprise. As politician/superhero Nathan Petrelli's surrogate father figure, Linderman explains in the following dialogue from episode 20, "0.07%," how his plan to destroy New York City constitutes an attempt to re-establish a socio-symbolic order that functions like the inherently frightening "big Other":

Linderman: People need hope, Nathan.

Nathan Petrelli: An explosion of that magnitude would destroy half the population of New York City like that. [snaps fingers]

Linderman: There's six and a half billion people on the planet. That's less than 0.07%. Come on, that's an acceptable loss by anyone's count.

Nathan Petrelli: By anybody's count?

Linderman: Look, I said people needed hope, but they trust fear.

Nathan Petrelli: This is crazy.

Linderman: This tragedy will be a catalyst for good, for change. Out of the ashes, humanity will find a common goal, a united sense of hope, couched in a united sense of fear. And it is your destiny, Nathan, to be the leader who uses this event to rally a city, a nation, a world. Now you look deep into your heart. You know I'm right.

Linderman's revelation of the nature of his scheme casts a new light on the season's larger narrative. Throughout the preceding eighteen episodes, the protagonists had been struggling to avoid the destruction of New York City, of which they were forewarned by a comic book artist's prophetic visions of the future. Following the series' mantra "Save the Cheerleader, Save the World," the main characters ultimately band together against what at that point appears to be the show's main villain: the former watchmaker Sylar (played by Zachary Quinto), who has been murdering other characters with supernatural powers in order to steal them and make them his own. Once it has been established that New York will be destroyed by a giant explosion caused by a mysterious "exploding man," the general assumption among the characters has been that Sylar will be responsible for this, and is therefore the one who must be stopped.

The above scene thus changes both the characters' and the viewers' understanding of the mechanisms that actually drive the plot. Firstly, this development establishes a direct connection with *Watchmen*, in which the character of Adrian Veidt reveals that he is responsible for the deliberate destruction of New York City as an attempt to restore balance to the world and thereby avoid an even larger apocalypse. Like Veidt, Linderman is also portrayed as the embodiment of global capitalism, his corporation a ubiquitous presence throughout the many levels of the narrative. But whereas Adrian Veidt was a member of the central superhero team in *Watchmen* and therefore a generational peer of the other protagonists in the story, Linderman functions as a surrogate father figure. He therefore represents a figure of patriarchal authority whose relationship to Nathan Petrelli is constituted in classically Oedipal terms. Like the figure of Ducard in *Batman Begins*, he provides a false father figure who must be resisted and ultimately defeated in order for the superheroic son to establish his own position in the "natural" patriarchal order. This essentialist and deterministic aspect of superhero fiction can thus be interpreted as a desire to restore a belief in the "big Other," and reconstitute a symbolic authority that structures reality for us.

The other main difference between Daniel Linderman and Adrian Veidt involves the outcome of their apocalyptic plots. For whereas the destruction of New York in *Watchmen* is orchestrated in a way that precludes any form of resistance (as explained in more detail in chapter 4), the similar disaster in *Heroes* is narrowly avoided. The television series thus rids itself of the catastrophic consequences of neoliberal capitalism, and thereby of the "moments of paradox and possibilities out of which all manner of alternatives [to capitalism], including socialist and anti-capitalist ones, can spring" (Harvey 2010: 216). And yet, one of the series' most confounding contradictions is the ambiguous, even contradictory nature of this disaster. The classic disaster film provided both spectacular images of mass destruction and a last-minute happy ending that transforms the apocalypse into a redemptive new beginning. Similarly, *Heroes* repeatedly shows both the explosion and its aftermath in various forms, from the garish "future-vision" paintings to CGI footage of skyscrapers falling before a billowing dust cloud. It therefore offers a different way of navigating back and forth between representations of catastrophes that have already occurred, and

Visualizing the destruction of New York in *Heroes*.

the nostalgic desire to return to a point in history where they can still be avoided, but also enjoyed.

Unwriting the Present: The Historical Vacuum of 9/11

The strange ambiguity in the series' representation of this central moment of apocalyptic spectacle revolves around *Heroes'* participation in discourses of neoliberalism and post-9/11 disaster capitalism. As I argued in previous chapters, central elements within this form of discourse are constituted by the attacks' singularly traumatic effects, the resulting emphasis on cultures of surveillance and panoptic control, and a redefinition of the global postmetropolis (signified by New York City) as the commodified "Ground Zero" of postmodern culture and identity. The apocalyptic narrative of *Heroes* brings these elements together: firstly, by presenting the consequences of an attack on New York as deeply traumatic; secondly, by introducing numerous organizations (both corporate and government-controlled) that secretly govern characters and events via panoptic control; and thirdly, by equating the destruction of the postmetropolis with the end of the world (an alternate, more accurate wording of the series' catchphrase would have been "Save New York, Save the World").

Episode 20, "Five Years Gone," establishes these elements, and thereby the season's relationship to its historical context of post-9/11 neoliberalism, most dramatically. In this installment, Hiro and Ando accidentally travel five years forward in time, finding themselves in a future in which the attack they have been trying to prevent has already occurred. In this future New York, both the city and the series' other protagonists are portrayed as physically and emotionally scarred: downtown Manhattan is still in ruins, slowly undergoing reconstruction; the government has developed into a totalitarian police state; suspected terrorist and "illegals" are routinely tortured by state agents; and the surviving protagonists have become cynical and embittered.

Within this dystopian environment, Hiro works together with his future self to mobilize the other protagonists and assemble a team that can send him back in time to the series' temporal "present" in order to prevent this future from happening.

This narrative device, which draws on popular Reagan-era time-travel narratives such as *The Terminator* (dir. James Cameron, 1984) and *Back to the Future* (dir. Robert Zemeckis, 1985), involves a complex relationship between the text and its historical context. For example, *Back to the Future* contrasts its narrative present of the mid-1980s with representation of the 1950s that is clearly preferable, while *The Terminator* offers a similar indictment of postmodernity by revealing that its present will lead inevitably to an apocalyptic future. Each in their own way, these cultural artifacts embrace Jameson's "nostalgia mode" by glorifying an unhistorical sense of "pastness": "they show a collective unconscious in the process of trying to identify its own present at the same time that they illuminate the failure of this attempt, which seems to reduce itself to the recombination of various stereotypes of the past" (1991: 296). *Heroes* demands to be historicized in a similar way, especially because its first season (and this episode in particular) represents a post-9/11 New York as the kind of future that must be avoided at all costs, while the stereotypes of the past must be brought to life once more.

This becomes most explicit as "Five Years Gone" reaches its climax during the ceremony to commemorate the five-year anniversary of the explosion that devastated the city. In this scene, Nathan Petrelli (who is President of the United States in this alternate future) ascends a podium constructed at Ground Zero, the scene's staging an obvious recreation of George W. Bush's commemorative speech on the occasion of the five-year anniversary of the 9/11 attacks.

Not only is the mise-en-scène an uncanny reminder of the real-world events organized at Ground Zero in New York City after 9/11, but Petrelli's speech also echoes the familiar War on

The presidential podium at Ground Zero in *Heroes*.

Terror rhetoric that came to define the post-9/11 policies of the Bush Doctrine:

> My fellow Americans, fellow New Yorkers. Please let us take a moment to remember the men, women and children who were taken from us five years ago: five bells for the five years of sorrow. [A bell tolls five times]
>
> Sacrifice: something we are all too familiar with. We've all lost, we've all mourned, and we've all had to become soldiers—heroes—protecting one another from the great danger. This is a battle none of us wanted. One that we entered with a heavy heart, knowing that the enemy was ourselves. We've won battles the world over, not only against those that would do us harm, but against poverty, reclaiming the environment...
>
> But we do not forget the price that we've had to pay, the laws that we've had to pass to keep our citizens safe, to preserve our way of life.

In Petrelli's earlier conversation with his surrogate father, Linderman argued that the attack would bring the people together in "a united sense of hope, couched in a united sense of fear." This later speech demonstrates that this goal was never achieved, and has led instead to a culture of fear and a "battle that none of us wanted." As in previously discussed examples such as *Batman Begins* and *Superman Returns*, the narrative therefore comes to revolve around finding a way to retroactively avoid the traumatic events of 9/11, and to restore the socio-symbolic order that had been disrupted by them.

What is therefore most problematic about *Heroes*, as well as the many other superhero narratives that deal with this central concern, is that this repeatedly involves the attempted restoration of the "big Other" and the patriarchal symbolic order for which it stands. When these narratives reject father figures, it is because they are revealed as inauthentic, even perverse embodiments of patriarchy who use their status to point the heroic protagonists in the wrong direction (e.g. Ducard in *Batman Begins*, Obadiah in *Iron Man*, Magneto in *X-Men*, etc.). Unlike the authentic fathers, who consistently represent values associated with modernist entrepreneurial capitalism, these false bearers of patriarchy are explicitly aligned with postmodern global capitalism, which is thereby identified as the apocalyptic threat that has already occurred, and which yet must somehow also be avoided.

This final interpretive step, which reveals the true threat behind the false, empty father figure, ultimately short-circuits the ideological framework that informs these postmodern narratives. For if the fear of the monstrous cause of the apocalypse in the disaster movie, in *Heroes* as much as in *Cloverfield*, is the Lacanian Thing ("das Ding") that points towards what lies in the unknowable void of the Other, the real source of this Thing must ultimately—and paradoxically—be found within oneself. It constitutes the excess within the subject that triggers the drive towards *jouissance*:

The subject of drive is grounded in a constitutive *surplus* — that is to say, in the excessive presence of some Thing that is inherently "impossible" and should not be here, in our present reality — the

Thing which, of course, is ultimately *the subject itself*. (Žižek 1999: 371)

What seems like a strange contradiction here, locating the unknowable void of the Other within the subject itself, makes more sense when we start applying this to the narratives in the examples discussed previously in this chapter. For in all cases, the story logic creates a short circuit that interrupts the process of othering, pointing back towards the subject itself.

In the dialectical structure of the 1950s disaster film, the formal protagonist is traditionally the scientist-hero, joining forces with the military in order to fight off the apocalyptic threat of some monstrous Thing that is wreaking havoc on the modern city. But as I discussed in the first section of this chapter, what initially appears to be an inhuman monster turns out to be the result of human scientific experimentation, making the scientist-hero ultimately responsible for its actions. Furthermore, the monster in these films provides the central point of audience interest in the film, its destructive capabilities embodying our own unleashed drive towards unmediated *jouissance* as it acts out our secret fantasies and allows us to revel in spectacular images of mass destruction.

Cloverfield incorporates many elements of continuity as part of this genre tradition, from its spectacular set pieces of New York City under attack by a giant visual effect to its small group of protagonists on an impossible mission to rescue one of their own from the creature's onslaught. But the film's departures from genre conventions tell us a great deal about historical processes, changes in ideology, and the postmodern dissolution of older notions of the "big Other." For whereas the socio-symbolic order associated with patriarchal traditions was always restored at the end of the 1950s disaster film, *Cloverfield* ends in a vacuum, the image fading to black as the final two protagonists perish in Central Park. If the monster represents a threat to the existing symbolic order, then this film is remarkable for the way in which it deliberately rejects the notion that this order will always be restored.

Similarly, the change of perspective from that of the traditional scientist/hero to a small group of young "neo-yuppies" is significant. For not only does this limit our perspective to that of individual subjects undergoing the experience without the resources to contextualize or explain events; it also demonstrates how our notions of the "big Other" have shifted from an archaic belief in scientific progress towards the invisible, all-encompassing power of global capitalism. If the traditional disaster film therefore acted out anxieties relating to the increasingly unstable perceptions of Enlightenment values in the atomic age, then we can see how *Cloverfield* corresponds uncannily with similar anxieties relating to the status of capitalism in the postmodern risk society:

> What happens today, with the "postmodern" risk society, is that there is no "Invisible Hand" whose mechanism, blind as it may be, somehow re-establishes the balance; no Other Scene in which the accounts are properly kept, no fictional Other Place in which, from the perspective of the Last Judgement, our acts will be properly located and accounted for. Not only do we not know what our acts will in fact amount to, there is even no global mechanism regulating our interactions — this is what the properly "postmodern" nonexistence of the big Other means. (Žižek 1999: 412)

This perspective on the structure of the postmodern disaster film, in which disastrous events are presented as kinetic, frightening experiences without explanation or the traditionally redemptive resolution, clearly connects with Žižek's compelling description of the postmodern nonexistence of the big Other. At the same time, the fact that the protagonists of *Cloverfield* are presented as caricatures of postmodern capitalists illustrates how this shift has relocated responsibility for disaster to the ongoing crisis of late capitalism. In the perpetual present of postmodernity, our lack of historicity has reduced all such events to mere commodities: "in a world bereft of historical bearings even the most awful events inevitably offer themselves up as pure spectacles" (Rozario 6-7).

This ambiguous relationship with these catastrophic images also informs the narrative logic (or lack thereof) in the first season of *Heroes*, which similarly becomes easier to understand once we locate the source of this (self)destructive drive within the subject. The main narrative, centering on the explosion that will destroy New York City, follows a causal chain of events that is initiated by "future Hiro's" appearance before Peter Petrelli, instructing him to avoid disaster with the words "Save the Cheerleader, Save the World."

This curious narrative bootstrapping of "future Hiro" and his initial appearance to Peter Petrelli in episode 5, "Hiros," is mirrored by "present Hiro" and his trips into the future. As early as the second episode, he accidentally time-travels a month forward in time, where he witnesses the explosion as it occurs, while his extended stay in the future New York of five years after the disaster in episode 20 makes up a crucial phase in his "hero's journey": only after witnessing the lasting and traumatic repercussions of the catastrophic explosion is he able to develop the necessary skills and motivation to travel back in time to avoid it. As in *Batman Begins*, *Superman Returns*, and *Spider-Man*, *Heroes* thus comes to relate explicitly to the historical events of 9/11 as an overwhelmingly traumatic singularity that eludes symbolization, and from which the only escape comes in the form of historical regression.

This is perhaps the key reason why the superhero genre has proved so popular in post-9/11 popular culture: it has provided images and events that offer viewers the opportunity to "traverse the fantasy" that underlies our fascination with the 9/11 attacks while keeping intact the historical vacuum that contributed to the cultural trauma they caused. As archetypal examples of postmodern commodity culture, these superhero franchises offer endlessly adaptable templates for mass entertainment that mobilize the quintessential antinomies of postmodernity: its worlds are constantly being destroyed, yet never end; its characters have long and complex histories, yet they never age; and an absolute dividing line between good and evil is constantly being established, only to be re-defined as historical circumstances change. Like the other superhero films that have dominated popular culture franchises after 9/11, *Heroes* brings together the strands of apocalyptism and postmodern culture that have come to define our contemporary episteme of neoliberal capitalist realism.

Hiro's main narrative therefore reflects the contradictory position the 9/11 attacks have taken up historically as a singularity that was experienced outside of any form of socio-political context. Peter Petrelli's character arc meanwhile comes to embody the disturbing paradox that the deeper cause of this crisis lies within ourselves. Peter's power as a superhero is his ability to absorb other characters' gifts, which makes him an obvious symbolic representation of the endlessly adaptable shapelessness of capitalism:

> [Capitalism] is a system which is no longer governed by any transcendent Law; on the contrary, it dismantles all such codes, only to re-install them on an *ad hoc* basis. The limits of capitalism are not fixed by fiat, but defined (and re-defined) pragmatically and improvisationally. This makes capitalism very much like the Thing in John Carpenter's film of the same name: a monstrous, infinitely plastic entity, capable of metabolizing and absorbing anything with which it comes into contact. (Fisher 2009: 6)

And while Peter Petrelli's "infinitely plastic" nature therefore articulates some of the most fundamental aspects of deregulated capitalism, it should come as no surprise that the central villain Sylar has identical powers: like Peter, he incorporates the abilities of other characters. The only difference is that Peter adopts others' powers by simply coming into contact with them, thus embodying the myth of benevolent capitalism as a painless, "natural" development. Sylar on the other hand takes those powers by force, his violence an uncanny reminder of the monstrous violence and destruction inherent in the capitalist system.

If we therefore identify Peter Petrelli as one of the series' nominal protagonists and Sylar as his main antagonist, we come to recognize how *Heroes'* seemingly contradictory logic in fact perfectly reflects both the central antinomies of postmodern capitalism and the "There Is No Alternative" mantra of neoliberalism. For not only does *Heroes* repeat the typical ambivalence of the disaster film towards its protagonist; it also suggests that both sides in the War on Terror are part of the same system, and that they use identical methods to achieve opposite goals. In his book *Terror and Consent: The Wars for the Twenty-First Century*, Philip Bobbitt explains how contemporary market state terrorism is radically different from the older forms of nation state terrorism:

> In the twenty-first century, terrorism presents a different face. It is global, not national; it is decentralized and networked in its operations like a mutant nongovernmental organization (NGO) or a multinational corporation; it does not resemble the centralized and hierarchical bureaucracy of a nation state ... It will operate in the international marketplace of weapons, targets, personnel, information, media influence, and persuasion, not in the national arenas of revolution and policy reform. (84)

Bobbitt's insightful analysis of the nature of 21st-century terrorism thus emphasizes how forces such as Al Qaeda, which are consistently presented as the polar opposite of Western democratic values, at a deeper level in fact operate according to the same logic that drives the "states of consent" of neoliberal democratic multiculturalism. As in the narrative logic of the disaster film, the monstrous Other that threatens and attacks us is thus revealed as emanating from the very same subject that sees it as an absolute challenge to its identity.

While it would go much too far to describe a television series like *Heroes* as an insightful critique of the contradictory logic of late capitalism after 9/11, its narrative patterns and seemingly incoherent causal logic do reflect the ideological frameworks and historical short-circuits of the series' cultural-historical context. Within the post-9/11 narrative of *Heroes*, we can thus identify what Slavoj Žižek has described as the postmodern nonexistence of the "big Other": on the one hand, the lack of strong patriarchal order that allows the characters to place the ongoing events in a coherent, meaningful context; on the other hand, the desire to find a way to restore the very same patriarchal order, acted out by the multitude of father figures that secretly orchestrate the events in *Heroes*. In both instances, these popular texts can be viewed as a symptom of the cultural dominant of neoliberal capitalism.

Conclusion

During the final days of the George W. Bush presidency, after Barack Obama had roundly defeated Republican candidate John McCain in the 2008 elections, *Der Spiegel* revisited the 2002 "Bush Warriors" cover that had sought to parody the superheroic rhetoric with which the government had started the War on Terror. The cover image that I referenced in the opening passages of my introduction portrayed prominent members of the Bush administration as comic book superheroes and action movie icons. Of those original five politicians, only Bush, Dick Cheney,

The superheroic Bush Administration in 2008: "End of the Engagement" (27-10-2008).

and Condoleezza Rice remained; Colin Powell had abandoned the stage, leaving behind an empty Batman suit, and "Rumsfeld the Barbarian" is visible only as a battered, muscular arm, symbolizing his ignominious departure from the Bush cabinet. The remaining "warriors" are bruised and battered after six years of seemingly fruitless and increasingly unpopular wars in Iraq and Afghanistan, the president whose popularity had soared in the wake of 9/11 now serving as the punchline to a bad joke. Fittingly, the cover's design mirrors that of an aging movie poster, a banner across it announcing the "end of the engagement."

This magazine cover is but one of many cultural indicators that the end of the George W. Bush presidency signaled the end of an era. Just as the 2001 attacks had created the illusion of an historical rupture that now divided history into pre- and post-9/11, the 2008 elections were presented again in terms of their epochal qualities. But as events in the subsequent years have shown, Fredric Jameson's truism that "historical events are never really punctual" and that cultural life does not turn on a dime continues to hold true (2002a: 301). The anxieties that fuelled 9/11 discourse are not removed by a change in government, for their roots lie neither in the supposed trauma of the attacks themselves nor in the ongoing military conflicts and government policies that followed in their wake. As the case studies in this book have shown, the deeper cause of these symptoms is located in the system of neoliberal capitalism and commodity culture that makes up the Lacanian Real underlying these fantasies.

It is therefore not surprising that the utopian fantasy of a post-racial, non-partisan America that informed Barack Obama's successful presidential campaign has not materialized under his actual administration. Indeed, the rhetoric and aesthetics of his campaign depended on the very same cultural logic that is so often associated with the neoliberal policies of his predecessor: from the icons and slogans that transformed the presidential candidate into a marketable brand to the superheroic fantasies that quickly accumulated around his public persona as a near-messianic figure with comic book appeal.

President-elect Obama as superheroic fantasy on the cover of *Amazing Spider-Man* #539 (January 2009).

The superhero movie genre meanwhile has maintained its central position within contemporary popular culture, providing images and events that offer viewers the opportunity to traverse the fantasy that underlies our fascination with the 9/11 attacks while keeping intact the historical vacuum that contributed to the cultural trauma they caused. Even as critical voices continue to predict that the now ten-year-old phenomenon of the superhero movie must finally be nearing its end, companies like Marvel and DC/Warner are in fact successfully transforming themselves from comic book publishers to multimedia conglomerates on the basis of their ongoing superhero chronologies. Individual films in established franchises increasingly serve as platforms to advertise upcoming ventures, like for instance the critically disparaged but commercially successful *Thor* (dir. Kenneth Branagh, 2011). And while attempts are also made to reinvigorate the genre with fresh approaches such as *Kick-Ass* (dir. Matthew Vaughn, 2010) and *Scott Pilgrim vs. The World* (dir. Edgard Wright, 2010), their general lack of mainstream success seems to confirm the absolute hegemony of the superhero genre as a form of commodity culture that trades exclusively in repetitive formulas and astronomic budgets.

As an ongoing indicator of shared cultural anxieties and public fantasies, the superhero movie would thus seem to indicate that little has changed since the establishment of neoliberalism as a hegemonic framework. The dramatic contradictions that continue to define American culture, its dominant role in global politics and entertainment, and the popular methods of symbolically representing its role in the global arena still result in an intensely polarized national culture. The postmodern erosion of the boundaries between history and representation, politics and entertainment, and the real and the virtual, has resulted in a situation in which the terms of the political debate are now defined to a large extent by television personalities like Glenn Beck, Sean Hannity, Jon Stewart, and Stephen Colbert. The Tea Party movement may be the most alarming manifestation of this kind of hyperreality, its resolute, intensely nostalgic embrace of comic book vocabulary identifying new heroes and villains as in the self-evident moral logic of a superhero narrative.

The central themes discussed in this study also continue to suture the gap between fiction and history by providing fantasies that disguise their ideologically defined contours. The subjects of origin stories, trauma, the city, surveillance, and apocalyptism that I have described individually in the preceding chapters remain the central nodes around which forms of contemporary subjectivity are constructed. Just as the events of 9/11 did not constitute a moment of historical rupture, the end of the George W. Bush presidency has not ushered in a sudden change in the social and cultural vocabulary. For in the same way that the effects of 9/11 can be viewed as an intensification of neoliberal capitalism, the issues surrounding the presidential elections and the Obama administration revolve around the same concepts that make up the Real of globalized capitalism. All the attempts to enter into a bilateral form of communication between the United States government and Islamic states notwithstanding, the dominant narrative of American identity remains that of the traumatized victim: the "common-sense" history of 9/11 is still repeated as one of a trauma narrative in which an evil aggressor had attacked a self-evidently innocent larger "us."

Although this book has shown that there are also instances in which the superhero figure has lent itself to negotiated readings of contemporary culture, the overwhelming majority of narratives and characters analyzed here points toward a more disturbing worldview in which the nostalgic desire for an earlier form of modern capitalism is accompanied by patriarchal forms of authority. These figures display an attitude towards other cultures and ethnicities that is usually patronizing at best, and openly racist at worst. And although these franchises certainly provide the individual subject with a site where the contradictions of postmodernity can be negotiated metaphorically from within the safety of an unrealistic, allegorical context, it does so in a way that is entirely dictated by the text's status as a branded commercial commodity.

Endnotes

1. One could argue that several other narrative cycles and genres, from James Bond to Jason Bourne and Jack Bauer, could in many ways be seen as types of superheroes, especially at the syntactic level. But since they lack the semantic elements that make them instantly identifiable as such, they are rarely identified as superhero movies by audiences at the pragmatic level.

2. Altman introduces this problematic in relation to *Star Wars* (dir. George Lucas, 1977) and debates surrounding its generic identity: "When *Star Wars* took American theatres by storm, many viewers recognized in its structure the familiar epic configuration of the Western. In fact, some critics described *Star Wars* as a Western. Their desire to integrate this film into the corpus of the Western did not hold sway, however, for the general tendency of genre theorists and the popular audience alike is to recognize genre only when both subject and structure coincide" (24).

3. As Slavoj Žižek has observed about the public's ever-growing fascination with these "making-of" films: "far from destroying the 'fetishist' illusion, the insight into the production mechanism in fact even strengthens it, in so far as it renders palpable the gap between the bodily causes and their surface effect" (1997: 129).

4. See, for instance, books like Tom Soffard's insufferable and shortsighted *Hollywood 9/11: Superheroes, Supervillains, and Super Disasters*.

5. The best-known examples from a long list of mainstream film genres include *Midnight Cowboy* (dir. John Schlesinger, 1969), *The Omega Man* (dir. Boris Sagal, 1971), *The French Connection* (dir. William Friedkin, 1971), *Soylent Green* (dir. Richard Fleischer, 1973), *The Prisoner of Second Avenue* (dir.

Melvin Frank, 1975), *The Warriors* (dir. Walter Hill, 1979), *Hardcore* (dir. Paul Schrader, 1979), *Escape from New York* (dir. John Carpenter, 1981), *Fort Apache: The Bronx* (dir. Daniel Petrie, 1981), and *Prince of the City* (dir. Sidney Lumet, 1981).

6. Both parts of the publicity campaign were immediately withdrawn following the events of 9/11.

7. In addition, *24*'s real-time formula, along with its iconic visual motif of the recurring digital clock, can be seen as a typical branding device that contributes to the series' success as a recognizable global entertainment commodity.

8. This applies not only to the film's theatrical run and its use of IMAX screens; its also translates to its position in home video technology, with its 2008 Blu-ray release setting a sales record for the high-definition digital video format that remained unchallenged until the home video release of *Avatar* (dir. James Cameron, 2009) in April 2010 (Fritz n. pag.).

9. This moment has been interpreted by some as a form of legitimization for the Bush administration's controversial policies: "Like [George W. Bush], Batman sometimes has to push the boundaries of civil rights to deal with an emergency, certain that he will re-establish those boundaries when the emergency is past" (Klavan n. pag.).

10. This formula holds true for all the key 1950s monster movies mentioned above: the paleontologist-hero of *The Beast from 20,000 Fathoms*; the doctor-hero of *Invasion of the Body Snatchers*; the rocket scientist-hero of *Earth vs. The Flying Saucers*; the marine-biologist-hero of *It Came From Beneath the Sea*; the medical scientist-hero of *20 Million Miles to Earth*; and so on.

Works cited

9-11 – September 11th 2001: Artists Respond, Volume One. Milwaukie: Dark Horse Comics, 2002.

9-11 – September 11th 2001: Artists Respond, Volume Two. New York: DC Comics, 2002.

Ackerman, Spencer. "Batman's 'Dark Knight' Reflects Cheney Policy: Joker's Senseless, Endless Violence Echoes Al Qaeda." *The Washington Independent.* 21 July 2008. Accessed: 12 March 2010. <http://washingtonindependent.com/509/batmans-dark-knight-reflects-cheney-policy>

Altman, Rick. *Film/Genre.* London: BFI Publishing, 1999.

Amis, Martin. *The Second Plane.* London: Jonathan Cape, 2008.

Balio, Tino. "'A Major Presence In All Of The World's Important Markets': The Globalization of Hollywood in the 1990s." Neale and Smith 58-73.

Barthes, Roland. *Image, Music, Text.* Trans. Stephen Heath. London: Fontana Press, 1977.

—. *Mythologies.* Trans. Annette Lavers. London: Vintage, 1972.

—. *S/Z – An Essay.* London: Farrar Strauss Giroux, 1991.

Baudrillard, Jean. *The Illusion of the End.* Trans. Chris Turner. Cambridge: Polity Press, 1994.

—."The Precession of Simulacra." *The Norton Anthology of Theory and Criticism.* Ed. Vincent B. Leitch. New York: Norton, 2001. 1732-41.

—. *Simulacra and Simulation.* Michigan: University of Michigan Press, 1995.

—. *The Spirit of Terrorism.* Trans. Chris Turner. London and New York: Verso, 2003.

Bazin, André. *What is Cinema?* Ed. and trans. by Hugh Gray. Berkeley: University of California Press, 1971.

Benjamin, Walter. "From *The Arcades Project.* Bridge and Watson, 393-400.

—. *The Work of Art in the Age of its Technological Reproducibility and Other Writings on Media*. Michael W. Jennings, Brigid Doherty and Thomas Y. Levin, eds. Cambridge, MA: Belknap, 2008.

Bennett, Tony and Janet Woolacott. *Bond and Beyond: The Political Career of a Popular Hero*. Basingstoke: MacMillan, 1987.

Bennett, Tony, Colin Mercen and Janet Woolacott, eds. *Culture, Ideology and Social Process*. London: Batsford, 1981.

Bobbitt, Philip. *Terror and Consent: The Wars for the Twenty-First Century*. New York: Alfred A. Knopf, 2008.

Booker, M. Keith. *Monsters, Mushroom Clouds and the Cold War: American Science Fiction and the Roots of Postmodernism, 1946-1964*. Westport: Greenwood Press, 2001.

Bordwell, David. "Superheroes for Sale." *Observations on Film Art*. 16 August, 2008. Accessed: 10 March, 2010. <http://www.davidbordwell.net/blog/?p=2713>

Bowles, Scott. "Comic-Con Illustrates Genre's Rising Influence." *USATODAY.com*, 25 July 2004. Accessed: 10 August 2009. <http://www.usatoday.com/life/movies/news/2004-07-25-comic-con-side_x.htm>

Bridge, Gary and Sophie Watson, eds. *The Blackwell City Reader*. Malden: Blackwell Publishing, 2002.

Broe, Dennis. "Fox and its Friends: Global Commodification and the New Cold War." *Cinema Journal* 43:4 (2004), 97-102.

Brooker, Will. *Batman Unmasked: Analyzing a Cultural Icon*. London: Continuum, 2000.

Bukatman, Scott. *Matters of Gravity: Special Effects and Supermen in the 20th Century*. Durham: Duke University Press, 2003.

Campbell, Joseph. *The Hero with a Thousand Faces*. London: Fontana Press, 1993.

Cadorette, Guylaine. "Films Postponed after 9/11 Flop at Box Office." *Hollywood.com*. April 10, 2002. Accessed: 15 February 2010. <http://www.hollywood.com/news/Films_postponed_after_911_flop_at_box_office/1107516>

Canavan, Gerry. "Person of the Year: Obama, Joker, Capitalism, Schizophrenia." *Politics and Popular Culture*. Leah A. Murray, ed. Newcastle upon Tyne: Cambridge Scholars Publishing, 2010.

—. "Terror and Mismemory: Resignifying September 11 in *World Trade Center* and *United 93*." *Portraying 9/11: Essays on Representations in Comics, Literature, Film and Theatre*. Véronique Bragard, Christophe Dony and Warren Rosenberg, eds. Jefferson NC: McFarland, 2011: 118-33.

Caruth, Cathy. *Unclaimed Experience: Trauma, Narrative and History*. Baltimore: Johns Hopkins University Press, 1996.

De Certeau, Michel. *The Practice of Everyday Life*. Berkley: University of California Press, 1988.

Chaw, Walter. Review of *Cloverfield*. *Film Freak Central*. 26 June 2008. Accessed: 1 June 2010. <http://filmfreakcentral.net/dvdreviews/cloverfield.htm>

Collins, Jim. "Batman: The Movie, Narrative: The Hyperconsciousness." Pearson and Uricchio 164-81.

—. "Television and Postmodernism." In Robert C. Allen, ed. *Channels of Discourse, Reassembled*. 2nd Edition. London: Routledge, 1992. 327-49

—. *Uncommon Cultures: Popular Culture and Post-Modernism*. New York and London: Routledge, 1989.

Cook, David A. *A History of Narrative Film*. 3rd Ed. New York: W.W. Norton and Co., 1996.

Cooligan, J. Patrick. "Obama Goes Gloves-Off, Head-On." *Las Vegas Sun*. 14 January 2008. Accessed: 27 April 2010. <http://www.lasvegassun.com/news/2008/jan/14/obama-gloves-off/>

Copier, Laura. *Preposterous Revelations: Visions of Martyrdom and Apocalypse in Hollywood Cinema 1980-2000*. Sheffield: Sheffield Phoenix Press, 2012.

Debord, Guy. *The Society of the Spectacle*. New York: Zone Books, 1995.

DeLillo, Don. *Falling Man*. New York: Scribner, 2007.

—. "In the Ruins of the Future: Reflections on Terror and Loss in the Shadow of September." *Harper's* Dec. 2001: 33-40.

—. *White Noise*. London: Penguin Books, 1999.

Dittmer, Jason. *Captain America and the Nationalist Superhero: Metaphors, Narratives, and Geopolitics*. Philadelphia: Temple University Press, 2012. Ebook file.

Donnelly, K.J. "The Classical Film Score Forever? *Batman*, *Batman Returns* and Post-Classical Film Music." Neale and Smith 142-155.

Dubose, Mike S. "Holding out for a Hero: Reaganism, Comic Book Vigilantes, and Captain America". *The Journal of Popular Culture*. 40.6, (2007): 915-35.

Ebert, Roger. Review of *Superman Returns*. RogerEbert.com, June 27, 2006. Accessed: 30 January 2012. <http://roger ebert.suntimes.com/apps/pbcs.dll/article?AID=/20060626/REV IEWS/60606009/1023>

Eco, Umberto. "The Myth of Superman". *Dialectics* 2.1 (Spring 1972): 14-22.

Eaglestone, Robert. "'The Age of Reason is Over… an Age of Fury was Dawning': Contemporary Anglo-American Fiction and Terror". *Wasafiri* 22-2 (July 2007): 19-22.

Elsaesser, Thomas. "Specularity and Engulfment: Francis Ford Coppola and *Bram Stoker's Dracula*." Neale and Smith, 191-208.

—. "Trauma: Postmodernism as Mourning Work," *Screen* 42/2 Summer 2001, 193-201.

—. "'Where Were You, When…,' or 'I Phone, Therefore I am'," *Publication of the Modern Language Association* (January 2003) 120-122.

Emerson, Jim. "Opening Shots: *The Dark Knight*." *Jim Emerson's Scanners*. 26 February, 2009. Accessed: 10 March, 2010. <http://blogs.suntimes.com/scanners/2009/02/opening_shots_t he_dark_knight.html>

Fisher, Mark. *Capitalist Realism: Is There No Alternative?* Hants: Zero Books, 2009.

—. "Gothic Oedipus: subjectivity and Capitalism in Christopher Nolan's *Batman Begins*." . *ImageTexT: Interdisciplinary Comics Studies*. 2.2 (2006). Dept of English, University of Florida. Accessed: 28 May 2008. <http://www.english.ufl.edu/imagetext/archives/v2_2/fisher>

Foucault, Michel. *The Archaeology of Knowledge*. Trans. A.M. Sheridan Smith. London and New York: Routledge, 2002.

—. *Discipline and Punish; The Birth of the Prison*. New York: Vintage, 1995.

—. *The History of Sexuality: 1. The Will to Power*. Trans. Robert Hurley. London: Penguin Books, 1978.

—. "Of Other Spaces (1967), Heterotopias." Trans. Jay Miskowiec. *Foucault.info*. Accessed: 10 August 2010. <http://www.foucault.info/documents/heteroTopia/foucault.heteroTopia.en.html>

—. *The Order of Things*. London: Routledge, 1989.

—. *Power/Knowledge: Selected Interviews and Writings 1972-1977*. Colin Gordon, ed. New York: Pantheon Books, 1980.

Fritz, Ben. "'Dark Knight' Blu-ray Sales Stay Ahead of 'Avatar.'" *Los Angeles Times*, 26 April 2010. Accessed: 3 May 2010. <http://latimesblogs.latimes.com/entertainment-newsbuzz/2010/04/updated-dark-knight-bluray-sales-stay-ahead-of-avatar.html>

Fukuyama, Francis. "The End of History?" *National Interest*, vol. 16 (Summer): 3-18.

Gibbons, Dave. *Watching the Watchmen*. London: Titan Books, 2008.

Gordon, Ian, Marc Jancovich and Matthew P. McAllister, eds. *Film and Comic Books*. Jackson: University Press of Mississippi, 2007.

"Gotham Rises" (Supplementary material on DVD release of *Batman Begins*). DVD. Warner Home Video, 2006.

Gramsci, Antonio. *The Antonio Gramsci Reader: Selected Writings 1916-1935*. Ed. David Forgacs. New York: New York University Press, 2000.

Hall, Stuart. *Culture, Media, Language: Working Papers in Cultural Studies, 1972-1979*. London: Hutchinson, 1980.

—. "Encoding, Decoding." *The Cultural Studies Reader*. 2nd edition. Ed. Simon During. London: Routledge, 1999. 507-517

—. *The Hard Road to Renewal: Thatcherism and the Crisis of the Left*. London: Verso, 1988.

Haraway, Donna. "A Cyborg Manifesto: Science, Technology, and Socialist-Feminism in the Late Twentieth Century," in *Simians, Cyborgs and Women: The Reinvention of Nature*. New York: Routledge, 1991. 149-81.

Hardt, Michael and Antonio Negri. *Empire*. Cambridge: Harvard University Press, 2001.

Harvey, David. *A Brief History of Neoliberalism*. Oxford: Oxford University Press, 2005.

—. *A Companion to Marx's* Capital. London: Verso, 2010.

—. *The Condition of Postmodernity: An Enquiry into the Origins of Cultural Change*. Oxford: Blackwell, 1990.

—. *The Enigma of Capital and the Crises of Capitalism*. London: Profile Books, 2010.

—. *Spaces of Global Capitalism: Towards a Theory of Uneven Geographical Development*. London: Verso, 2006.

Heller, Dana, ed. *The Selling of 9/11: How a National Tragedy became a Commodity*. Basingstoke: MacMillan, 2005.

Heroes. Vol. 1, No.1. New York: Marvel Comics, 2001.

Heuring, David. "Batman Looms Larger." *American Cinematographer* 89:7 (July 2008). Accessed: 3 May 2010. <http://www.theasc.com/magazine_dynamic/July2008/TheDarkKnight/page1.php>

Horkheimer, Max and Theodor Adorno. *Dialectic of Enlightenment: Philosophical Fragments*. Gunzelin Schmid Noerr ed. Trans. Edmund Jephcott. Palo Alto: Stanford

University Press, 2002.

Hughes, Jamie A. "'Who watches the Watchmen?': Ideology and 'Real World' Superheroes." *The Journal of Popular Culture*. 39.4 (2006): 546-57.

Huntington, Samuel P. "The Clash of Civilizations?" *Foreign Affairs*, summer 1993, 7:3: 22-49.

Jameson, Fredric. *Archaeologies of the Future: The Desire Called Utopia and Other Science Fictions*. New York: Verso, 2005

—. "The Dialectics of Disaster." *South Atlantic Quarterly*. 101:2 (Spring 2002): 297-304.

—. *The Geopolitical Aesthetic.* Indianapolis: Indiana UP, 1992.

—. *The Political Unconscious: Narrative as a Socially Symbolic Act.* London: Routledge, 1981.

—. *Postmodernism, or, The Cultural Logic of Late Capitalism.* Durham NC: Duke University Press, 1991.

—. "Postmodernism and Consumer Society." Hal Foster, ed. *The Anti-Aesthetics: Essays on Postmodern Culture*, New Press, New York, 1998, pp. 111-125.

—. *The Seeds of Time.* New York: Columbia University Press, 1996.

—. *A Singular Modernity.* New York: Verso, 2002.

— and Masao Miyoshi, eds. *The Cultures of Globalization.* Durham, NC: Duke University Press, 1998.

Jeffords, Susan. *Hard Bodies: Hollywood Masculinity in the Reagan Era*. New Brunswick: Rutgers University Press, 1994.

Jenkins, Henry. *Convergence Culture: Where Old and New Media Collide*. New York: New York University Press, 2008.

Kauffmann, Linda S. "In the Wake of Terror: Don DeLillo's 'In the Ruins of the Future,' 'Baader-Meinhof,' and *Falling Man*." *MFS Modern Fiction Studies*, 54-2 (Summer 2008): 352-77.

Kermode, Frank. *The Sense of an Ending: Studies in the Theory of Fiction*. Oxford: Oxford University Press, 1968.

Klavan, Andrew. "What Bush and Batman Have in Common." *Wall Street Journal*, July 25, 2008. Accessed: 2 September 2008.

<http://online.wsj.com/public/article_print/SB12169424734348 2821.html>

Klock, Geoff. *How to Read Superhero Comics and Why*. New York: Continuum, 2002.

Koskela, Hille. "Cam-Era: The Contemporary Urban Panopticon." *Surveillance & Society* 1(3): 292-313.

Lacan, Jacques. *Écrits: The First Complete Edition in English*. Trans. Bruce Fink. New York: W.W. Norton & Co., 2000.

Lawrence, John Shelton and Robert Jewett. *Captain America and the Crusade Against Evil: The Dilemma of Zealous Nationalism*. Grand Rapids: Eerdmans, 2003.

—. *The Myth of the American Superhero*. Grand Rapids: Eerdmans, 2002.

Lee, Nathan. Review of *Cloverfield*. *The Village Voice*. 15 January 2008. Accessed: 5 June 2010. <http://www.villagevoice .com/2008-01-15/film/cloverfield-is-one-giant-incredibly-entertaining-screw-you-to-yuppie-new-york/>

Lefebvre, Henri. *Introduction to Modernity*, trans. John Moore. New York: Verso, 1995.

—. *The Production of Space*. Trans. Donald Nicholson-Smith. London: Blackwell Publishing, 1991.

Leman-Langlois, Stéphane. "The Myopic Panopticon: The Social Consequences of Policing Through the Lens." *Policing and Society*, 13 (1), 2003: 44.58.

Lyon, David. "9/11, Synopticon, and Scopophilia: Watching and Being Watched." In: Kevin Haggerty and Richard Ericson, eds. *The New Politics of Surveillance and Visibility*, Toronto: University of Toronto Press, 2006.

Lyotard, Jean-François. *The Postmodern Condition: A Report on Knowledge*. Manchester: Manchester University Press, 1984.

Maggio, J. "The Presidential Rhetoric of Terror: The (Re)Creation of Reality Immediately After 9/11." *Politics & Policy*, 35.4 (2007): 810-35.

Maltby, Richard. "'Nobody Knows Everything': Post-classical

Historiographies and Consolidated Entertainment." Neale and Smith, 21-44.

Manovitch, Lev. *The Language of New Media*. Cambridge, MA: MIT Press, 2001.

—. "What is Digital Cinema?" 1995. Accessed: 15 July 2009. <http://www.manovich.net/TEXT/digital-cinema.html>

Markovitz, Jonathan. "Reel Terror Post-9/11" Paper presented at the annual meeting of the American Sociological Association, Atlanta Hilton Hotel, Atlanta, GA, Aug 16, 2003. Accessed: 7 September 2009. <http://www.allacademic.com/meta/p108147 _index.html>

Mayer, Jane. *The Dark Side*. New York: Doubleday, 2008.

—. "Whatever It Takes: The Politics of the Man Behind *24*." *The New Yorker*. 19 February 2007. Accessed: 5 May 2010. <http://www.newyorker.com/reporting/2007/02/19/070219fa_f act_mayer>

McHale, Brian. *Postmodernist Fiction*. New York: Methuen, 1987.

Miller, Frank and David Mazzucchelli. *Batman: Year One*. New York: DC Comics, 1987.

— with Klaus Janson and Lynn Varley. *Batman: The Dark Knight Returns*. New York: DC Comics, 1986.

Moore, Alan. Interview with Jennifer Vineyard. "Alan Moore: The Last Angry Man". *MTV*. Accessed: 30 August 2006. <http://www.mtv.com/shared/movies/interviews/m/moore_al an_060315>.

Moore, Alan and David Gibbons. *Watchmen*. New York: DC Comics, 1987.

Moore, Alan and David Lloyd. *V for Vendetta*. New York: Vertigo, 1989.

Morris, Tom and Matt Morris, eds. *Superheroes and Philosophy; Truth, Justice and the Socratic Way*. Chicago: Open Court, 2005.

Morrison, Grant. *Supergods*. New York: Spiegel & Grau, 2011. Kindle ebook file.

Neale, Steve and Murray Smith, eds. *Contemporary Hollywood*

Cinema. London and New York: Routledge, 1998.

Newman, Kim. *Apocalypse Movies: End of the World Cinema*. New York: St. Martin's Griffin, 1999.

—. "Beauty in the Beast." *Sight and Sound*, 14:9 (September 2004): 50-51.

—. "Cape Fear." *Sight and Sound*, 15:7 (July 2005): 18-21.

Norlund, Christopher. "Imagining Terrorists Before Sept. 11: Marvel's *GI Joe* Comic Books", 1982-1994' in: *ImageText*, 3.1 (2006).

North, Dan. *Performing Illusions: Cinema, Special Effects and the Virtual Actor*. London: Wallflower Press, 2008.

Nowell-Smith, Geoffrey. "Cities: Real and Imagined." Shiel and Fitzmaurice, 99-108.

Page, Max. *The City's End: Two Centuries of Fantasies, Fears, and Premonitions of New York's Destruction*. New Haven: Yale University Press, 2008.

Pearson, Roberta E. and William Uricchio, eds. *The Many Lives of the Batman: Critical Approaches to a Superhero and his Media*. New York: Routledge, 1991.

—. "I'm Not Fooled by That Cheap Disguise." Pearson and Uricchio 182-213.

Petras, James and Steve Vieux. "Neo-Liberalism and Daily Life." *Economic and Political Weekly*. Vol. 31, No. 38 (Sep. 21, 1996): 2594-97.

Pistelli, John. "*The Dark Knight*: Hollywood's Terror Dream." *Dissident Voice*. 26 July 2008. Accessed: 10 March 2010. <http://dissidentvoice.org/2008/07/the-dark-knight-hollywood's-terror-dream/>

Procter, James. *Stuart Hall*. London: Routledge, 2004.

Purvis, Trevor and Alan Hunt. "Discourse, ideology, discourse, ideology, discourse, ideology…" *The British Journal of Sociology* 44:3 (1993): 473–499.

Reynolds, Richard. *Superheroes: A Modern Mythology*. Jackson: University Press of Mississippi, 1992.

Rozario, Kevin. *The Culture of Calamity: Disaster and the Making of Modern America*. Chicago and London: University of Chicago Press, 2007.

Sabin, Roger. *Adult Comics: An Introduction*. London: Routledge, 1993.

Said, Edward. *Orientalism*. 25th Anniversary Edition. New York: Vintage Books, 2004.

—. "Orientalism once more." *Development and Change* 35.5 (2004): 869-79.

Sanders, James. *Celluloid Skyline: New York and the Movies*. New York: Alfred A. Knopf, 2002.

Scott, Catherine. "'Events Occur in Real Time': 24, Masculinities, and the War on Terror" Paper presented at the annual meeting of the ISA's 49th Annual Convention, San Francisco, Mar 26, 2008. Accessed: 17 April 2010 <http://www.allacademic.com/meta/p251753_index.html>

Segal, Victoria. Movie review: *V for Vendetta*. *New Statesman*, 20 March 2006: 47.

Seitz, Matt Zoller. "Superheroes Suck!" *Salon*. 6 May 2010. Accessed: 8 May 2010. <http://www.salon.com/entertainment/movies/film_salon/2010/05/06/superhero_movies_bankrupt_genre>

Shiel, Mark. "Cinema and the City in History and Theory." Shiel and Fitzmaurice, 1-18.

— and Tony Fitzmaurice, eds. *Cinema and the City: Film and Urban Societies in a Global Context*. Oxford: Blackwell, 2001.

Simmel, Georg. "The Metropolis and Mental Life." Bridge and Watson 11-19.

Soja, Edward W. *Postmetropolis: Critical Studies of Cities and Regions*. Oxford: Blackwell Publishing, 2000.

—. *Postmodern Geographies: The Reassertion of Space in Critical Social Theory*. London: Verso, 1989.

—. "Six Discourses on the Postmetropolis." Bridge and Watson, 188-96.

—. *Thirdspace: Journeys to Los Angeles and Other Real-and-Imagined Spaces*. Oxford: Blackwell Publishing, 1996.

Sontag, Susan. "The Imagination of Disaster." *Commentary*, October 1965, 42-48.

Spigel, Lynn. "Entertainment Wars: Television Culture After 9/11." Heller 119-54.

Stearn, Gerald Emmanuel. *McLuhan Hot & Cool*. London: Penguin Books, 1968.

Straczynski, J. Michael, with John Romita Jr. and Scott Hanna. *Amazing Spiderman Vol. 2: Revelations*. New York: Marvel, 2002.

Strauven, Wanda, ed. *The Cinema of Attractions Reloaded*. Amsterdam: Amsterdam University Press, 2006.

Suvin, Darko. *Metamorphoses of Science Fiction*. New Haven: Yale University Press, 1979.

Tenenbaum-Weinblatt, Keren. "'Where is Jack Bauer When You Need Him?' The Uses of Television Drama in Mediated Political Discourse." *Political Communication*, 26:4 (2009), 367-87.

Tomasovic, Dick. "The Hollywood Cobweb: New Laws of Attraction. (The Spectacular Mechanics of Blockbusters.)" Strauven, 309-20.

Travers, Peter. Movie review: *Spider-Man. RollingStone.com*. May 23, 2002. Accessed: February 15, 2010. <http://www.rolling-stone.com/reviews/movie/5947695/review/5947696/spiderman>

Trimarco, James and Molly Hurley Depret. "Wounded Nation, Broken Time." Heller 27-53.

Turnau, Theodore A. III. "Inflecting the World: Popular Culture and the Perception of Evil." *The Journal of Popular Culture* 38.2 (2004): 384-96.

Vågnes, Øyvind. "'Chosen to be Witness': The Exceptionalism of 9/11." Heller 54-74.

Virilio, Paul. *Ground Zero*. Trans. Chris Turner. London: Verso, 2002.

—. *Open Sky*. Trans. Julie Rose. London: Verso, 1997.

Vu, Ryan. "Heroes We Deserve." *American Stranger*. August 7, 2008. Accessed: March 10, 2010. <http://traxus4420. wordpress.com/2008/08/07/heroes-we-deserve/>

Wolf-Meyer, Matthew. "The World Ozymandias Made: Utopias in the Superhero Comic, Subculture, and the Conservation of Difference." *The Journal of Popular Culture* 36.3 (2003): 497-517.

Williams, Evan Calder. *Combined and Uneven Apocalypse*. Hants: Zero Books, 2011.

Wloszczyna, Susan. "'Spider-Man' spins Towering Tribute to New York." *USAToday.com*. 18 April 2002. Accessed: 15 February 2010. <http://www.usatoday.com/life/lphoto.htm>

Wright, Bradford W. *Comic Book Nation: The Transformation of Youth Culture in America*. Baltimore and London: Johns Hopkins University Press, 2001.

Xenakis, Nicholas J. "T for Terrorist." *The National Interest*, Summer 2006: 134-8.

Zacharek, Stephanie. Movie review: *Hellboy II: The Golden Army*. *Salon*, 11 July 2008. Accessed: 12 May 2010. <http://www .salon.com/entertainment/movies/review/2008/07/11/hellboy _ii/index.html?CP=IMD&DN=110>

Žižek, Slavoj. "Against Human Rights." *New Left Review* 34 (July/August 2005): 115-31.

—. *First as Tragedy, Then as Farce*. London and New York: Verso, 2009.

—. *In Defense of Lost Causes*. London and New York: Verso, 2008.

—. *Iraq: The Borrowed Kettle*. London and New York: Verso, 2004.

—. *Living in the End Times*. London and New York: Verso, 2010.

—. "The Matrix, or Two Sides of Perversion." *Philosophy Today*. Vol. 43 (1999). Accessed: 6 May 2010. <http:// www.egs.edu/faculty/slavoj-zizek/articles/the-matrix-or-two-

sides-of-perversion/>

—. *The Parallax View*. London and Cambridge, MA: MIT Press, 2010.

—. "Passion: Regular or Decaf?" *In These Times*. 27 February 2004. Accessed: 4 May 2010. <http://www.inthesetimes.com/article/146/>

—. *The Plague of Fantasies*. London and New York: Verso, 1997.

—. *The Sublime Object of Ideology*. London and New York: Verso, 1989.

—. *The Ticklish Subject: The Absent Centre of Political Ontology*. London and New York: Verso, 1999.

—. *Welcome to the Desert of the Real*. London and New York: Verso, 2002.

Zukin, Sharon. "From *Landscapes of Power: From Detroit to Disney World*." Bridge and Watson, 197-207.

Contemporary culture has eliminated both the concept of the public and the figure of the intellectual. Former public spaces – both physical and cultural – are now either derelict or colonized by advertising. A cretinous anti-intellectualism presides, cheerled by expensively educated hacks in the pay of multinational corporations who reassure their bored readers that there is no need to rouse themselves from their interpassive stupor. The informal censorship internalized and propagated by the cultural workers of late capitalism generates a banal conformity that the propaganda chiefs of Stalinism could only ever have dreamt of imposing. Zer0 Books knows that another kind of discourse – intellectual without being academic, popular without being populist – is not only possible: it is already flourishing, in the regions beyond the striplit malls of so-called mass media and the neurotically bureaucratic halls of the academy. Zer0 is committed to the idea of publishing as a making public of the intellectual. It is convinced that in the unthinking, blandly consensual culture in which we live, critical and engaged theoretical reflection is more important than ever before.